MW01253018

TRUTH AND NORMATIVITY

Beginning by posing the question of what it is that marks the difference between something like terrorism and something like civil society, Brassington argues that commonsense moral arguments against terrorism or political violence tend to imply that the modern democratic polis might also be morally unjustifiable. At the same time, the commonsense arguments in favour of something like a modern democratic polis could be co-opted by the politically violent as exculpatory.

In exploring this prima facie problem and in the course of trying to substantiate the commonsense distinction, Brassington identifies a tension between the primary values of truth and normativity in the standard accounts of moral theory which he ultimately resolves by adopting lines of thought suggested by Martin Heidegger and concluding that the problem with mainstream moral philosophy is that, in a sense, it tries too hard.

ASHGATE NEW CRITICAL THINKING IN PHILOSOPHY

The Ashgate New Critical Thinking in Philosophy series brings high quality research monograph publishing into focus for authors, the international library market, and student, academic and research readers. Headed by an international editorial advisory board of acclaimed scholars from across the philosophical spectrum, this monograph series presents cutting-edge research from established as well as exciting new authors in the field. Spanning the breadth of philosophy and related disciplinary and interdisciplinary perspectives *Ashgate New Critical Thinking in Philosophy* takes contemporary philosophical research into new directions and debate.

Truth and Normativity
An Inquiry into the Basis of Everyday Moral Claims

160901

IAIN BRASSINGTON
University of Manchester, UK

ASHGATE

Published by
Ashgate Publishing Limited
Gower House
Croft Road
Aldershot
Hampshire GU11 3HR
England

Ashgate Publishing Company
Suite 420
101 Cherry Street
Burlington, VT 05401-4405
USA

Ashgate website: http://www.ashgate.com

British Library Cataloguing in Publication Data
Brassington, Iain
    Truth and normativity : an inquiry into the basis of everyday moral claims. – (Ashgate new critical thinking in philosophy) 1.Normativity (Ethics)
    I.Title
    170.4'4

Library of Congress Cataloging-in-Publication Data
Brassington, Iain.
    Truth and normativity : an inquiry into the basis of everyday moral claims / Iain Brassington.
        p. cm. – (Ashgate new critical thinking in philosophy)
    Includes bibliographical references and index.
    ISBN–13: 978–0–7546–5874–0 (hardcover : alk. paper)
    1. Ethics. I. Title. II. Series.

    BJ1012.B634 2007
    170'.44–dc22

2006018031

ISBN: 978–0–7546–5874–0

Printed and bound in Great Britain by Antony Rowe Ltd, Chippenham, Wiltshire.

Contents

Preface

The arguments in this book started life as a PhD thesis written at the University of Birmingham between 1999 and 2003. The thesis was, I think, reasonable, but needed alteration before it was suitable for publication; the result of this modification is an improvement, but I have no illusions that the arguments in this book are perfect. As such, this book should not be taken as articulating my definitive position on any matter.

Several people deserve acknowledgement. Primarily, Iain Law deserves massive credit for his role supervising and supporting my PhD research. Nick Dent also deserves credit for this. Richard Norman and Joss Walker made valuable comments. Much of the work towards the revision of the original thesis has been done using office space at the Centre for Professional Ethics and at the School of Medicine, both at Keele University: I am particularly grateful to Steve Wilkinson for lending me his office for 18 months, and to Angus Dawson for allowing the library to think that I was a member of staff. Credit is also due to the staff and students at Newcastle-under-Lyme School, who tolerated me using their word processors for my work when I should have been planning lessons; it was the fact that marking would eat into research time that stopped me setting any homework at all during my spell as a teacher there.

On a more personal level, I am immensely grateful for the continued support – financial and moral – of my family and friends, without whose encouragement I would have abandoned the project and entered the real world ages ago.

Chapter 1

'There Are No Innocents':
Why we Should be Worried
about Moral Philosophy

Peradventure there be fifty righteous within the city: wilt thou also destroy and not spare the place for the fifty righteous that are therein? That be far from thee to do after this manner, to slay the righteous with the wicked.

Genesis 18: 24–25

Making Moral Arguments

Philosophy, along with any number of other intellectual disciplines, is concerned with solving problems. Moral philosophy is about solving problems of conduct: problems such as what I should do and what sort of person I ought to be. It is also about getting people to change their behaviour: implicitly, in saying that something is impermissible, we're also making a claim that other people should stop doing it forthwith.

So, implicit in making a moral claim, there is a number of things going on. In the first place, we have to think that a claim to the effect that an action is permissible, admirable, or whatever, is *true*: we have to think that it really *is* permissible, admirable, or whatever. I shall call this a 'first-order' feature of moral debate. It is a belief that my point of view has first-order features that allows me to think that a moral debate is capable of settlement in the first place, too; this is a belief that I must have *ab initio* if I am to think that it is worth trying to convince anyone of my point of view. In the second place, we have to believe that the truth of our moral claim is going to have some sort of normative clout. We want people to believe us, *and* we want them to change their behaviour as a result. I shall call this a 'second-order' feature of moral debate. It is the balance of these two features that I want to investigate here. Now, there is a further debate to be had about whether, if a moral claim can alter behaviour, it can do so because it is *sufficient* to do so, or whether it needs to be supplemented by some further disposition to be influenced by moral claims: it might be that a person assents to the claim that this or that is wrong, but still has no corresponding desire not to do it (just as we might acknowledge that visiting the dentist would be a good idea, but still not go). I shall not touch on this problem of moral psychology here.

Another way of making the same point is to say that, in making a moral claim, we want people to change their behaviour (a point that corresponds to the second-order features of a moral claim), but we want them to do so *for the right reason* (a point that corresponds to the first-order features of a moral claim). I could change your behaviour by putting a gun to your head: this would give you a very good reason to do as I said, but it would not be a *moral* reason, and the moral point would remain unmade. (The same applies to any argument: it is not enough to the mathematician that his colleague should stop disputing his conjecture; what is also necessary is that he should stop disputing it *because he sees its merits*.)

What these accounts of the mechanics of a moral claim have in common is this: for my moral argument to work *as* a moral argument, I have to be able to convince you not only that you should perform or avoid some behaviour; but I have also to offer some account of why this is – that it is *true* that this behaviour is admirable, impermissible, or whatever. To win a moral argument, I have to be able to convince you that your claims are erroneous and that mine are compelling in their own terms.

The claim that motivates this book – at least, the first sixty per cent of it – is that traditional moral thinking faces a problem in reconciling first- and second-order features of moral claims. It is difficult to balance the need for truth in moral claims with the need for them to influence the way that we act. Roughly, I shall argue that the moral strategies that might be best placed to change behaviour – that is, that display second-order characteristics as I used the term above – are the least good at establishing first-order claims to truth, and that those that are most likely to be able to sustain a truth-claim can do so only by letting go of any normative aspect compelling enough to make our claims recognisably *moral* in the first place. My claim is that moral theory – at least as it is traditionally done – is in trouble, and that if it *is not* in trouble, then it *ought* to be. Although commonsense moral discourse appears to have both first- and second-order moral features, extant explanations of how this might be fail.

It is worth glossing my claim a little. If I were concerned to convince you that something is permissible, admirable, or whatever, and that you should do it, you might well ask me why you should believe me. And in answering this question, if I wanted my claim to be true *and* compelling (as I must), I would have a serious problem were I to rely on traditional moral tools. I will have difficulty accounting for its truth, for there is a big problem associated with the idea that there is a thoroughgoing standard of *truth* for moral statements. It is easy enough to check on the veracity of many statements – if I insist that snow is usually green and warm to the touch, it is easy enough to check. But moral statements are different. It is difficult to see how we could check the veracity of a claim that, say, terrorism is wrong.

This is not a new problem, and several attempts have been made to explain how moral statements might be related to notions such as truth. However, the problem that I shall point out in Chapter 3 is that, if I try to solve this problem and provide some plausible criterion for truth in moral statements, I will end up with a claim that is normatively anaemic. A metaphysically plausible account of the truth of a moral claim can provide a description and venture an explanation of people's moral reactions to an act or event, but it cannot tell a recalcitrant why he should think otherwise than he does. The dilemma is that an authoritative moral theory involves metaphysical extravagance, but that an attempt to become more metaphysically thrifty leaves moral thought impoverished of one of the things that make it characteristically *moral* in the first place.

One response to this argument is to slide into moral nihilism. If I am right in my claim that none of the foundations upon with the moral statements that we make every day is able to take the weight that we put on it, we might well throw up our hands in despair. If we imagine a commonsense moral claim such as 'terrorism is wrong', and imagine further that none of the candidate methods for making this claim work is sustainable, then there would seem to be little to stop us deciding that the rule is not so compelling after all. This is something I think I can avoid: the last two chapters of this book are directed at showing how we can keep hold of commonsense morality.

I shall explain my strategy for avoiding nihilism more nearer the time. Still, I can afford to spend a little time sketching out the position I will adopt. By the end of the book, I will be in a position that, I believe, will allow us to keep hold of the truth that we want from a moral claim without having to pay a prohibitively high metaphysical price. Moreover, the method that I shall use to establish the truth of moral claims should also provide normativity. Essentially, I shall claim, it is convention that bankrolls the truth of moral statements; however, I am reluctant to talk about 'mere' convention: at least *some* conventions have serious normative authority. The picture is obviously in need of a good deal of development, but it gives a good enough idea of what is to come for the moment. At least in terms of the *content* of commonsense morality, I am willing to go along with Wittgenstein's thought that philosophy 'leaves everything as it is';[1] unless there is something problematic about having a contentful morality per se – and it is not my intention to argue this – I want to leave it alone. Indeed, in relation to this last point, if my arguments in Chapter 4 succeed, contentful morality will not be a problem at all: in fact, I will have to foreclose the possibility of a superabundance of moral content.

The upshot will be that a moral dispute is something that will bear settlement – that there is a sense in which a moral judgement can be true or false *and* compelling – and what is definitive in providing settlement is the correct application of a moral convention common to the disputants. Only in circumstances in which there is no common convention am I forced to say that moral disputes are not amenable to settlement. But I shall examine the problems posed by this sort of relativism later on, in Chapter 5.

One point that needs to be faced down before proceeding any further is this: is it not simply a little 'emperor's-new-clothesy' to claim at the outset that I shall keep hold of commonsense morality but try to find a new means of sustaining it? Ought not I simply to accept that, if there is a problem with moral philosophy, good faith

---

1   Wittgenstein, 2001, §124.

demands that, at the very least, we suspend our commonsense moral claims? There is something bogus about starting with a moral conclusion (say, 'terrorism is wrong'), casting about for an argument to support it, and then, in a fit of dogmatism, claiming that it does not matter if there turns out to be no support after all, since we can just re-tailor the theory to fit. A sustained defence of my strategy will only be attempted in Chapter 4 – for the moment, it is enough to point out that my strategy follows an illustrious precedent: Kant's moral thought, too, begins with an attempt to ground common moral understanding;[2] whatever the differences between his thought and mine, this is not one of them. He, too, seems to use something like commonsense morality as his starting point and construct a moral theory from there.

Although I am mainly concerned with theory, it is also inescapable that claims about theory impact on claims about practice. There is something to be said for treating practical and theoretical questions separately, but there is also something to the idea that it is not possible to keep the two entirely segregated. Thus, what I have to say has practical implications – indeed, I will be using a practical problem to force my way into the theoretical problem in a few paragraphs' time. There is a range of reasons that we might give for thinking this. For example, it might turn out that there is no particularly good justification for the content of whatever moral thoughts I think. My belief that this or that is permissible might rest on only the shakiest of foundations. This does not mean that I should abandon my point of view: to have no reason to think that an action is morally acceptable does not imply that I should *not* think that it is morally acceptable. But good faith would seem to demand that, if I was to come across someone whose moral beliefs included the claim that the action I have in mind is wrong, and he was able to cite a steadier foundation for those beliefs, I should adopt his view as my own.

Thus, when serious disputes arise about the content of systems of morality, this leads implicitly to the possibility of questioning the authority of those systems. If someone makes a series of outrageous moral claims, we might well wonder whether something was seriously amiss with the moral understanding that informs them. And if it turns out to be difficult to pinpoint exactly what has gone wrong with this person's moral sensibilities, we might be forced to interrogate our *own* foundational beliefs. This allows for the orthodox assumption that metaethical investigation – theorising about the validity of moral claims – is content-neutral (after all, it is possible for someone to make an error of reasoning and so reach an erroneous moral conclusion from sound premises), but it also recognises that the form and the content of a person's set of moral beliefs do impinge on each other at least some of the time, and that investigation of one might justify investigation of the other.

This last point stands in relation to claims of a much more general sort as well as those that we make in relation to particular cases. For example: if we can show that disinterestedness is a virtue, we are not told what this might mean in practice – but we do have ammunition that we can use against someone who advocates egocentricity. And, to work the other way, we might be able (at least sometimes) to

2   Kant, 1993, Section 1, *passim.*

suggest a content for moral beliefs that is suggested by their form. As an example of this, we might point to the way in which Hobbes's understanding of the laws of nature as determining behaviour leads to a system of imperatives in *Leviathan*. The way in which we think about the world can, and often does, influence the way that we think about the moral status of actions. If a moral claim can be shown to rest on unreliable metaethical premises, we might suspect the content of that claim; and our understanding of metaethics might, in certain circumstances, make a positive difference to our normative beliefs. Either way, it is worth iterating that, although there is a difference between the content of a moral theory and its form, it is not too radical a difference: metaethical questions shade into normative questions. (This is a claim that foreshadows arguments that I shall present in Chapter 5, albeit subject to many qualifications that I shall make closer to the time.)

The example I shall use to show how practical questions can shade into theoretical questions is one that concerns the sustainability of the commonsense judgements that we might make concerning the difference between civil social practices and terrorism (although there is any number of other examples that I might equally well have used). I shall use this example to inform my wider claim about the problem of reconciling first- and second-order features of moral discourse. Commonsense morality says that there is a serious distinction to be drawn between terrorism and democratic, civil-social political engagement; I shall suggest that the distinction is much hazier than we might imagine, and that this gives us a good reason to question the metaethical assumptions upon which claims about a distinction might be made.

If it is possible to raise questions about the impermeability of the apparent moral boundary between terrorism and democracy, and to do so without stepping outside the considerations of commonsense morality, then there is scope to doubt just how good moral philosophy is at what it is supposed to be doing. In the example I shall develop in this chapter, I am specifically *not* challenging one moral paradigm with another: I am suggesting that the features of democracy and terrorism are such that it does not matter what flavour of moral reasoning we use – whether we are a deontologist, utilitarian, or whatever: we cannot make sense of the apparently startling moral difference between plebiscites and Armalites. So it will not do to try to fit commonsense morality to any extant moral theory: rather, we must think quite seriously about what is going on in *any* moral judgement. In other words, it is not unreasonable to start questioning the faculty of moral judgement per se. Still, by the end of the book, I shall have presented a case for thinking that we can keep hold of the distinction between democracy and terrorism, arbitrary as it seems (and, in fact, is), and that the same applies to any number of commonsense moral beliefs. What we should be prepared to question quite radically is the reasons why we hold these beliefs. I do not suppose that what I am going to claim is definitive – there are, doubtless, gaps to fill and loose ends to tie. But I believe that the theory I am about to construct is worthy at least of serious investigation.

The Moral Terrorist?

How might we go about establishing the need for a look at metaethics? The strategy that I intend to pursue will revolve around looking at two things from opposite ends of the moral spectrum, and asking *why* they are at opposite ends. As I suggested a moment ago, I shall use as my moral termini democracy and terrorism. Commonsense morality says that terrorism is wrong and that democracy is right – or, if not exactly that, then something very much like it. However, once we begin to look at why this might be, it becomes apparent that, at least in practice, there is not so big a difference between these two forms of behaviour as there might appear to be at first. This being the case, we can either ditch the idea that there is a compelling moral difference between them, or we can try to establish why we draw the moral line where we do. As I said above: none of the extant ways of thinking about morality can answer this satisfactorily. Thus, if we were engaged in debate with a terrorist or advocate of terrorism, we would have a hard time in getting him to change his behaviour or beliefs *for the right reason* if all we had to hand was extant moral thinking.

The point that will occupy me for the rest of this chapter – and the first half of the book – is not so much that we should stop worrying and learn to love the bomb as that we should worry *even more* if we want to avoid having even to respect the bomb. The problem is structural, though: the same points will apply in some form in relation to other moral claims that we might want to make. The democracy *versus* terrorism example functions as a test case, and as such it will recur; however, there is no shortage of examples that we might want to use in its place.

A commonsense moral critique of terrorism will be aimed at establishing two things: that the terrorist should abandon his strategy; and that this rejection will be based on a recognition of the strategy's impermissibility. Yet, while a term such as 'terrorist' comes with plenty of moral baggage that is generally not shared by a term such as 'democracy' or 'civil society' (this is a point that will turn out to be important in the second half of the book), the distribution of that baggage is more even than might be thought; the civil-social or democratic *polis* and the terrorist carry similar weights. For this reason, if there is something about criticisms of terrorism compelling enough to make the terrorist abandon his strategy, then the *polis* should, for the sake of consistency, halt a good number of its functions.

The first point to make is that it is not as if terrorists have a categorical desire to do evil things: either they reject the idea that they do evil things, or they claim that what they do is undesirable, but unavoidable as a means of ensuring some future good. This I shall take as axiomatic. Either way, they operate morally rather as does the state, which also believes either that it does not do evil things, or that it does so only for the very best *raisons d'état*. Hence, either we have to revise the content of the commonsense moral intuition that distinguishes terrorism from democratic civil society, or else we have to find what it is that gives the distinction its authority, lest the terrorist reject it.

Émile Henry looks as though he might be a good example of a terrorist who denies that he does anything evil or wrong. Quite possibly, he would have claimed that he was doing something *right* – and not simply as a means to an end. His story is told, with slightly differing details, by Igor Primoratz[3] and Walter Laqueur.[4] The bones of this story are these: Henry was a young French anarchist who, in 1894, threw a bomb into the Café Terminus in Paris. At his trial he claimed that his intention had been to kill, and made the claim that gives this chapter its title: 'There are no innocents'. *Prima facie*, this is moral nonsense. However, I do not think that we should be so automatically dismissive.

For one thing, Henry does seem to have been speaking the language of commonsense morality, however badly. In claiming that there are no innocents, he seems to have qualified his own action: the implication is that, if there had been any innocents, he would have been less willing to throw his bomb. He would, I am willing to believe, have discriminated between the innocent and the not-innocent – he just did not find anyone who fitted into the former category. There is reason to believe, then, that Henry passes at least one moral and judicial test: that of applying the principle of desert. Whether or not he was particularly *good* at applying it is another matter. The point is that it would appear that he has a defence against the charge that he was acting at random. Henry cannot be immediately dismissed as a psychopath: there is a moral argument to be had with him.

This supposition seems to be supported by Laqueur's telling of Henry's story. According to his account, Henry's claim was that there are no innocent *bourgeoises*.[5] This further qualification makes a difference: we can imagine that Henry had in mind the idea that he was on some sort of a crusade against a moral iniquity for which the bourgeoisie was culpable. Nevertheless, there is a very obvious commonsense counterclaim to the contention: it would be simply that the 'bourgeoises' qualification is a smoke-and-mirrors job. Even if Laqueur's representation is accurate, Henry's claim still jars. After all, being bourgeois is a matter of fact and not act. One would have a hard time, as a result, if one wanted to argue that there is something culpable about the mere fact of belonging to a particular social class. By and large, one is born bourgeois: for every one person who joins the complacent middle classes by treading on the workers' faces, there are hundreds who find themselves on the same social level through accident of birth; and it is not really fair to say that one can be anything other than innocent simply because of the social status of one's parents. Moreover, we could even weaken *this* position, and still leave commonsense morality with a reasonably strong argument against Henry's claim.

Concede, for the sake of the argument, that being bourgeois involves more than simply having been born in the leafier parts of town. Imagine that it also involves a range of attitudes, patterns of behaviour and so on, and that this is what Henry found so offensive. Allow, too, that spending time in the Café Terminus is a sign that one is not only of bourgeois heredity, but that one engages in insidiously bourgeois behaviour as a matter of course. (Karl Marx, for example, might be cited by a latter-

---

3   Primoratz, 1990.
4   Laqueur, 1977.
5   Ibid.

day Henry as the sort of person who came from a bourgeois background but who managed to overcome this handicap through systematically bad behaviour around Europe.[6]) It is the bourgeois *behaviour*, and the negligent failure to notice and purge oneself of this behaviour, that makes one a legitimate target. Finally, imagine that everyone in the café was bourgeois – that we are in a world in which even being a waiter is a bourgeois occupation. In short, everyone in the café was bourgeois, and there really are no innocent bourgeois. But even in this imaginary world, commonsense morality is able still to point out that the concept of desert, to which Henry paid at least lip-service, is what I will call a 'simple' concept, that this can not be said of bourgeoisie, and that this makes a moral difference.

What do I mean by conceptual simplicity? Simplicity is a quality of a concept such that it does not admit of degrees. Being dead or being pregnant are simple concepts: you cannot be slightly deceased or a junior member of the pudding club. The same applies to desert: either you deserve something or you do not. Certainly, *what* you deserve is variable and in commonsense terms demands proportion; but the fact of whether or not it is deserved is not a matter of grey areas: you cannot slightly deserve the death penalty, even though it may or may not be the death penalty that you deserve. Someone who commits a minor misdemeanour does not deserve to be treated in the same way as a major criminal. Henry claimed that 'There are no innocents', and further, that his intention was to kill. Even if we go along with the claim, we can do so with reservations: admitting that there is something culpable about being bourgeois might mean that one deserves *something* (this is why I am willing to suppose that Henry paid lip-service to the principle of desert), but it does not follow that that something is death by bomb.

By contrast, even if being bourgeois is culpable, I do not see why we have to think that it is simple. If there is no such thing as a 'good' bourgeois, the point can still be made that one person could be more intolerably bourgeois than his neighbour. Imagine, analogously, a den of thieves: it might be that each thief is a black-hearted scoundrel; but it is equally possible that black-heartedness is only a feature of one or two. Perhaps the others' hearts come in a range of shades of grey. If being bourgeois implies a mode of (bad) behaviour, we might be able to say something similar about those who are. Wasting time in cafés might be a bad thing, but owning a factory that oppresses the labourers and pollutes their water is worse, and there is enough of a discrepancy between the two to mean that Henry had made a serious error in treating all bourgeois alike. There are, then, two questions to be put. *How* bourgeois is this person (akin to asking how ruthless a thief is)? And does being bourgeois (or committing a theft) deserve killing?

I suspect that all could agree that, if being bourgeois involves a range of behaviours, one can be more or less (reprehensibly) bourgeois than one's neighbour; but it is equally plausible to suppose that no degree of bourgeoisie is enough to make a café bombing anything like deserved. This is enough for our moral intuitions to tell us that Henry did something very wrong.

---

6   Cf. Wheen, 2000, for a biography.

None of this deals with the important issue, though: so if this is the strongest argument that commonsense moral thought can offer against someone like Henry, it is still in a weak position. It does not really get around the fact that *Henry still seems to have been reasonably conversant with an important moral principle based in an understanding of the concept of desert.* The worst that we can say of him is that he was not very good at recognising desert and terribly misguided in responding to it. Applying some sort of moral standard such as justice or desert means making some sort of discrimination between people who may have widely different levels of implication in a given state of affairs: Henry could surely have recourse to an argument that he had made an *error* in the discrimination that is morally expected, but that he was still (in principle) discriminating. Allowing that Henry spoke some of the language of commonsense morality and justice does not commit anyone to agreeing that he spoke it particularly well – we might say that he had got the syntax roughly right, but simply did not understand the semantics – but it does mean that he has some claim to have been working within a moral paradigm with which we tend to be reasonably happy.

Other Terrorists

So this would seem to be one instance in which a terrorist would seem at first glance to be irreconcilably at odds with commonsense morality, but who emerges as someone who, albeit with difficulty, might be accommodated within some version of commonsense moral thought. However, this is not always the case with terrorism: it might be possible to entertain the possibility that Henry was something of an anomaly – if he was a terrorist, he was a terrorist of a more or less unique stripe.

A more familiar model of terrorism – bearing in mind that the concept of terrorism is notoriously difficult to pin down – is that which defines the terrorist as the sort of person who embarks on a programme of politically motivated and violent coercive intimidation.[7] Such intimidation is at its greatest and most effective when it is the innocent who are targeted specifically *because* of their innocence. The terrorist's main weapon is not explosive; it is terror, as the word 'terrorist' implies.[8] There

---

7   Primoratz, 1990, p. 130.

8   Attacks on the police or armed forces are frequently labelled as terrorist, but with only dubious legitimacy – after all, a person who carries out such an attack need not intend to *terrorise* anyone. Strictly speaking, given the volunteer status of the people targeted, the British government was mistaken when it condemned Irish sectarian attacks against non-civilian targets as terrorism rather than as political assassination. However, a title such as 'terrorist' has the political function of foreclosing any legitimacy that an assassin might have: his targets are quite precise, and so he is not as easy to condemn outright as the terrorist.

At the same time, an organisation that aims to induce an atmosphere of fear might be terrorist, regardless of the number of attacks it carries out and against whom it directs them. And inducing this atmosphere could, I think, count as violent – psychologically violent, that is – quite easily.

are two reasons why this strategy might be embarked upon, though the difference between the two is hazy. One reason for terrorism is that it should lead to the overthrow and replacement of the state or force an important modification of the way that a state works (for example, its tolerance of a particular form of perceived injustice); the other is the overthrow of *states*. Into the first category, which I will call 'archist', we might place organisations such as Umkhonto we Sizwe, whose aim was to overthrow the South African government and replace it with another, more egalitarian government.[9] This is the sort of model that I think Ted Honderich has in mind when he talks about democratic violence.[10] At a push, groups such as the IRA, the Peruvian Sendera Luminoso or at least some Islamic groups might also fit into this category.

Into the second category, which I will call anarchist, we might place organisations such as the Baader-Meinhof group. The aims of such an organisation are more radical, in that they want to disrupt not just the mechanism of a state, but the whole system of states per se: the political colour of the government is not so important. An anarchist terrorist attempts to force the government into increasingly brutal retaliation, thereby awakening the political consciousness of the masses to the fundamental viciousness of the whole system,[11] or to the generalised inability of *poleis* to live up to what they promise in terms of guaranteeing justice and security (a point that owes much to one made by Walter Benjamin: 'violence, when not in the hands of the law, threatens it not by the ends that it may pursue but by its mere existence outside the law'[12]). A population shaken in this way would eventually realise the limitations not just of one *polis*, but of all *poleis* necessarily, and would choose to live in a world in which the political mechanism is replaced entirely by something radically different and which, perhaps, could not realistically be instantiated 'archically', let alone democratically. (Of course, there might be room for a *polis*-like institution, such as a cooperative or soviet, to deal with the realities of the world – say, to administer disaster relief. But a passing resemblance to the state, *ex hypothesi*, would be all there was to affairs so arranged.)

Either way, archist or anarchist, the terrorist attempts to force a situation by deliberately flouting justice and instilling fear into the population as a means to an end. This is certainly true of attacks on democratic societies, in which the feelings of the public are of direct political import. Indeed, terrorism has been identified by some commentators as more prevalent in democracies than under other political systems in which (*prima facie*, at least) there is a much bigger incentive towards radical political action. This idea holds to the extent that, In Lacquer's words, '[w]herever the means of repression has been most complete and perfect there has been no terrorism at all'.[13] A problem with this claim is that it seems to invite counterexamples: for

---

9   See Mandela, 1994, for a first-hand account of the organisation.
10   Honderich, 1989.
11   Laqueur, 1977a, p. 353.
12   Benjamin, 2000, p. 65.
13   Laqueur, 1977b, p. 142; cf also ch. 4, the conclusion, and 1977a, chs. 8–9.

example, a number of countries in Arabia and North Africa have suffered from terroristic insurgencies, although they do not have a strong liberal culture by any means. Thus we might be tempted to claim that Lacquer's point is informed rather too much by cold-war politics.

Nevertheless, there is still a nugget of accuracy in claims that, the more liberal the society, the more vulnerable it should be to terrorism: after all, creating public fear when the public has no official voice is not an obvious move for a political activist to take – we might note that al-Qa'ida activities in Saudi Arabia, for example, are aimed indirectly at America; and when the aim is to undermine the legitimacy of the state (at least in respect to some of its function – think of the animal rights activist who might well want only to undermine some aspects of state activity), terrorism might well be superfluous (if not counterproductive) when the legitimacy of the state is viewed suspiciously in the first place. However, there seems to be no good reason to suppose that democracy is the only form of government that responds to political violence: *any* rule which makes *any* claims to be recognisably just must be seen to respond to a threat to the 'innocent victims' of events, which means either accommodating the challenge or squashing it; any rule must at least *claim* to accord with justice as it is perceived by the *demos* lest it appear to give *carte blanche* to its opponents.

Yet the point remains that most terrorist groups have a sense of morality, and depend on commonsense morality. Their sense of morality is implied in the very fact that they think that the world should be thus and so, and set about to realise their vision. To this extent, it is possible to imagine a bomber who goes about his business with a heavy heart. Émile Henry (or someone like him) might have denied that what he did was immoral, but Henry is arguably not a typical bomber. In most cases, it is possible to imagine that the terrorist would concede that, seen in isolation, what he is doing is seriously wrong. But, he might add, we ought not to look at things in isolation: while, all else being equal, a given terror-tactic is unjust, and anyone engaging in it commits a wrong, and this injustice constitutes a serious (moral) reason not to do it, the point stands that all else is *not* equal, and that the reason not to engage in this particular activity is outweighed by a moral or instrumental reason *to* engage in it. Our hypothetical terrorist's claim might here be based on an appeal to future justice, national self-determination, or something like that. The immorality of bomb-planting is able to supply *a* reason not to plant bombs, but it is nothing like a compelling reason, and is outweighed by the moral advantages of whatever it is that the bomb-planting is supposed to achieve.

And there is more to be said, for not only might the terrorist make an appeal to a 'wide' account of what is morally permitted or even required: he might also turn out to rely on a version of commonsense morality *just so that he can violate it*. This is implicit in the idea that part of the way that terrorism works is through terror. If a group chose methods that did not generate outrage, it would not be terroristic: terrorists need outrage to make their point. For this reason, they need commonsense morality.

Imagine, for example, two organisations which bomb buses as a means of making their political presence felt. One targets school buses; the other, prison buses transporting paedophiles. The latter group is unlikely to disrupt the mechanism of the state or to generate the public opprobrium that is, in practice, necessary to force the political pressure for change, and this is not just because there are fewer paedophiles than schoolchildren. The child is seen as morally different. It is innocent and certainly does not deserve to be at the receiving end of political violence. Hence bombing children represents a severe injustice. Of course, the paedophile does not deserve *political* violence either: depending on your view of motivational psychology, it is possible that he does not *deserve* much *at all*.[14] But a disjunction between the paedophilia and the politics is unlikely to cause too many sleepless nights to the public at large: the violence would not be strictly appropriate punishment, but as long as the public mood is hostile to the paedophile, it'd probably be considered churlish to get too picky. As far as the *demos* is concerned, the paedophile is either not as innocent as the child, or not relevantly innocent.

This is not a radical proposal for penal reform: the point is simply to illustrate that, despite appearances, a terroristic programme actually does not eschew commonsense notions of desert. Whatever other considerations there may be, the paedophile is seen by the public at large as deserving some kind of retribution, but it is almost certain that we'd try to prevent children being bombed. An organisation that threatens credibly to injure children unless we give it what it wants seems more likely to succeed, rightly or wrongly, than one that threatens to kill a paedophile a week until its demands are met – we might be willing, as a *demos*, to let it get on with it. The terrorist's hope is that he can force the *demos* at least to listen. A principle based in the concept of desert plays a part in this transaction, but only as something that is deliberately transgressed. There is a sense of morality behind the terroristic act: partly because the act is motivated by a belief that the world should be thus and so, and partly because the effect of terrorism has to play on the public's sense of decency. Put another way: a commonsense criticism of terrorism might well display first-order, truth-based, characteristics: but it might lack second-order, normativity-based, characteristics entirely.

Having said this, though, there are still likely to be limits to the moral transgressions which will be contemplated by at least some terrorists. Archist terrorists, who have no fundamental problem with the state as long as it is run in a certain manner, cannot afford to alienate themselves from the possibility of public sympathy: for example, an organisation that ostensibly wants to bring democracy cannot realistically afford to be seen as having maimed or killed a large part of the *demos*. There is, then, a need to keep the *actual* injustice to a minimum, compared to the *perception* of the threat

---

14   Someone might claim, for example, that he can neither help nor control his desires: he was just born that way. He would have quite a serious claim not to deserve imprisonment according to commonsense moral thought. However, he would be vulnerable to the equally commonsense counterclaim that he should still be locked up in the interests of protecting the public. The end result, at least in relation to what I'm arguing here, would be the same.

thereof – and even this perception would have to be limited. For this reason, it does seem legitimate to agree with David Mapel that a terrorist would welcome civilians' survival as much as would what he calls a 'tactical bomber', such as a member of the Air Force on a mission, after the military facility had been destroyed.[15]

Perhaps this sort of argument would be less compelling to the likes of Ulrike Meinhof: she might have responded with an argument to the effect that seeking not to enrage the public is tantamount to pandering to exactly the kind of bourgeois prejudice that was at the root of the dispute. Nevertheless, in the *samizdat* pamphlet *The Bomb Throwers*, the self-described revolutionary anarchist 'R.A.T.' concedes that the terrorist must balance the creation of a sense of menace with a minimisation of actual danger.[16] Spilling *some* innocent blood might be necessary, but too much is likely to be counterproductive. Note, though, that the tone here is one in which the morality of the tactic is confronted only in relation to its pragmatic value. The question is one concerning the *extent*, not the *adoption*, of injustice.

The point of the past few paragraphs has been to argue that commonsense morality does have a handle on the terrorist. In the first place, there is a debate to be had in principle about whether an outcome is sufficient warrant for a given tactic – and this is not unlike the kind of debate that goes on in government departments and in seminar rooms all around the world. In the second, the terrorist depends on the strictures of commonsense morality just so that he can transgress them. The problem here is that, while it is not at all difficult to say that there is something wrong about what this person does and thereby to offer a moral critique, it is equally plain that the critique is, pretty much, irrelevant. It will make no difference at all to the terrorist, who is deliberately being immoral, although he might not be pursuing a programme of systematic immorality for its own sake. Either way, it is likely that a terrorist could agree that what he was doing was *ceteris paribus* immoral. But he does not thereby have to agree that it is immoral in this case; and, even if he does agree with this, it might be that this is why he's doing it in the first place.

In a sense, it turns out that the terrorist can claim to be a sort of utilitarian. What he does would count as a moral mortgage: in the short term, there would be a serious moral debt accrued; but the hope would be that this would turn out to have been an investment in a morally better world. In this context, the bomber might cite the idea that 'however unhappy about it he may be, the utilitarian must admit that … he might find himself in circumstances in which he ought to be unjust'.[17] If this is right, then he can at least make an attempt to place his activity on a moral par with any number of activities with which we might have no intuitive problem. That the terrorist could

---

15   Mapel, 2001, p. 259.

16   'R.A.T.', 1971.

17   Smart in Smart and Williams, 1993, p. 71. As it happens, it is odd for a defence of any form of consequentialism to take this form. I am not happy with the coherence of the thought that one *ought* to be unjust: 'ought' is a strong word; and since for the utilitarian the justice of an action lies *only* in its results it is either questionable or question-begging how unjust the compelled injustice truly *is*. But this is a problem with *utilitarianism*, rather than with the adoption of given tactics by certain individuals.

do this is not necessarily a proof against consequentialism; it might just as easily be an argument for toning down our intuitive condemnations of the terrorist.

Besides: the terrorist need not be a consequentialist. It is not inconceivable, for example, that some agents might recognise a *prima facie* duty to behave in a certain way that clashes with another *prima facie* duty to act in another. Such a person might recognise that he has a duty not to kill, but might also think that he has a duty to end injustice by whatever means necessary (or whatever), and that, *in this instance*, the second duty trumps the first. Moreover, it seems possible that even a Kantian could embrace violence, in at least some forms. Kant himself can be seen as an advocate of some kinds of violence: he is not averse to the idea that there might be such a thing as a just war, nor to the idea that some people might make themselves morally outlaw. All a Kantian has to do is to believe that he is engaged in a just war, then, or to convince himself that the people whom he attacks are morally outlaw, in order for him to be able to engage in activities that are contrary to commonsense morality with a fair degree of moral self-assurance.

Terrorism and the Democratic State: Unelected Affinities

So far, the argument has been roughly this: that something intuitively morally bad such as terrorism turns out, at least notionally, to be able to make some sort of claim for backing on moral ideas that are recognisable to commonsense. When the focus is on someone like Émile Henry, there is a powerful argument for thinking that we ought to concede at least a theoretical compatibility of his actions with commonsense morality. Any modifications that we might want to make to a Henry-like maxim would be modifications in content rather than in form. In relation to terrorists and terrorist organisations in the more 'traditional' mould, be they archist or anarchist, there is also a compatibility with some (different) aspects of moral thought. Some groups can draw on a form of consequentialism, and, whatever might be our feelings about consequentialism, and whether or not it succeeds as a moral theory, we have to admit that we cannot criticise it for being unrecognisably *outré*. Other groups are not necessarily consequentialists, but there is nevertheless a sense in which they still rely on commonsense moral rules, even if only in that they can be broken in order to make an impact – strategically, as it were.

If there is anything to be said about the argument of the last few pages, then it looks as though the terrorist might have a stronger entitlement to claim the support of commonsense morality than commonsense itself would be immediately willing to allow. At the very least, a moral understanding of terror-tactics does not always mean having to relinquish commonsense morality; and quite often, we can only understand these tactics on the basis of a grasp of commonsense morality. Having raised questions along this route, I want to shift focus now, from one of my moral termini to the other. I want to question the moral reliability of a concept that commonsense morality would probably accept happily: the democratic state. The terrorist seems to be catching up with democracy's moral head start; it is time to see whether civil society can be given a helping hand.

Roughly speaking, one of the functions of the *polis*, and one of the reasons for the formation of *poleis*, seems to be the guarantee of justice and the application of the demands of commonsense morality: at the end of the *Oresteia*, with the Furies buried beneath Athens, the brute force of moral bad luck is subdued by the power of the *polis*, and this ending is intuitively satisfying. This point holds even though we might have differing concepts of what justice actually is. This is a picture that I will have to revise fairly radically in the penultimate chapter of the study, but for now it will do. It is a picture that seems to be that relied upon by thinkers such as Locke and the restatement of Lockean political thought presented by Nozick.[18] For thinkers of this stripe, we need (and can justify) a *polis* because often justice is a feature that is notably lacking from the world. There are, we may point out, certain moral demands that we are entitled to make of each other – but it is equally plain that there are circumstances in which this moral demand is not, and cannot be, met. For example, I might be robbed in the street. Even if I knew my attacker's identity, it is not always the case that I would be able to retrieve my wallet as easily as all that: my robber might count boxing among his hobbies. In reality, it is highly likely that I simply will not know who my attacker is, nor will I have the ability to find out. Either way, there is an incentive to join what Nozick calls a 'protective association':[19] a body that can act on my behalf to rectify such eventualities, if not prevent them altogether. Though not yet quite a *polis*, this association is certainly a *polis*-like institution, and so I do not think that I'm making too many sacrifices by treating it in roughly the same way.

Still, the moral status of the *polis* is questionable: its relationship with justice isn't necessarily as cosy as all that. By Nozick's own lights, the protective association must be limited; he thinks that '[i]ndividuals have rights'[20] – these are the first words in *Anarchy, State and Utopia* after the contents page – and that any *polis* that is more than minimal is unacceptable because it violates these rights. The subtext here is that even the 'minimal state' has something morally fishy about it insofar as it is a threat to the rights that Nozick is so adamant that people have, but that it is (just about) redeemed by being, at the very least, better than the alternatives.

By no stretch of the imagination is this a massive vindication for the moral probity of the protective association. Now, it is possible that this is simply a problem with the account that we might get from someone like Locke or Nozick of how states get their legitimacy. However, the wider point is that, whatever their intellectual affinity, one of the big moral worries that supporters of the democratic *polis* must allay is the thought that it does, in a disguised form, something rather similar to what is done by the terrorist. Obviously, the idea that the *polis* may act to restore or to guarantee justice is an idea that can be claimed by at least some terroristic organisations, so we

---

18   See, for example, the discussion of Locke in Nozick, 1974, pp. 11 ff.
19   Ibid., pp. 12 ff.
20   Ibid., p. ix.

have a reason to think that the difference between the terrorist organisation and the *polis* might not be quite as large as we might have thought. In addition, it is worth bearing in mind Primoratz's definition of terrorism as coercive intimidation.[21] If we allow that it is an accurate definition, even if it is not exhaustive, it captures a good deal of what terrorism seems to be about. But it is not madness to contend that there is a good deal of coercive intimidation in the modern democratic state as well. For example, the police force is equipped with high-visibility clothing and vehicles. Part of this is for the sake of safety, admittedly. But it is arguably also true that a highly visible police force is one that can make its presence felt without really having to exert itself too much: the population is herded into behaving in a certain manner simply though being aware of the presence of the policeman.

Perhaps I am being a little paranoid here. But there are examples that might be stronger: the CCTV camera in the town centre is justified on grounds that it is something that will help *prevent* crime, not that it will aid identification once a crime has been committed. In other words, there seems to be an intention to influence patterns of behaviour through awareness of visibility. This could certainly be construed as coercive, and arguably as intimidation; it is quite insidious as well. Another example might be the road signs that warn of speed-cameras: 'Don't speed, lest you be fined,' they hint. Well: 'Give us what we want, or we shall injure you,' hints the terrorist. The degree of severity is different, but the moral grammar appears to be exactly the same. Along similar lines, Foucault offers a critique of the 'panoptical society' in *Discipline and Punish*[22] and talks of the regulatory power of the psychiatrist in *Madness and Civilisation*.[23] In both cases, an important part of the argument is that 'modern' and 'civilised' methods of behaviour modification, intuitively more morally secure than those used before the Enlightenment, hide methods that are just as coercive, albeit differently so, than those that they replaced. If modern, Westernised 'civil society' can be coercively intimidating, what is the moral (rather than pragmatic) difference between its methods and those of the terrorist?

One obvious answer is that the terrorist, whatever his justification, tends to be a representative of a radicalised minority, whereas the democratic *polis*, whatever its strictures, represents the will of the majority. However, drawing this distinction is not enough to make the moral difference all that convincing. If it is to have any hope of doing the work expected of it, the defence must be able to point out what difference this makes to *me*, the individual who is having his behaviour modified by forces beyond his control. What difference does it make whether I am coerced by one very powerful person (such as a terrorist with a bomb) or by a very powerful collectivity (such as a *polis* with a democratic mandate)? Indeed: *why should* it make a difference?

It is not obvious that there really is much of a difference at all – certainly not unless we propose an a priori rule to the effect that there just *is* something morally

---

21   Primoratz, 1990.
22   Foucault, 1991.
23   Foucault, 1997a.

right about majorities (and what might entitle us to make any such claim is part of what I will be looking for in the next three chapters). The famous illustration in the 1651 edition of Hobbes's *Leviathan* is instructive here:[24] the sovereign is depicted as the incorporation of *hoi polloi*. In the end, many individually weak people incorporated mean more or less the same as one strong person. The strongest argument that might be put would be one that moulds right and wrong according to the will of the majority: one that democratises morality. But, if this is the case, there are a couple of arguments against it.

The first is to subject it to a *reductio*. Suppose, for example, that Hitler's electoral success had been genuine: would this provide moral backing to the machinery of the Nazi state? Anyone who is even willing to entertain the possibility that the answer might be 'no' needs to come up with a better argument in favour of the moral strength of democracy than simple majoritarianism: the concession must be made that right cannot rest in strength of numbers alone. The second argument is based around the idea that it is circular to justify the rule of the majority by means of an appeal to the will of the majority. So, even if we are willing to accept the *reductio*, simple majoritarianism is still not much of an argument. The point is that there really is no enormously compelling difference between being told what to do by tens of big swords and being told what to do by tens of millions of rather smaller ones. This represents a chink in the supposedly sturdy wall separating civil politics from violence.

The Ship of State and its Galley Slaves

Another defence of civil society is that it represents government by consent. Even if my behaviour is coerced by the wishes of the masses in a way that I personally would not have chosen, the obvious difference is that within civil society these are the rules under which I have chosen to live: in entering the protective association, I have taken the gamble that, even with all the factors that count against it, my life in general will be better than it would be outside. I might occasionally have to act against my wishes or conscience, and very occasionally the clash might be deep and serious. But this is the contract into which I entered, and this is something I must grin and bear. In a similar way, I enter a game of roulette in the full expectation that I will come out of it rather better off than I was when I went in; but if the fall of the ball is against me, then this is how it goes, and I must accept this fate.

This is all very well for roulette – but the analogy with the state is rather fatuous. Importantly, I *chose* to enter the game for whatever reason; and I *chose* to risk everything on the little ball stopping on the zero. But this is not the case with membership of the *polis*. Hume, I think, has a knock-down argument here:

---

24   Hobbes, 1999, pp xciii.

We may as well assert that a man, by remaining in a vessel, freely consents to the domination of the master; though he was carried on board while asleep, and must leap into the ocean and perish, the moment he leaves her.[25]

Political obligation is somewhat akin to galley-slavery. I was *born* into the *polis* in a way that is not at all true for games of roulette, and – importantly – I can always leave the game if I choose. But I cannot leave the *polis*: where would I go? We'd have to look long and hard to find somewhere that was not likely to subject me to some sort of control but which could offer a reasonable life. A hermitic life in a largely empty country such as Mongolia might be suggested, but I would still be in Mongolia, a recognised and discrete political entity, and so the in-principle problems with living within a country and under a government would not have been avoided. There is no part of the dry surface of the planet that has not already been claimed by someone.[26] Besides this: why should it be *me* who's forced to move? Because I cannot help having been born in a particular place at a particular time, it seems unreasonable that the onus should be solely on me to do anything about it.

Someone might argue that political consent does not have to be explicit: it can be tacit. By choosing to remain within a certain *polis*, I have implicitly decided to abide by the rules of the political game. *Contra* Hume, I *could* have chosen to leap from the ship of state if life aboard was so intolerable – but I chose not to. Hence there *was* consent, and Hume was in error after all. However, there are plenty of reasons to think that tacit consent is bogus. The first argument is that it mistakes accordance for compliance. It is entirely possible to suppose that one might live one's whole life according to the laws of a given *polis* without ever once thinking that they are legitimate. For example, I might freely choose to drive on the left and to interpret a red light at a road junction as an instruction to proceed no further until it turns to green. However, this does not mean that I am tacitly allowing that the highway code has anything to it that might count as binding; it does not even mean that I am aware that there is such a thing as the highway code in the first place. It is just that I am aware that, if I want to keep my car (and myself) in reasonably good shape, it pays to comply with certain conventions. Similarly, I may get insurance because I feel that, were I to run someone over, I would have a moral duty to compensate them – or simply because I recognise that my life is easier with this kind of cover. This does not *begin* to mean that I have tacitly accepted the traffic laws. Or, to continue Hume's analogy, a galley slave might (bizarrely) enjoy the physical exercise of rowing, and might have chosen to spend his life doing something that looked like galley-slavery. This does not mean that he is no longer a slave, though, or that he would consent to *this* life on *this* ship.

There are other reasons for thinking that tacit consent is a sham. Notably, it seems plain that an unwillingness to comply with the wishes of the state will land

---

25   Hume, *Of the Original Contract*, in Barker, 1960, p. 156.

26   I suppose that there might be the odd rock in the Pacific Ocean, but what kind of life would this be? There is little doubt that it would be all but impossible – and this rather makes Hume's point for him.

us in trouble. There is not only a pragmatic reason to consent tacitly, but also a prudential one. However, consent on this basis is deeply unreliable: it is not anything like a free choice. Imagine that I happen to run a business in territory that is 'owned' by a certain criminal mastermind. He lets me know that I can do as he says – pay him protection money, refrain from entering the waste disposal business (which he controls) and so on – or I can suffer the consequences of his anger. If I choose to play along, he will not only leave me unscathed, but he will also see to it that no one else will threaten my property: if I am burgled, he assures me, I need only ask him for help and he will put his goons at my disposal. I choose to play along and enjoy his protection as a result; he claims that, having accepted his largesse (not breaking my legs, putting his goons at my disposal should I ever need them), I have accepted the situation as a business proposition between friends and partners. Unequal partners, maybe; but partners none the less.

Does this mean that I have consented to living under the law as dictated by Tony Soprano? Not at all. I have just tried to avoid having my legs broken. Receiving the benefits of a protection racket does not make this any more of a willing transaction; a promise that no one *else* will threaten my property is not much of a promise. Commonsense morality tells me that I'm entitled to expect that no one *at all* would threaten it. If I agree that I have entered into a partnership with him, this is only because I had no real choice in the matter. It is a partnership without any of the characteristics of a partnership.

Is the *polis* so different? Or is Cosa Nostra a *polis*-like institution? Arguably the latter. It demands that I pay my protection money – taxes – and that I refrain from entering the security-provision business – which it controls – lest I suffer consequences such as imprisonment. It claims that my acceptance of its benefits means that I am obliged to it. I make use of the streetlights, the roads, the schools and so on. I therefore must obey rules such as handing over taxes. But what else am I supposed to do? How can I get to the record shop *without* using roads?[27] Can I really expect streetlights to go out as I pass under them? (What if I'm walking with someone who willingly pays taxes? Would they dim to half their brightness?)

Perhaps my use of the police and fire brigade might be slightly different; insofar as I could choose not to use their services, perhaps their standing in relation to my having bought into the system tacitly is different. On the other hand, these only tend to get called on when the world is already suboptimal, and so their value as freely chosen must take this into account. Moreover, it would be at least notionally possible to pay for their services on an ad-hoc basis: £5 to have a policeman tell me the proper Greenwich time, £300 for rescuing my cat from a tree, and so on. We could buy insurance policies to cover these costs: but the crucial part is that they would be

---

27   The BBC used to run an advertisement in which a man leapt across the rooftops of London in order to be back home in time for an evening in front of *EastEnders* (a UK soap opera). Or someone might invest in some sort of jetpack that can get him from door to door without ever touching any public highway. I suppose that these might be alternatives, but I am going to pretend that they are not. I do not think that I have to pretend very hard.

chosen rather than *imposed*. That these ideas are of Heath-Robinson impracticality does not dent the *moral* argument for them. That a morally optimal world is equally impossible does not ameliorate the moral problems with the world as it stands.

If there is an obvious difference between the *polis* and the Mafia, it would seem so far to be one of degree rather than of kind. The difference is that leg-breaking is (I assume) more immediately threatening and more painful than a term in prison. However, the underlying idea – do *x* lest unpleasantness befall you – is the same in both cases. From a *moral* point of view, then, there is not much yet to differentiate the two: we must concede either that the Mafia is a *polis*-like institution, or that the *polis* is morally dubious. This, then, seems to represent another fault line in the moral bedrock of the *polis*. Although it is not directly related to the problem of terrorism, the argument still suggests that the *polis* might be something that, properly considered, ought to be treated with moral suspicion.

There is yet another route that might be able to legitimise the *polis* and rescue me from galley-slavery. This route depends on a distinction being drawn between tacit and implicit consent. Some people might have implicitly, rather than tacitly, consented to political membership: the most obvious class of person to whom this might apply is the immigrant. There would seem to be a good argument to say that immigrants chose to be there, and so *have* entered into a contract, albeit one that is so informally drawn up that it does not require verbalisation. Their allegiance is not forced upon them. But there are problems even with this view: it would seem to compel us to say that *only* people such as immigrants have any duty to obey the law, for example. Further, they might have come (say) to Britain without intending to become British. There is a difference between choosing to come to Britain and choosing to go to the most convenient place that springs to mind that offers a decent life: they might have every intention to return 'home' the minute it stops raining bullets or can afford to educate their children. People who arrive through desperation do not look like contractors. Hence expectations of consent from *anyone* seem to be in need of serious scaffolding; the most we can expect is that the social contract is something that could only be signed by those who, for whatever reason, have made an uncoerced and unforced decision to relocate from the place of their birth to another. So few are these people that the idea of a social contract being at the heart of social relations is absurd.

The Blurred Borders

There are two further defences available to the *polis*. The first would be to argue that, whatever its demerits, membership of a *polis* does, at least, offer the hope of a restoration of the moral balance at some time in the future. Maybe tacit consent is a sham; maybe implicit consent is not much better; maybe there is no contract; maybe the *polis* does intimidate coercively. But it allows peace and a medium in which humans, qua moral agents, can flourish. This is an argument that I shall allow to be restated in Chapter 3 in relation to Aristotelian ethics. The argument, though, would have to take a form along lines like these: that the *polis* is *uniquely* capable of preparing the ground upon which justice can come to fruition *sufficiently to outweigh the moral problems of political membership.* The problem with this argument is that it is heavily dependent on pretty dubious support. For one thing, it demands that we accept that the *polis* really will be vindicated in whatever actions it takes now. There is no obvious reason even to think that this might be possible, let alone to think that it will happen; hence it is a sizeable task to show that in the future, let alone at the present, there is justification of the state along these lines.

The other belief that we have to swallow is that the terrorist *cannot* promise future compliance with our commonsense moral expectations. This second belief asks even more than the first. Why should we distrust, a priori, the claims made by the terrorist? I have already argued that there is plenty of mileage in the thought that a terrorist might make some kind of appeal to deferred justice. Granted: he might not be able in practical terms to meet the target he has set for himself, but the same surely applies to the *polis* in a relevantly similar measure. And there are other reasons to reject the idea that we should, a priori, distrust the terrorist. Consider, for example, the assassins who shot Reinhard Heydrich in 1942 or those who tried to kill Hitler in 1944. Under normal circumstances, their actions might be considered as terroristic: certainly the assassination of Aldo Moro or of Louis Mountbatten was seen as such. However, circumstances were *not* normal, and it would be difficult to prove that the assassination had no moral backing. The assassins believed that they were acting to help bring about a better world: there is precious little reason to think that they were misguided in their beliefs; and even if they *had* been misguided, we would still have to deal with the possibility of their having committed a noble error. The same might well be said of at least some terrorists.

Hence appealing to deferred justice as a defence of political existence over political violence is not much of an appeal, and does as much damage to the *polis*'s case as it does to the terrorist's. The best for which the *polis* can hope when it argues along these lines is that it makes itself look as *bad* as the terrorist organisation – but it might equally well end up making the terrorist look as *good* as the *politikon zōon*. Hence, after all, this attempt to draw a clear distinction between the *polis* and the terrorist turns out to be not as clear as all that. And, besides: even if the argument *does* work against the terrorist, it can do so only on condition that we look at matters consequentially. A Kantian would not care that the *polis* can offer deferred justice: what matters is the maxim that informs an action – and there is no necessary reason to think that the *polis* will be particularly well served by Kantian considerations.

Finally, the civil society might be able to offer one more, last gasp, difference between itself and terrorism. This is roughly that it does not contravene the principle of desert. This is not so strong an argument as it may seem at first, for the very simple reason that Émile Henry did not contravene the principle (or, at least, did not think he did), and the other type of terrorist is, in a sense, vaccinated against the argument (as I have outlined above); the importance of desert is not a necessary component of accounts of political action, and so it is something that can be discounted in at least some situations. Let us not strain a weak argument. Let us act as if it is strong: as if Henry clearly did contravene the principle of desert, and as if making this point to Ulrike Meinhof would give her pause. Even so, there is *still* no reason to think that the *polis* is in a particularly strong position. This is a claim that rests on the relationship between desert and responsibility.

Commonsense morality would insist that the civilians killed in a bombing did not deserve to be killed. But for them not to have deserved to be *killed* does not vitiate the idea that they might rightly have been held jointly responsible for the perceivedly unjust actions of the state. Commonsense morality would insist that this, too, is not the case: that there is no moral trickledown from the state to the citizenry. However, for this to be true, it would have to be proven that they had *nothing at all* to with the state's actions. This claim is only sustainable if we abandon the idea of tacit consent: a population that consents tacitly to a government or set of governmental actions should be willing to take responsibility for having permitted that government or those actions. But a *polis* that is willing to abandon tacit consent in this sort of circumstance must obviously have abandoned its confidence in tacit consent per se.

The *polis* thus faces a dilemma. The first horn of the dilemma can appear in one of two forms, and is this: it must admit either (a) that *every one* of its citizens has consented to its existence and is therefore jointly responsible for it, or (b) that, irrespective of consent, a person's public existence is inseparable from his private existence,[28] in which case everyone is complicit to some extent and therefore is a legitimate target (and there really are no innocents: no one, that is, wholly innocent of state activities as long as they are enfranchised) – and settling on either version of this horn destigmatises the terrorist. The only alternative open to the *polis* is to settle on the other horn of the dilemma, and admit that it is making claims over, and demands of, its population that are unwarranted – which stigmatises civil society.

Overall, then, the picture that remains is one in which another of the boundaries between the *polis* and the terrorist is not as clear as it might have appeared. Retaining a precise distinction means that the *polis* has to sacrifice one of its own claims to legitimacy. The problem can be put more crudely: if government is by, of and for the people, then a dispute with the government must be, de facto, a dispute with the people.

Perhaps there is a difference between children and adults. But if this is the only difference, it does not seem to give us what commonsense morality demands. It is counterintuitive to think that anyone to whom the franchise has been extended is a fair target. Commonsense wants a tool that it can use against terrorists of all kinds, not just some terrorists on some occasions. I suspect that it would be unwilling to accept the proposition that the only thing that is wrong with terrorism is that it harms the disenfranchised. In short: what I hope I have shown over the last few pages is that there are plenty of circumstances in which the arguments that commonsense morality might offer against terrorism could be turned against something as intuitively morally acceptable as the democratic *polis*. Similarly, the commonsense moral arguments that might be offered on behalf of civil society could also be used by the terrorist as

---

28   See the position described in Dworkin, 1992, pp. 216 ff.

something that might work in his own favour. There is nothing obvious that could secure the moral border between the two political phenomena. The question, then, is whether there is *anything* to back up the moral intuition that there is a serious difference between the *polis* and political violence. *What* might back up a moral claim about the *polis* and terrorism?

Opening the Question

If things that are supposedly as obviously different as terrorism and civil society can be shown to have serious moral similarities, then it is not unreasonable to begin to question whether a claim such as 'terrorism is wrong' really is true. But, because it is self-evident to commonsense morality that terrorism really *is* wrong, it seems that we also ought to be asking very serious questions about what it is that allows us to make that sort of judgement in the first place: what might give *any* moral claim its truth. If we can be so deeply mistaken about the moral values of terrorism and civil society, it behoves us to look at our ability to make reliable moral judgements *period*. Note that this is something that seems to hold irrespective of whether or not 'terrorism is wrong' turns out to be true after all – the mere fact that there is a putative ambiguity to the statement is enough to cause problems. The question of terrorism translates very quickly to a wider question about the justifications of commonsense moral intuitions.

So; is there anything that might be able to offer us a basis for a moral belief? What is it – if anything – that informs the moral claims and judgements that we make and guarantees the possibility of their accuracy? This is the problem that will occupy me for the remainder of this study. The explicit question of terrorism will take a less dominant position from here on, but this is deliberate: I have been using it to jemmy my way into wider moral questions about what, if anything, might back up commonsense morality per se. If I can find nothing to back up these intuitions in general, then there is obviously nothing that can back up intuitions on any number of particular questions. Having said this, the problem of terrorism will recur as a testing-board fairly frequently.

As I hinted above, my argument in the next couple of chapters is that there *is* nothing in mainstream metaethics that can give much of a bulwark to commonsense morality. This is not a problem with the *content* of commonsense morality; *whatever* our moral thoughts, they would have precious little to sustain them. With this in mind, the thematic first half of the study will proceed roughly as follows.

First, Chapter 2 will look at a line of thought that I shall call 'independentist'. Independentism holds that at least some acts and events have a property or set of properties such as to bestow on them a moral value, and that these properties obtain irrespective of any fact about the observer; the truth of a moral claim is a function of how well it reflects that property. Independentism can take one of two forms. In its realist form, independentism amounts to the claim that these value-bestowing properties would be in principle detectable in an act or event even in an otherwise empty universe. In its idealist form, independentism denies that there is anything *real* about the moral characteristics of an act or event, but it insists that all the same thinking about certain acts or events is constrained in such a way as to make it inconceivable for them not to have their particular moral value. For neither the realist nor the idealist does the identity of the individual have any impact on truth of a moral claim. The foci of the chapter will be Plato and Kant, but the use that I make of them will be synecdochial – the more general intention will be an examination of the notion that there is definitively a right and a wrong way to behave that is not at least partially based on the propensities of any given agent.

I will argue that this approach simply does not work: whatever norms independentism might be able to provide are untrustworthy and unsustainable because of their metaphysical commitments.

Then, having rejected 'independentist' approaches to normativity, I will shift my focus in Chapter 3 to 'dependentist' approaches. Dependentism holds that at least some acts and events have a non-moral property or set of non-moral properties such as to make them apt to have a moral value attributed to them. The truth of a moral claim is a function of an agent's response to those properties. Dependentism, like independentism, can take one of two forms, which I shall call Aristotelian and Humean. The Aristotelian approach is predicated upon beliefs that an agent may have about himself or the object of his concern; the Humean approach is predicated simply on the desires and preferences of the agent, and he need have no particular beliefs about himself. Either way, the claim is that the content of a concept like 'good' depends on the context in which it is conceived and who is conceiving it.

Dependentism is an inversion of independentism, and this inversion translates to the critique I will offer. Dependentism tries to get around the metaphysical weaknesses of independentism, but it is far better at describing norms and moral expectations than it is at making anything particularly substantial of them. The dependentist's norms lack bite: if two people disagree in good faith about the truth of a moral claim, he has no obvious way to tell who has made the error, or even (in some cases) whether there has been an error made at all – and without this, there is scant hope for the possibility of compelling norms. Any attempt to solve this problem relies on the dependentist smuggling in independentism's assumptions; this is metaphysically odd if it is done unconsciously; and if done consciously it is an act of bad faith.

In other words, the argument will be that, in independentism, one can have morality that is metaphysically untrustworthy and the claims of which are only dubiously 'true', and that dependentism gets around the problem of metaphysical untrustworthiness only by sacrificing the normative power that is one of the defining characteristics of morality.

By the end of the first part of the study, I think that things will look pretty bleak for anyone who wants to be able to back up commonsense morality. I make no claim that I can give a definitive refutation of traditional approaches to metaethics, of course: there is always going to be a possibility that someone could solve the problems that I set out. However, solving the problems with an approach is not the same as vindicating it: after having shown that their approaches *could* support commonsense morality, the defenders of independentism and dependentism alike would *still* then have to show that their approach *is* what underpins it.

I hope that I can circumvent this. I shall not spend too much time giving all the details of the arguments that might be mooted in favour of one approach or another, because I shall be suggesting that there is no *need* to go into such detail. Chapter 4 will put forward a way in which we can understand the basis for commonsense morality and provide it with normative bite without the problems: extravagant defences of independentism and dependentism are unnecessary. For Ockhamite reasons, this feeds into a powerful intuition that there is no need to mount them. Admittedly, my suggestion will mean a certain re-evaluation of moral philosophy, and so I will have to sacrifice *some* of my plan to leave moral philosophy as I find it: I will deal with this as and when it is important. This will come to a head in the final chapter, when I will demand a serious rethink of what ethics is about; but even here, I will simply be drawing on other people's work. I will still be leaving things as I find them – I will simply be finding different things. I will only really explain the last two chapters when I get to them, though: for the time being, I think that this would just confuse matters. But first: mainstream moral philosophy and commonsense.

Chapter 2

Independentism: Moral Truth
and the Lack Thereof

So what is it that backs up moral intuitions such as that which tells us that the *polis* is morally better than violence and that statements to this effect are true and compelling? There is a good deal of overlap between how the two might be evaluated: in the most practical and down-to-earth terms, the terrorist and the democrat might well share moral beliefs and aims. Hence the intuition, which I think fair to ascribe to most, that there is a substantial moral difference between them is not as easy to substantiate as one might think it to be at first glance. We can't easily say that terrorists are bad people and democrats are good people and then stand by our judgement without due diligence as to what a term such as 'good' might mean and to what grants accuracy in its application. If it is true that terrorism is wrong and democratic politics is not (as) wrong, we still have to find some basis for this thought.

We can look at the problem this way: perhaps we could say that terrorism kills, that killing is wrong, and that therefore terrorism is wrong. But the question that we might then face is one concerning whether it is *true* that killing is wrong. Granted that, if true, such a claim might be normatively compelling, upon what basis might we accept it *as* true? (I will leave to one side the points that democracies can kill – some have the death penalty – and some people think that it is worth killing in the name of democracy.)

Independentism and Dependentism

I'm going to capitalise on what appears to be a fairly natural division of traditional moral thinking into two classes. This chapter will deal with (and problematise) the mode of thought that I have named 'independentist'; predictably enough, the next chapter will deal with (and problematise) the class that I have named 'dependentist'. I have taken the liberty of coining my own names for the classes because I'm not quite sure that the existing terminology will provide me with what I want. I considered using 'moral realism' to suggest that there are real criteria somewhere 'out there', but this would have ruled out Kant, who is germane to what I want to argue in this chapter. I could have used 'moral objectivism' for one chapter, and 'moral subjectivism' for the other. However, had I chosen this route, I think that Aristotle would have been pertinent to both, and to have him straddling two chapters in this way would have been to complicate matters unnecessarily. (Admittedly,

Aristotle will make a cameo appearance in this chapter, but no more.) A word like 'deontology' would have meant forcing Plato into the next chapter, which would disrupt the structure of the argument I want to put. Finally, I rejected a 'naturalism' *versus* 'non-naturalism' format because the position I will be advocating in Chapter 4 could be seen as non-naturalist, and I do not think that it would really have been wise to run the risk of arguing against a position with which I will later claim some affinity. 'Independentism' *versus* 'dependentism' it is, then.

The basic hope of moral theory of both the independentist and dependentist stripe is to find the characteristic that gives an action or class of action its moral status so that moral assertions about it can be true and, on that basis, potentially compelling. Independentism wants that characteristic to be built into the object of our moral judgement, so that when we make such a judgement, we're talking about an action or class of action rather than about *our responses* thereto. Independentism itself can be divided into two subtraditions. On the one hand there is a realist version, which suggests that there is a self-contained fact of the matter woven into the fabric of reality that can serve as a foundation for moral thought, and which I shall call 'realist independentism', or 'RI' for short. Some things just *are* right or wrong, good or bad by virtue of some characteristic or property that they possess in and of themselves. These characteristics would provide a source for accurate moral evaluations even if there was no judge nearby; and, were there a judge, his evaluations, made correctly, would represent more than matters of taste: there would be a moral touchstone outside of us. On the other, there is an idealist version of independentism – 'II' for short – that suggests that certain moral conclusions are inescapable and woven into the fabric of thought about the world, rather than the world itself (which, certainly if we're Kantians, might be unknowable in any sense).

I shall take Plato as an exemplar of the realist tradition; his contention (most explicit in the *Republic*) is that the features of the observed world are traceable back to a reality that lies behind those appearances. This reality, the suprasensible world of Forms, is what allows objects to take on an appearance in the first place[1] and 'give objects of knowledge their truth and the knower's mind the power of knowing'.[2] Essentially, appearances give a clue about reality, and the possibility of making a true statement about moral matters (or anything else) rests on learning to see the world aright. We can use those appearances to help us get to grips with the truth, but we should, of course, be aware that they might be misleading. Still, there is a reality – a moral fact of the matter – to be found if we want it.

On this sort of basis, something can truly be said to be good if it has Goodness as an inbuilt characteristic, separate from the display of goodness. I shall discuss Plato more later; however, we should be wary of thinking that Plato represents all realist independentist possibilities. Other realists are not – or, at least, claim not to be – so metaphysically extravagant; moreover, even those who can tolerate the metaphysical cost of the Platonic picture need not accept its content: a hedonist could be a kind

---

1   Plato, 1987 , 509b.
2   Ibid., 508e.

of Platonist, for example. All the hedonist has to share with Plato is the opinion that there is something about the way the world works that determines what the good is, irrespective of whether there is any sentient being in the universe to experience it. For the hedonist, it could be a fact of the world that pleasure is the highest good. Plato would dispute this. But he would do so by positing that it is a fact of the world that something else is the highest good: he would not dispute that there is a moral fact of the matter.

For Plato, the hedonist, and any other person inclined towards RI, there is something about moral inquiry that bears an analogy to research into, say, the Hubble constant: just as cosmologists might dispute *what* the constant is, but are all, at root, chasing the same thing, so philosophers might disagree whether something is good, but still have in common the idea that there is a way to definitively settle such arguments, and that this way will be by reference to an accurate account of the thing in question. Having said all this, I do not think that it is really necessary to spend too much time on RI; for my purposes, a fairly basic exposition will be enough. It won't take long to show what problems face the realist independentist and that it takes a lot to get around them.

As hinted above, distinct from the realist approach, there is an idealist approach. This approach, and the account that it gives of the truth of a moral claim, is slightly more complicated. For idealist theorists, there is no moral characteristic that obtains separately from the moral agent. Hence, ontologically, an idealist moral theory such as Kant's is ostensibly not independentist: in a world without creatures of the right sort, there would be no moral truths to be had. However, if we look at matters in another way, there is easily enough to justify the contention that idealists can be independentist, since they do not think that ontological independence is all that important. What *is* important is that the *content* of any given moral scheme is and must be independent of the individual moral theoretician. Without the theoretician, there is, *stricto sensu*, no moral scheme; but what goes into that moral scheme, once its construction gets underway, is not something that depends on the theoretician, since its content will be determined by the rules of thought, rather than by the proclivities of the thinker. As the content of a moral scheme is unravelled, it will be revealed to be the same as every other scheme, and the theoretician will learn something about the world around him not just as it seems to him, but as it must seem to any agent.

Hence *whenever* and *wherever* there is a creature with the right intellectual capacities (and there is no reason to think that this creature has to be human), so will there be not only *a* moral law, but *the same* moral law, and this law will provide the test of the truth of a moral statement (again, I shall probe this more later). The content of moral theory is the same for all, independent of all, and demands the agreement of all. However, I hope to show later in this chapter that idealist independentism, to be particularly strong, needs support that is metaphysically questionable. By the end of the chapter, I hope to have raised enough problems with independentism of both varieties to justify looking elsewhere for support for commonsense moral intuitions.

Realist Independentism

The first candidate metaethical theory that I shall examine is realist independentism. RI contends that moral values are both real and valid independently of the observer – that is, that there is a criterion by which we might judge the truth or falsity of a moral statement that obtains irrespective of any facts about the person doing the judging. Indeed, the thought is that, even if no one is doing or even *prepared* to do any judging, the moral characteristics, qua characteristics, would be there all the same. In other words, the claim is that there is a free-standing moral reality, that, since appearance might differ from one observer to another, the association between reality and appearance is not necessary, and that a true moral statement is possible if it captures the moral features of the world accurately. It is the moral reality of matters that allows the possibility that any particular action could be right or wrong.

Just as a hackneyed statement such as 'snow is white' is true if and only if snow is white when 'is white' means something like 'is apt to reflect light of all wavelengths in the visible spectrum equally', so a statement such as 'terrorism is wrong' is true iff terrorism is wrong when 'is wrong' means 'has inbuilt characteristics of a certain moral sort'. So, given the problem of terrorism outlined in Chapter 1, RI would offer the possibility of a solution based on an appeal to some independent reality: an irreducible fact about the world and the things that go on therein, or about the people who act in the world. Naturally, in order to avoid the charge of begging the normative question, it might be necessary for the RI theorist to concede that investigation of the moral realities could reveal there to be *no* significant backing for any number of commonsense moral claims – including the claim about the difference between terrorism and civil society – but, even here, at least we could admit that we had settlement on the issue: either the true moral status of terrorism accords with commonsense morality, or it does not. If it does, then this is a boon for commonsense morality. If it doesn't, then this is just too bad. Commonsense needs reform.

Moreover, establishing the truth of a claim that something is right or wrong or that a person really is good or bad would give normative weight to our moral statements. If it can be shown that a certain action, kind of action, or person has a certain definitive moral characteristic, then it looks as though a participant in a notional moral argument has armed himself with the means to provide agents with a reason to act or not to act in such and such a way. This reason may not yet be *sufficient* to guarantee behaviour, but it would seem, intuitively at least, to be a big factor. Thus realist independentism seems to be able to furnish moral statements with both first- and second-order moral features as I described them in the last chapter.

However, despite its promising appearance, the RI account is unlikely to succeed because the truth-claims that it wants to make are, in the end, unsustainable. In addition, I think that there are problems about normativity in RI theory, but, by and large, I shall let these pass: I do not think that I need to worry too much about them given that I am going to argue that there is a good reason to doubt the truth of the moral claims upon which any norms might be based. Were someone to draw on RI to say to the notional terrorist that his actions are wrong or that he is a bad person, he would be able to allow that, should the claim be substantial, it might impact on his behaviour; but I think that there would be no requirement for him to accept the claim as substantial. And this makes it normatively weak by default.

To begin with, things do look promising for RI. The realist account is, roughly, that the world at least appears to contain moral features, and that the best explanation for the appearance of these moral features is that they are provided by something specifically and irreducibly *moral*. (This contrasts with a feature such as a colour, which, although a feature that the world appears to contain, is reducible to the surface characteristics of the object at which we are looking, and so is not 'real' in a strong sense.) There is a class of characteristics that can bestow virtue or vice upon an act or event. Moreover, the realist claims that, in Alexander Miller's words:

> we can view moral properties as part of the natural fabric of the world for the same reason that we can view, for example, physical, chemical or biological facts as part of the fabric of the natural world, namely, *that they pull their weight in explanatory theories*.[3]

According to the realist claim, an account of the world that has room for real moral properties is better at explaining the world as we find it than is any account that does not make room for such properties.

A parallel is often drawn with certain experiments in physics – notably experiments with Wilson cloud chambers.[4] Here, observed phenomena could be explained in a number of ways, including the way that attributes them to the existence of protons. In a sense, the existence of protons has a kind of causal influence on the formation of our beliefs – these beliefs about the world are at least partly prompted and underwritten by the actual existence of such things as protons. Of course, the evidence for the existence of protons is indirect, and the possibility can never be wholly discounted that our proton-beliefs may be funded by some essential misunderstanding of the world. However, this is not in itself something about which we need to worry too much. After all, it is true, but only trivially so, that *every* account of the world is equally framed by the limits of our knowledge; what counts is that, given that the world appears to be thus-and-so, certain accounts are better than others at explaining that appearance.

Moreover, and more importantly, proton-beliefs gather support from a range of sources. Other observations in other contexts sustain a belief in (things like) protons that can be brought in to support the proton-explanation for cloud-chamber phenomena; that is, the (things like) protons hypothesised by other areas of physical research can solve problems in cloud-chamber research, so that, even if the belief in protons was not independently viable, we would have enough circumstantial evidence to put together a pretty strong case for their existence. Such circumstantial evidence can deal with the point that particle physics can hypothesise that there are such things as protons, but if the only evidence for such things were the phenomena of the cloud chamber, we would not be in a good position. After all, it is not inconceivable that

---

3   Miller, 2003, pp 140.
4   Ibid., *passim*; see also, *inter alia*, Wiggins, 1987, Sturgeon, 1988, Wright, 1992.

some people may attribute the cloud-chamber phenomena to the activities of pixies: the existence of protons could therefore also have a causal influence on our belief in such beings, inasmuch as someone could still cite cloud-chamber phenomena as evidence for their existence and activity, and, *ceteris paribus*, do so with just as great a claim to credibility as anyone else. Similarly, there would be no a priori reason not to think that the observed phenomena might simply be illusory. But, of course, pixie-theorists lose plausibility when we widen our focus: the account of what goes on in cloud-chambers is not the end of the story.

Cloud-chamber observations, then, are not taken in isolation – many other observations either contribute directly to the theory that protons exist, or serve as indirect support. The beliefs of particle physics lend support to each other, and, though the whole network *may* one day collapse, such doubts could, with justification, be taken as hyperbolic, for every new observation adds a little to strengthen the whole lot. By contrast, there have been (as far as I am aware) no other observations that could lend comparable support, direct or indirect, to the pixie theory of cloud-chamber phenomena. For example, while one might seek to measure the charge of a hypothesised proton and subsequently slot this information into the structure of the proton-explanation of cloud-chamber phenomena, one could not perform the same measurement with a pixie – any plausible tests that one could carry out along these lines would do little more than draw us to the conclusion that whatever is referred to by the word 'pixie' is the same thing as is referred to by the word 'proton' in standard English. Equally, though physicists have, at times, been taken in by illusion – Blondlot's contagious belief in N-rays might serve as a salutary lesson here[5] – the fact that the belief in protons meshes well with other beliefs suggests that the illusion-theorist is in a considerably weaker position than the proton-theorist.

Overall, the point is that an account of the world that hypothesises real things – protons – is better at explaining the world as it is presently understood than a hypothesis that puts the phenomena in the cloud chamber down to the activities of pixies, or that insists that those phenomena are merely illusory. *Per analogiam*, says RI, an account of the world that hypothesises real moral characteristics is better at explaining the world as it is currently understood than is the best of the other alternatives. Hence, for the realist independentist, in what I shall call the RI-argument:

---

5   René Blondlot was the head of physics at Nancy University, and in 1903 published a paper in which he claimed to have discovered a new form of radiation: N-rays. This was not, in itself, an implausible claim, especially given the youth of research into radiation at the time, and it was taken seriously in the scientific community. There are, of course, no such things as N-rays: Blondlot had been taken in by an optical illusion, and his N-ray hypothesis did a less good job of explaining the observed world than did the theory that the eye contains rods and cones that respond differently to normal light. N-ray theory was condemned to fail because there was no supporting evidence. However, the falsity of the theory did not prevent a flurry of research into the phenomenon. For a fuller account of the story, see Chapter 4 of Paul Collins' *Banvard's Folly*.

P$_1$ P is a real property iff P figures ineliminably in the best explanation of experience.

P$_2$ Moral properties figure ineliminably in the best explanation of moral experience.

C   Therefore moral properties are real properties.[6]

And, as Nicholas Sturgeon points out, although notionally real moral principles may lack support when considered on their own, there is reason to think that real moral properties figure in the best explanation of experience because we can 'allow ourselves, as we do in the scientific case, to rely on a background of other assumptions of comparable status'.[7]

Moreover, moral realism gives us a strategy for dealing with moral statements that are counterintuitive and for deciding whether it is the intuition or the statement that is at fault. Again, the analogy is with natural science. A freshman's unexpected and counterintuitive chemistry result may appear to present a problem for the atomic theory of gasses, but it would do so only if it was taken in isolation. However, because it the atomic theory of gasses sits comfortably in a protective belt of supplementary theories and observations (including, we must admit, the belief that freshmen are more likely simply to have fouled up the experiment than discovered something earth-shattering), it is possible to say that the counterintuitive result is, in all probability, false. Moral claims, RI theory says, are testable in roughly the same way: it is easy to derive tests that allow us to strip the deadwood from any *set* of moral claims, and it is the fact that we are dealing with *sets* of moral claims that is important. For example, a claim to the effect that Hitler was morally admirable, taken alongside 'a modest piece of moral theory to the effect that no morally admirable person would … instigate and oversee the degradation and death of millions of persons' allows us to draw the testable conclusion that Hitler did not do this. But, testing the conclusion (say, by adverting to history books), we learn that Hitler *did* do this, which means that, according to the rules of deductive reasoning, we must ditch one of our premises. And it is not difficult to figure out which of them it is that has to go.[8] Hence a fairly elementary set of moral principles allows us to reach moral conclusions about persons, acts and events that are true, or, at the very least, truth-tracking: a claim that Hitler was an admirable human being is, we might allow, plausible in isolation, but, taken alongside other beliefs about the criteria for moral admiration, can be shown to be untenable. But, the RI theorist will claim, the possibility of untenability in such a claim implies that there is a moral fact of the matter.

> We find it easy to conclude from the evidence not just that Hitler was not morally admirable, but that he was morally depraved. But is not it plausible that Hitler's moral depravity – the

---

6   After Miller, 2003, pp. 140–41.

7   Sturgeon, 1988, p. 231.

8   Ibid., p. 232.

fact of his really having been morally depraved – forms part of a reasonable explanation of why we believe he was depraved?[9]

Sturgeon thinks so.

Would we be correct to agree? It is not at all clear that we would, and there is a range of reasons for rejecting realist independentism. The first reason is, broadly, that it is metaphysically extravagant: in fact, its affinities with Plato's theory of the Forms are unavoidable. Both theories imply that appearances imply a reality that it irreducible *to* those appearances, and that they may nevertheless provide a clue about that reality when they are treated in the right way. But the correlate of this is that, for more or less the same reason that most of us are suspicious of Platonic Formalism, so we ought to be suspicious of RI. The defender of RI theory may want to respond, of course, that whatever affinities with Platonism his thought has are incidental; he is likely to insist that RI has much more in common with natural science, and that, in arguing against RI, one is implicitly also arguing against a great deal that is not problematic at all – in fact, I am adopting a sceptical line that leaves our understanding of the world a good deal worse than it actually is. However, I think that there is a serious difference between the functioning of an RI theory of morality and that of natural science (to the extent that a version of Platonism in natural science is still acceptable), which I shall outline in a little while. However, this difference leads to my second broad reason for rejecting RI theory, which is this: however extravagant RI theory might be, the possibility that it does provide the best possible explanation of moral experience all the same is unlikely. Against RI, I shall ally myself with those who argue that, far from providing the best possible explanation of moral experience, the ascription of moral experience to moral 'reality' contributes *nothing at all* to the explanation of that experience except, perhaps, to shuffle things around a bit. Therefore the extravagance cannot be presented as a simple, albeit large, investment that will pay comparably large dividends: there never will be any return.

Realist Independentism and Queer Science

Pivotal to RI is the idea that is expressed in the first premise of the RI argument above: that P is a real property iff P figures ineliminably in the best explanation of experience. What is important to note here is that a distinction is drawn between the experience and the explanation of the experience – that is to say, between experience and what causes that experience. This distinction is what makes RI distinctively *realistic*: in the absence of such a distinction, whatever remained of RI would be something to which an idealist – especially an idealist of the Berkeleyan mould – could happily subscribe. In other words, the point that is being made by the RI theorist is that the object of moral enquiry is not limited to the 'mere' moral experience; rather, there is something ineliminably moral 'behind' that experience

---

9   Ibid., p. 234.

capable of explaining it that is worthy of investigation. (Presumably, of course, even if there is no moral experience, this will not tell against the possibility of something having a moral property or set of moral properties: it just means that, for whatever reason, no one has noticed them yet.)

So, it is the moral reality behind moral experience that provides that experience, and an account that includes moral reality is more reliable than its rivals such as idealism, in rather the same way that the proton hypothesis provides a better explanation of cloud-chamber experience than does the pixie hypothesis. What is striking in the first place about this account is just how similar it is to that offered by Plato. He, too, is willing to draw a serious distinction between our experience of reality and that reality itself – between, that is, the 'intelligibility of the objects of knowledge' and 'their being and reality'.[10] In Plato's thought, it is reality that bankrolls all experience (or, at least, all 'genuine' experience: plausibly we can discount illusion, although, like the shadows on the wall of the cave, even that would owe its provenance ultimately to a reality that has simply been misperceived). Without an underlying determinate reality, cashed out for Plato in the currency of the theory of the Forms, appearances would be neither apparent nor intelligible;[11] it is the Forms that 'give objects of knowledge their truth and the knower's mind the power of knowing'.[12] In terms of broadly ethical concerns, Plato's claim is that Formal moral 'reality' can be inferred 'to be responsible for whatever is valuable and right in anything'.[13]

Although Plato seems to think that there is just one Formal standard of Virtue that underpins all apparent virtue and there is no reason to suppose that RI must be so reductive, the point should be clear: when the RI theorist talks about experience and the explanation of experience, it is moral reality that bankrolls moral experience in roughly the same way as it is Plato's Forms that bankroll experience per se. From the supposition that experience must be causally attributable to *something*, we get the idea that it is causally attributable to substantial *reality* – in other words, that there is something *really there*. (I should point out that this assumption also drives dependentism and is something that I shall challenge in Chapter 4.)

The question that this supposition prompts concerns the ontological and epistemological status of real moral properties: just what *are* they, and how are they discerned? The problems are very well put in Mackie's 'argument from queerness':[14] *concesso non dato*, if there *were* real moral characteristics, it would still have to be explained what kind of thing they were and how they were possibly knowable. The idea that moral characteristics are discoverable through the conventional five senses is difficult to accept; characteristics such as the loudness of the aircraft passing overhead or the squareness of the picture-frame in my study are all things

---

10 Plato, 1987, 509b.
11 Ibid., 509b.
12 Ibid., 508e.
13 Ibid., 517c.
14 Mackie, 1977, *passim*.

about which we learn empirically. Yet there is no analogue with values: it is only metaphorically that evil has a stench.

Here, at least, the RI theorist would seem to be able to draw a clear distinction between his thought and Plato's. By insisting that the apparent world is merely a shadow or manifestation of Formal reality, Plato does not have to worry about how real values can inhere in the real world: the real world is no more amenable to sensory knowledge than is any notional real moral characteristic perceived therein, and correctly deciding something's moral value presents no greater difficulty than does accounting for the fact that there is a thing there in the first place. But there is little likelihood that the RI theorist will want or need to adopt such a radical solution to the problem he faces: Plato is far too willing to invent new levels of reality willy-nilly, and there is no reason why the RI theorist should feel any desire to follow this precedent.

A reasonably sophisticated proponent of RI theory might well admit that real moral characteristics are not observable directly, but have to be inferred from what we *do* see: a moral quality *an sich* may be something that we can only come to know intellectually. But, he can claim, this is not the same as admitting to metaphysical witchcraft. After all, the same can be said of a good deal of natural science, and this is a discipline that is not usually accused of witchery. All the RI theorist has to do is to point out the there is plenty that we can claim to know about the world that is not accessible through the conventional five senses, but which is no less real (or plausible) for that. This is, in a sense, the point of the cloud-chamber analogy; we may never see a proton, but this does not make it occult, and the same might go for any number of other things. Indeed, many theoretical physicists are happy to admit that our common-or-garden conception of reality is impoverished to the tune of six or seven *dimensions*; and while a ten-dimensional universe certainly is *queer*, that queerness does not on its own right provide us with a reason to dismiss post-Einstein cosmology, and there is enough evidence that can be extrapolated from the world as we *do* experience it to warrant an investment in queerness. The point is that theoretical entities such as strings or gravitons or extra dimensions are quite unlike anything in the familiar universe, and require methods of discovery quite unlike anything in the familiar universe. But this is not something about which we need to worry: such queerness does not mean they do not exist – it simply means that the universe is more queer than we might at first have thought. On reflection, we might even admit that this is not something that should surprise us.

And, in roughly the same way, understanding the nature and structure of the universe might require that we adopt some fairly queer ways of thinking. Hence, the RI theorist might say, if it is possible to hypothesise and to learn about *some* apparently bizarre aspects of the universe through thinking in a new way, then surely the same sort of account is at least plausible for moral theory. Through thinking about the world aright we can come to understand the moral realities that are waiting to be discovered therein.

In fact, and in no pejorative or problematic sense at all, Plato serves as the forerunner to this kind of account. Superficially, his claim is that the world of appearance is merely illusory, and that reality is by definition not accessible empirically: '[p]hilosophy … persuades the soul to withdraw from the senses *in so far as it is not compelled to use them*'[15] and that the trained philosopher will 'lift [his] mind's eye to look at the source of all light, and see the good itself'.[16] This reading supports a traditional attack on Plato along the lines that he is much too happy to invent whole new realms of being; however, is not the only possible reading: we might imagine that Plato is simply saying that, if we want a full and proper picture of the way that the world really is, it is necessary for us to abandon the idea that the evidence of the senses is able to tell us the whole story. All it does is set the scene, and the intellect allows us to go behind these appearances and explain *them*. (It is perhaps worth noting at this stage that John McDowell thinks that Plato is *not* guilty of the metaphysical hocus-pocus with which he is often charged. 'Plato is a naturalist of the Aristotelian sort,' he suggests, 'with a penchant for vividly realised pictorial presentations of his thought.'[17] Gadamer seems also to think that the differences between Plato and Aristotle are not as great as the tradition would have it.[18] As it happens, I disagree with this interpretation – however, it is certainly not an implausible reconstruction of Plato's position, and I will allow it room to breathe here.)

The point would be, then, that the reality of the moral characteristics of an action, class of actions or actor may be not all that unbearably queer after all. Certainly, moral realities demand that we approach them in a particular way, but this is not too big a deal – so does a range of other things, and there is nothing terribly occult about *them*. Perhaps we need a special training in order really to get to grips with moral reality – Plato thinks that his guardians will have to train until the age of fifty in order to be able to rule a city well[19] – but, again, this is not a point about which we should worry too much: a physicist will need years of special training to be able to appreciate cloud-chamber phenomena and Heisenberg's uncertainty principle for what they are. In other words, even if RI is Platonic, and even if natural science is also, in a sense, Platonic, this is not always too bad a thing, and we can allow ourselves to salvage a kind of Platonic reasoning. Ever-closer observations can lead us to an understanding of the world and the genesis of those observations that is, itself, unobservable without intellectual input.

The Rejection of Realist Independentism

Does this, then, mean that we have to admit that the metaphysical problems that we might be tempted to associate with realist independentism are not all that problematic after all? At first blush, perhaps. However, there is a serious disanalogy between what

---

15 *Phaedo* in Plato, 1981, 83a–84a; emphasis mine.

16 Plato, 1987, 540a.

17 'Two Sorts of Naturalism' in McDowell, 1998, p. 177n.

18 Gadamer, 1986.

19 Plato, 1987, 540a.

the RI theorist is doing and what the natural scientist is doing. Natural science takes observed phenomena as its starting point, but subsequently brings something new to the picture – roughly speaking, we can imagine someone gazing at a cloud chamber and asking himself whether the phenomena might be best explained by a particle of some sort. The RI theorist, though, cannot be thought of as reasoning along these lines. And, as such, he fails to establish realism: real moral characteristics do not feature in the best explanation of observed phenomena because they do not really feature in *any* explanation of observed phenomena. And this means that, even if my charge of Platonism fails, still there is no particular reason to accept RI. In fact, there is a reason *not* to accept it.

To see why this is, consider again Sturgeon's Hitler argument. The Hitler argument comprises two elements: the idea that we can draw on elementary moral theory to conclude that, among Hitler's moral characteristics, was depravity; and the idea that the word 'depravity' describes something irreducible and therefore *real* about Hitler. I have no desire to doubt the conclusion of the argument – that is, that Hitler was morally depraved: there should be nothing problematic about this for anyone. All the same, we can still ask what a term like 'moral depravity' means, and what its 'reality' might indicate. My guess is that the realist will want it to have quite a strong meaning – something like 'the possession of, or disposition to possess, a particular characteristic that is inescapably morally vicious in character'; indeed, the idea that a moral property should inhere *ineliminably* – and thereby, it is safe to assume, *irreducibly* – in the nature of moral experience backs this up. But the realist account does not exhaust the possibilities.

We can prick the realist balloon in a number of ways: by suggesting, for example, that 'moral depravity' might also simply mean that a person is seriously insensitive and antagonistic to moral considerations, however those considerations might be funded, we would force the RI theorist to show, in the first place, *that* there is something missing from our account such as to make it a less-than-complete description of the state of affairs that obtains, and, in the second place, to suggest *what* that something is. The difference is more than terminological. The non-RI interpretation does not rely on the supposition that moral considerations are about irreducibly *moral* characteristics and it is compatible therefore with an account that claims that morality is nothing more than a set of social conventions. In other words, insensitivity and antagonism towards expected behavioural norms may well be real characteristics of Hitler's psyche, but these characteristics do not have to be thought of as *moral* in any way that would satisfy the RI theorist. Hitler's depravity *may* be explained by a real moral characteristic – 'real' in the strong sense, that is, that there really was some irreducibly moral feature, depravity, that we can include in the inventory of the things inside his head – but 'depravity' may also be a portmanteau term that is cogently explained by, say, a full account of psychological, neurological and socio-historical factors, the moral aspect of which depends on our reaching a moral judgement of approval or disapproval.

If we can entertain the possibility that Hitler's moral depravity was a function of these factors that made him insensitive and antagonistic to moral considerations, we will not be committed to the idea that Hitler was morally depraved in the sense that would be meant by the RI theorist: we might equally well think that there was something in some sense wrong with or about him in a radical and terrifying, but ultimately not irreducibly moral, sense. A term like 'depravity', then, would not add anything to the explanation of his behaviour. Rather, it would serve as a mnemonic for all the things that made him what he was. It seems quite easy to suppose that a formula such as 'Hitler's depravity' describes real features about him, but that the *moral* dimension of his depravity is something that has to be projected by the observer. Brian Leiter makes the point in an impressively acid manner when he suggests that:

> if I were seeking an explanation for Hitler's conduct, and was offered the explanation 'He was morally depraved', I would take such an answer to be a bit of a joke; a repetition of the datum rather than an explanation.[20]

Neither impressiveness nor acidity, it should be noted, is a real characteristic of the comment. My description of it thus would lead one to learn something about the conventions of the elegant put-down, not its pH. The same applies to statements about Hitler: this, though, is a supposition that is directly antagonistic to that which has to be made by the RI theorist.

The question that needs to be asked at this point is, then, whether our claim that Hitler was depraved is most adequately described by an appeal to moral reality, or by an appeal to psycho-social facts. And it is the latter option that is better. Not the least of the reasons for this is that the psycho-social facts are independently testable in a way that, contrary to the implicit demands of the RI theorist, moral facts are not. We could imagine putting Hitler through various psychological tests and comparing him with others who have similar mental features but have been brought up in different circumstances to see what moral and behavioural differences there might be. (Having said that, of course, if Hitler was found to be unique, it would not necessarily be because he was the only one of our experimental set to have the relevant moral characteristic – it could simply be that anyone who occupied *exactly* the same neuro-psycho-social terrain would simply *be* Hitler.)

By contrast, the only way to test for a moral fact or real moral characteristic such as depravity would be to look at persons generally agreed to be depraved and then try to sift out the unifying factor. There is no reason to think, though, that there would be such a factor, save for the experimenter's propensity to call them all depraved – especially given the possibility that a person's depravity may be channelled only in one specific direction – and this seems simply to beg the question. With notional moral realities the evidence for the depravity (or virtue, or whatever) is taken to be depraved (or virtuous, or whatever) behaviour. In other words, the evidence for a person, act or event having a given real moral characteristic is, for the realist, nothing but the fact that it has that characteristic. This is a point that is different from, but fairly closely related to, that made by Leiter. Judging that a person, act or event

---

20 Leiter, 2001, p. 94.

has a characteristic of a certain kind presupposes already having decided that that characteristic is there *to* find; inferring the presence of a proton is not vulnerable to this circularity, though, since the inference is not based on the observation of protons, but on an observation of a quite different phenomenon, and nor is the physicist guilty of trying to find a way to show that his *ab initio* belief in protons was all right all along. After all, the evidence for the proton is not that there is a proton there – it is that certain things happen in a cloud chamber from which we can infer the presence of a proton. So when the RI theorist ropes in natural science to provide an analogical basis for his argument, he is trading on a fallacy.

Similarly, we can separate the question of the plausibility of a moral claim from the question about the reality that it is supposed to describe. We can say that a moral claim is plausible or implausible, accurate or inaccurate, without having to refer to any moral 'reality': when we reject the claim that Hitler was an admirable human being, we need not think of ourselves as rejecting it on the basis of real characteristics that we know to be there; we could equally well simply be pointing out that, given our expectations concerning the way in which the term 'admirable human being' tends to be used, and given our knowledge of Hitler's biography, the claim that he was an admirable human being is simply unsustainable. The fact that we can say with a reasonable degree of certainty that a moral claim is simply *wrong* does not imply that we are measuring it against a specific moral reality. It is not too gross a simplification to suggest that RI tells us nothing about the content of the world: all it does is show us how to do things with words. All RI establishes is that certain statements have more plausibility within a given moral discourse than do others – a thought that is surprising only in how unsurprising it is.

As things stand, then, I am in a position to claim that the RI theorist will fail in his claim that the supposition of real moral characteristics provides the best explanation of moral experience or of what might serve to make a moral statement *true*, notwithstanding whether or not we agree with his avowal that terrorism is wrong (or whatever). Because the account looks Platonic, it is somewhat less than the best one possible, since it seems vulnerable to a queerness argument; and the claim that it is only Platonic or queer to the same extent as something uncontroversial like natural science also fails. Even if we're feeling concessive, the very best that we can say about realist independentism is that it adds nothing to the debate. Granted, a rebuttal of RI leaves open the question of what basis there might be for moral appearances and moral appeals – for the moment at least – and this is unsatisfactory. But such dissatisfaction does not amount to a rearguard defence of RI, and nor does it give us a reason to try to mount one. In other words, *even if there is such thing as a real moral characteristic, RI has not established that we ought to believe in it*. And this means that accepting the truth of a moral claim based on RI is likely to be a tall order.

Moreover, as I hinted above, this is not the end of RI's trouble: I think that there is a normative problem, too. This is not essential to my dismissal of RI – it will suffice to show that RI's claim to found the truth of a moral claim fails – but it is worth airing.

The RI theorist wants to be able to bridge the fact–value divide by means of a claim to the effect that values are actually facts of a certain kind. But if this is the case, they have nothing to recommend them. That is to say, by pointing out that x really is right or wrong or that y really is good or bad, there is no particular reason for us to expect that we can change a person's behaviour. And, this being the case, at least some versions of RI theory fail not only the truth test, but also the normativity test.

To begin to understand the problem, I shall return to Sturgeon, whose claim is that, given a conflict between a particular moral claim and the prevailing body of moral claims, it is not difficult to decide which is recalcitrant and therefore the one that we should ditch. (I ought to make it clear that I have not taken particular exception to Sturgeon: it is just that his account of realism is pithy and allows me to make the important points in as efficient a manner as possible.) This, in itself, is questionable: it is not difficult for *us* to decide, but this is simply because we're wholly inculcated into a particular way of thinking. To rest a moral deduction on a statement such as 'no morally admirable person would instigate and oversee the degradation and death of millions of persons' is cheating, though. For one thing, a word like 'degradation' is loaded, and so begs the question to at least some degree. More importantly, a genuine *naïf* might simply not see any particularly compelling reason to accept the statement a priori. It is difficult for us to disagree with the claim that Hitler was not admirable; but, while this is something that we may earnestly believe, it is bizarre, but not paradoxical, to imagine a person who cannot see a problem reconciling Hitlerian actions with admirability – I shall say more on this in Chapters 4 and 5; even if it is impossible for us to square genocide with virtue *morally*, it is not impossible *logically*.[21]

Moreover, Sturgeon is presupposing a norm to the effect that, given the need to decide between a claim and a body of claims, one ought to lean towards accepting the body of claims. But what is the origin of this norm? Such a norm might imply a 'meta-claim', to the effect that claims that are consonant with a wide range of other claims are more worthy of acceptance – or, in common language, *better* – than those that are not. But is this meta-claim true? And if it is, why so? Is it because claims that are consonant with a wide range of other claims are so because they have 'betterness'

---

21 To make the point, consider this Sturgeon-like argument: a claim to the effect that Jemima is morally admirable, taken alongside a modest piece of moral theory to the effect that good girls would never have sex with a person before marrying him allows us to draw the testable conclusion that Jemima did not do this. But we learn that Jemima *did* do this, and according to the rules of deductive reasoning, we must ditch one of our premises. And it is not difficult to figure out which of them it is that has to go. Except, of course, that it *is* difficult. I would reject one premise; most people from my grandparents' generation, and a good number of people presently living today, would ditch the other. A deductive argument will not show us who is in error here; the same applies to the Hitler. The argument tells us nothing about Jemima's moral characteristics: it tells us about *ours*. *Mutatis mutandis*, however sincerely we might believe that Hitler was not admirable, our failure to be able to square admirability with overseeing genocide tells us about *us*, not about Hitler.

as a real characteristic to a greater degree than claims that are dissonant? This being the case, we have simply shunted the problem around, and we can do away with the idea of consonance being the marker of how one claim can be said to be better than another. And if we can do away with the idea of consonance, then there seems no particular need to bring it to bear on the claims of people who are unsure of whether or not Hitler was an admirable human being. Smith might think that Hitler was admirable, and Jones might reject that view. But if consonance is redundant, the question of how we might resolve the dispute remains open.

If, on the other hand, the claim is better simply because it is consonant with the way that we argue, we have relinquished any purported attachment that *any* norm needs to reality – again, we simply have to appeal to convention. Certainly, the meta-claim describes a norm the like of which we are used to following – but this is not enough to show that we aren't mistaken in our judgements or our willingness to follow it. A person who claims that Hitler or a given act of terrorism was morally admirable is making a claim that we think to be false (assuming that our interlocutor is speaking standard English), and we can back up an appeal to falsity by pointing out that the claim seems to be completely *outré*. But simple strength of numbers will not bring us close to moral reality, any more than Galilean theories are closer to the realities of the solar system than Ptolemaic theories *just because* we're more *au fait* with heliocentrism. Even if most people *rightly* tend towards heliocentrism, or the belief that Hitler was depraved, or the belief that terrorism is generally a bad thing, these beliefs do not have any bearing on the fact of the matter. A belief, however strongly it might be held, will not generate reality.

RI theory's problems on the normative front are much wider than this, though: the problem with Sturgeon's argument points the way to a deeper question. It seems safe to assume that the RI theorist wants his real values to be action-guiding. Whether or not this desire is likely to be fulfilled is the fuel of the debate between internalists and externalists; it is not a debate on which I want to concentrate here. What I *do* want to suggest, though, is that, even if real moral characteristics were there to be found, there would be no particular reason to expect anyone to look for them. They would not be attractive to an unbiased agent.

Let us allow that something like terrorism has a specific moral characteristic, or that all terrorists have such a characteristic. Let us also imagine Smith, who is considering performing a terroristic act of some sort, and Jones, who holds commonsense moral beliefs and also thinks that they can be founded in appeals to real moral characteristics. Let us imagine too that Smith and Jones share a commitment to rational discussion. Finally, since I have no reason to cast Smith as a psychopath, let us imagine that, although Smith grants that there is *something* wrong with terrorism, he does not see it as possessing any moral insuperably vicious characteristics. Jones's challenge, then, is to make Smith come to see the world not just in his way, but in a way that accords with how, as far as he is concerned, it *really is*: that is, to convince Smith that he has missed a serious aspect of the moral reality of terrorism. My claim is that Jones will not be able to do this.

The reason for this is that, even if we allow that a moral characteristic is sufficient to change behaviour, it will do so only if a person is convinced that a given act or event bears the hallmarks of that characteristic. In the example, Smith is willing to be convinced that there might be evidence to the effect that terrorism is insuperably wrong, but he simply doesn't see it at the moment. Jones's problem is that nothing he could say could serve to change Smith's mind, and this would be the case even if Smith was sympathetic to realist independentism. The normative failure is attributable to the simple fact that, without already being sympathetic to Jones's point, Smith will have no reason to take seriously the idea that he should look beyond the moral appearances as they present themselves to him. But convincing Smith that he ought to do this will involve convincing him that he has misperceived affairs – and it is unclear why he should think that this is.

The situation is not one in which either Smith or Jones is seeking an explanation of observed phenomena, as it would be if they agreed that the terrorism was seriously wrong but disagreed as to why; it is about those phenomena *simpliciter*. Now, for many things, it may be possible to point out that a person has misperceived something. For example, Smith might be a hiker who thinks that the building on the horizon is a church with a tower when it is, in fact, a church with a spire. If we were concerned to disabuse Smith of his mistake, though, we would be able to do this in a number of ways – not the least of which is that we could take him to the building for a closer look. In doing so, we would attempt to change his perspective and, by doing so, force upon him a change in his perceptions and beliefs about those perceptions. Nothing similar would be possible with the moral status of terrorism, though: the only way Jones could get Smith to change his perspective would be to get him to alter his beliefs. In other words, in respect of towers, a change in beliefs might require a shift in perspective; but, in respect of morality, the direction of fit is different: a shift in perspective requires a change in beliefs.

Now, if Smith has a history of apparent moral misperception – say, if he was consistently at odds with the rest of us over the morality of terrorism, abortion, veganism, and other things – we might be tempted to take this as evidence that he has misperceived the situation in this case. And we might think, from this, that our moral eyesight is simply better, and that Smith ought to take our word for it on moral matters. However, the problem here is that we are subtly shifting our ground in a manner that I noted a moment ago: rather than making an appeal to moral reality, we are making an appeal to moral orthodoxy; and, although we might hope that a given *doxa* is correct, this tells us nothing about reality: a social constructivist theory of morality could happily also accommodate the idea that moral 'correctness' is indicated by the orthodoxy of moral beliefs. In other words, then, adverting to a *belief* in the reality of something's moral characteristics will not give any opponent that we might have in a moral debate any reason to change *his* beliefs. That would rely on adverting to the moral reality itself – exactly the matter that is open to question as things stand. We can only give Smith a reason to look for the (supposedly) missing moral characteristics of terrorism if we can convince him that those characteristics

are there to find. But if we can convince him that they are there to find, we will have
no need to convince him that they are worth looking for.

The normative point is also not as straightforward as it might seem when it is
considered from another dimension. Think back to the comment by Leiter about
Hitler's depravity: this was a comment that I described as 'acid'. Let us suppose
that there was somehow some value – 'acidity' – that was a real characteristic. How
ought we to respond? It was, I hope, clear that I admired the acidity that I saw in the
comment. And if acidity is admirable, by RI lights, it is something worth pursuing,
and inalienably (even if not insuperably) worth pursuing. In other circumstances,
though, acidity may not be an admirable characteristic. Just because a comment has
a certain characteristic, then, we do not necessarily know what it means in practice.
(One possible response here would be that 'acid' actually refers to two quite different
real moral characteristics: perhaps a more clear language than English would have
an adjective – say 'pitimmeral'[22] – that accurately describes whatever it is that
is admirable about what I am forced to call an 'acid' statement; in other words,
Leiter's statement was not impressively *acid* but impressively pitimmeral. However,
this gives the game away, since it admits that there is no reliable clue to reality in
language, and that we are all floundering as a result.)

But if this point stands for acidity in comments, surely the same point would
also stand for other real value-bestowing characteristics. Would it not be plausible to
imagine that someone might find Hitler's depravity attractive or admirable? If not,
why not? Bringing the problem back to Smith and Jones, the worry might be that,
if Jones can convince Smith that his proposed terroristic action is seriously wrong,
this might (on the basis of considerations that I mooted in the last chapter) serve to
give him a greater reason to perform it. Hence, even if there is a normative aspect to
real moral characteristics, there is no guarantee that it is a normativity of the right
sort. Something might be deemed worth doing *just because* it is uncontroversially
vicious.

So, metaphysically, there is a range of problems with realist independentism and
its claims that the moral features of the world and the truth of a moral statement are
both attributable to a moral reality. Whatever the moral characteristics of a person,
act or event might be, we are not entitled to claim that they are the reflections or
manifestations of a specific moral reality: positing a real moral characteristic adds
nothing to the explanatory story (Hitler's depravity is not a property that he had so
much as it is a convenient metaphor for all the things that made him what he was
and/or our reaction to him); moreover, such a strategy begs the question by conflating
the phenomenon to be explained with the noumenon that is supposed to explain it
(Hitler's depravity is not explained by the fact that he was depraved). In addition,
at least in some versions of RI theory, any moral reality that we can establish seems
to be curiously lame, since there is nothing to recommend the integration of that

---

22 'Pitimmeral' is a word that I have invented and shall use again as a moral adjective
whose content is infinitely malleable according to my current needs. If I have accidentally
misused a real word, I apologise.

notional moral reality into behaviour without presupposing a norm that one ought to modify one's behaviour to track moral reality. But the origin of this 'ought' is unlikely to be clear to the RI sceptic, who will be unconvinced *ab initio* that such modification would *really* be a good thing.

Idealist Independentism: Kant and his Heirs

The failure of realist independentism to find a basis for commonsense moral thought that does not depend on the moral thinker or the circumstances of his thought is not enough to eliminate independentism wholesale. Not all independentism is realist independentism, and the idealist independentist, to whose claims I shall turn now, can legitimately aim to avoid anything so baroque as a person's, act's or event's inherently and irreducibly moral characteristics – although his success in meeting this aim is something that I shall question later. Whereas, for RI, moral standards and concepts are matters for discovery, Kant (with whom I will begin and upon whom I shall place most emphasis) and his idealist successors (not all of whom are Kantians) are happy to claim that such things have to be created by intellectually able creatures such as humans.[23] At the same time, though, the idea that moral standards are created by humans is not taken by the defender of idealist independentism – henceforward, 'II' – to imply that they are arbitrary. Nor does the abandonment of a realist position imply that a moral claim cannot be said to be true or false. II theory is characterised by the claim that moral thought needs a thinker, but that the *content* of that moral thought is independent of who is thinking. In effect, although moral systems and the foundations for moral claims that inhere therein are not self-sufficient, the content of those systems is still independent of *each* individual and of *all* individuals.

How, then, can a claim such as 'terrorism is wrong' be true, given that truth is supposed to have something to do with the classical *adaequatio intellectus ad rem*, if there is no *res*? There is still some sort of appeal to truth being made in any statement about the moral value of action or class of action, and there is more to a statement such as 'terrorism is wrong' than a simple expression of a range of feelings – at least, this is the hope of the II theorist, who wants to be able to say that the person who demurs from the claim has made a mistake. Thus the II theorist needs to be able to find some way to get the terrorist to accept that terrorism is wrong – or, more to the point, to get him to accept the truth of a statement to the effect that terrorism is wrong (which is not quite the same thing, but from which point acceptance that terrorism is wrong should follow in fairly short order).

In this section and for the remainder of the chapter, I shall concentrate on showing how in the first place Kant, and then other idealists, would set about establishing the truth of moral claims. I have selected Kant for a couple of reasons. The first

---

23 As an aside, and in an echo of the political problem that kick-started this investigation, one might note that the seat of the classical *polis* was Athens, and so relied on Athene, while the first *polis* to emerge after the Enlightenment originally placed its capital at Philadelphia, the city of *brotherly* love. Its legitimacy is a wholly *human* affair.

is that he provided the prototypical idealist theory, and his version of the theory is still, at the core, about as good as an II theory gets. Nevertheless, Kant is mistaken in a serious manner: his moral theory is beautiful, but beautifully wrong, like an intricately crafted clock whose maker miscounted the number of teeth on a vital cog. Further, while his mistakes do not mean the death of II, some of the reasons for Kant's failure are built into the presuppositions that II *must* make in order to earn its claim to independentism; hence an account of Kant's failure is a version of an account of the failure of II *in toto*.

So, then, how might we be able to substantiate a moral claim in an independentist idealist manner? In order to answer this question, it is going to be necessary to look at what morality *is* in an idealist account. Clearly, when an II theorist says that something is wrong, he cannot mean that there is some inbuilt characteristic without sacrificing his claim to idealism. What he must mean is that the *concept* of that thing brings with it the idea of wrongness. In other words, just as four-sidedness belongs to the *idea* of a square, and we do not need ever to have seen any real square thing to agree with this, so we ought in principle to agree with or reject the idea that value *v* belongs to action *A* simply from thinking about *A* aright. Put slightly differently, we do not correctly think that *A* is *v* when *A* is *v*; rather, we correctly think that *A* is *v* when we correctly think *period*. In more Kantian language, we do not say that action *A* is contrary to moral laws because it is wrong; we say that *A* is wrong because it is contrary to moral laws.

As such, it is up to us to attribute value by means of an intellectual exercise properly performed – although, of course, it is still an open question concerning what that exercise might be. Thus when we make a statement such as 'terrorism is wrong', and if we speak truly, that truth is *ideal* – the wrongness of the terrorism does not inhere in the activity itself, but comes from the way that we think about it.

That morality, or the truth of a moral claim, relies on a function of the mind secures II's claim to idealism, as I have just shown. But not just any function of the mind will do. We might all have the same emotional response to terrorism or to any other action, but this could be wholly a matter of coincidence: it is easy to imagine a person who does not share an emotional response to a given stimulus – some people might be outraged by action *A*, and others indifferent – but difficult to identify his mistake. But if it is not clear that a mistake has been made in a person's judgement of *A*, it is also unclear how a statement such as *A* has value *v* could be established as true or false. Emotions are fickle, and dependent on the agent; while looking at someone's emotional reaction to *A* might tell us truly what that person *thinks* of *A*, it won't tell us truly how *A* *ought* to be thought of. Emotions are therefore not the kind of thing in which II theorists are going to put any faith.

So, while the idealism criterion is satisfied by functions of the mind, to get independence, we need a function of the mind *of the right sort*. And to secure the claim to independence, and hence the claim that a moral statement may be said to be true or false without reference to personal or cultural contingencies, the 'correct' sort of intellectual faculty must be one that will guarantee that each agent will inevitably reach the same conclusions in matters of conduct. In practice, this means that II rests on reason and the cognitive skills of rational animals, since, the story goes, what we are told by reason is, uniquely, independent of the individual preferences of agents and of social or historical contingencies. In its turn, this means that any rational agent is able to take the place of any and all other rational agents when it comes to making moral decisions, as the rules of moral judgement track the rules of reason.

Hence, in terms of universality, idealists need make no weaker a moral claim than realists: there is still a sense in which at least some substantial moral claims are inescapable. If it can be shown that a statement such as 'terrorism is permissible' can only be made on the back of some error of reasoning, then it can also be shown easily that 'terrorism is permissible' is false, and it follows from that that 'terrorism is impermissible' – equivalent to 'terrorism is wrong' – is true, and that terrorism *is* wrong. The error made by the terrorist boils down to a mistake in reasoning and comes not from mismatch between a statement such as 'terrorism is permissible' and the world (encompassing terrorism's real characteristics) but from the process by which a particular conclusion might be reached.

We might cite the possibility that one could make a mathematical error as an analogy: the possibility that one might make a mistake in the solution of an equation does not depend on there being 'real' numbers – not even a mathematical realist has to subscribe to this position, since even a realist will feel entitled to demonstrate that '2+2=5' is false without having to worry about the ontology of fiveness – and, at least for a mathematical idealist, a statement such as 'there are infinitely many prime numbers' can be true or false without implying that there are infinitely many *real* prime numbers. Rather, truth or falsity in mathematics depends on the manner in which thinking about matters aright will lead one inevitably to a particular conclusion.

So, by scrutinising the procedure by which an agent came to his moral conclusions, we are able to say whether those conclusions are tenable or not. If they are tenable, then they stand a chance of being true; if not, then they cannot be true, and must therefore be counted as false. Working on the Sherlock Holmes principle, the next move is simply to say that, whatever remains after all the impossibilities have been eliminated, however improbable, must be the true account of what is permissible. In other words, if we get our procedure right, the results will follow as a matter of course. It is only in the wake of the provision of a reliable procedure for moral decision-making that it is possible to establish a moral scheme with reliable content; at the same time, though, once a reliable procedure for moral decision-making has been established, its content must be taken seriously. For this reason, even though values have their root in the mental activity of the individual rather than the world around him, it is still possible for the idealist independentist to come to a moral conclusion that he neither expects nor likes.

Still, it is not clear what it is we are reasoning *about*: that is, how reason tells us, or *can* tell us, anything morally interesting, let alone truth-apt. The mathematician reasons about numbers, and makes claims about the truth of numerical operations. But what about the moralist? We might imagine a person who wants to make a political point and believes that terrorist tactics are counterproductive, but who still adopts such tactics. With justification, this person might be said to be irrational, because he believes that he has a reason not to act as he does. But not all terrorists are irrational; our ascription of irrationality in this case does not signify the wrongness of terrorism so much as the ineptitude of the terrorist. The question stands: how does reason yield morality and true *moral* statements? It is on this point that Kant's version of II theory comes into its own.

The Importance of the Will

In order to get to grips with how a moral claim might count as being true in Kant's thought, I shall start from an unexpected angle: the question of why we ought to be moral at all.

Kantian thought leads us to think that, once we understand this question aright, it answers itself. It will also give us a handle on the possibility of moral truth. 'Why be moral?' requires that we understand what morality is. Clearly it has something to do with behaviour. But what? Well, behaviour might be determined by a few things. We might be caused to do something because of gravity or instinct. Thus the laws of physics, broadly construed, might influence our behaviour. But moral animals like humans also possess a will, Kant claims; and while we do not will that which we do through instinct, at least some of our behaviour – that which we will – is not determined by the laws of physics. Yet the will is not random; willed behaviour also conforms to laws. And these laws are *moral* laws.

So: 'why be moral?' could be expanded to mean 'why should we let morality determine our behaviour?' – but it turns out that the question is, in a sense, bogus, because 'morality' simply describes behaviour that arises from the operation of the will. But, of course, we might also wonder what the will is. And Kant's response is that it is practical reason.[24] But reason has laws that determine it, too – things like the principle of non-contradiction. So we can put all this together to say that, since moral laws determine the operation of the will, since rational laws determine reason, and since the will is practical reason, it must follow that 'morality' is the same as 'practical rationality'. We can also say that a contravention of the laws of practical rationality is a contravention of the laws of morality. This is exactly the move that Kant makes; moreover, it allows us to provide an account of how a moral claim might be true: if action *A* breaches the laws of practical reason, it is, *de facto*, in contravention of the laws of morality, and can therefore be said truly to be wrong, since wrongness simply means 'in violation of moral laws'. Similarly, *A* is permissible – and it is *true* that *A* is permissible – if it is compatible with the laws of morality; finally, *A* is obligatory or a duty if ~*A* violates those laws.

This is basically why Kant refers to the keystone of his moral theory as the Categorical Imperative. It is imperative because it determines action; it is categorical because it is woven into the very fabric of the will: it describes the bounds within

---

24 Kant, 1993, Ak IV, 412 ff.; cf. Kant, 2004, Ak V, 65.

which practical reason *must* work. Hence, when we tell a person colloquially that he *can't* do this or that, and we mean by this that he *oughtn't*, Kant thinks that our phrase hits closer to the truth than we might think. Understood metaphysically, a word like 'oughtn't' actually does mean something along the lines of 'cannot will rationally' – which boils down to 'cannot will'. Such a will is literally impossible: terms such as *permitted* and *forbidden* indicate that which is possible and impossible.[25] This reading of Kant puts meat on the bones of the claim that the moral *ought*, seen from the perspective of the intellect, is the same as a necessary *would*.[26] It is no more possible to countenance certain courses of action than it is to countenance a married bachelor.

Working the other way, granted that we can act in contravention of moral laws, it follows that this action is determined by non-moral considerations – perhaps desire or something like that, rather than the will properly understood. Now, since it at least looks as though at least some people might be rational and will their action without desiring it particularly, would this prove their terrorism permissible? Perhaps not. After all, one may rationally adopt evil means to achieve some end; but what is under consideration here is how we determine whether a given means is evil – that is, in violation of the laws of conduct – in the first place. As I have also noted, this is information that at least some terrorists need, as well – not so that they can *avoid* doing bad things, but just so they know what bad things to do. So how might we decide if action *A* is permissible?

Since II claims that the content of any moral scheme will be independent of the desires and biography of the agent or judge, it follows that the permissibility of *A* would be independent of these factors. At least as far as Kant is concerned, this line of thought leads directly to the conclusion that a determinant of the will must 'represent an action as objectively necessary in itself, without reference to another end'.[27] And this gives us the first, universalising, formula of the Categorical Imperative, which is this: 'Act only according to that maxim whereby you can at the same time will that it should become a universal law'.[28] Here, then, is our first test of the truth of a moral claim. If '*A* is permissible' is true, we should be able to imagine a world in which a maxim of *A*-ing determines action universally without irrationality. Hence if *A* stands for 'eating eggs', I ought to be able to imagine a world in which an egg-eating maxim determines action all the time; and I can imagine such a world: even though I dislike eggs, and think that such a world would be deeply unpleasant, it is still *possible*. If *A* stands for deceit, though, things are different. For my attempt to deceive you presupposes that I expect that you will believe me; but if deceit is universalised, all will expect it, so no one will believe anyone, and my attempt will fail because deceit will have become *impossible*. If a maxim passes the universalisation test, this is because it is permissible on the basis of a will that is

---

25 Kant, 2004a, Ak V, 11n; see also, e.g., Ak V, 69–70.
26 Kant, 1993, Ak IV, 455.
27 Ibid., 414; emphasis mine.
28 Ibid., 421.

formed *in abstracto*. If it fails the universalisation test, this entitles us to say that it is unwillable *in abstracto*; and, since unwillability implies incompatibility with the laws of conduct, thus impermissibility, this means that we are entitled to say that such a maxim would be wrong and that we have a duty to avoid it, and we would be entitled to think that we were saying something *true* thereby.

We can come at things from a slightly different angle, too. The truth of a moral claim, for Kant, need have nothing to do with the enduring features of the world outside the head. Indeed, the truth of *any* claim can be divorced from the world outside the head, and *must* be, given Kantian commitment to the idea that the world in itself is noumenal. Correspondingly, according to the argument put in the *Critique of Pure Reason*, a statement – including a moral statement – is false if it breaks the necessary rules of the understanding.[29] This formal demand is a *sine qua non* of truth, and since a moral claim is ostensibly not a claim about any empirical feature of the world, there is no a priori reason to demand more than the formal requirement of truth. As the *Critique of Practical Reason* puts it:

> If a rational being is to think of his maxims as practical universal laws, he can think of them only as principles that contain the determining ground of the will *not by their matter but only by their form*.[30]

Moral rules determine the rational will formally; hence we can derive the truth of a moral claim on purely formal grounds. And since 'deceit is permissible' offends against good form, it must be false.

At risk of saying too much about Kant particularly (rather than the II theory of which I take him to be an excelsior), this means that, when Kant claims that some maxim describes a duty, he is basing his claim on the idea that a duty is not something that we might take or leave: this is merely the 'anthropological' understanding of a duty. But this 'anthropological' duty owes its provenance to the concept of duty metaphysically understood. On this understanding, a duty is an 'action to which someone is bound [and] is therefore the matter of obligation'; and an obligation is the necessity of action under a categorical imperative of reason.[31] And this brings us back to the claim that 'moral actions' are simply those that are practically rational. We have a moral duty to do this or that in roughly the same way that we have a 'duty' to comply with, say, the principle of non-contradiction or a 'duty' to adhere to the laws of physics. Our moral duties are defined by what it is literally unthinkable for us not to do.

With this in mind, it is possible to attempt to give an account of how Kant would, and II could, attempt to demonstrate that terrorism is wrong and that civil society is, at worst, not *so* wrong. For the promise has been made of a way to establish whether

---

29 Kant, 2003, A59/ B83–84.
30 Kant, 2004a, Ak V, 27; emphasis mine.
31 Kant, 1998, Ak VI, 222.

'terrorism is wrong' is true – although the truth of the statement will have nothing to do with the *world* except that which we bring to it.[32]

One suggestion might be that the terrorist wills that persons be treated solely as means to an end, rather than as ends in themselves. But treating a person in this way cannot be universalised, since 'treat persons as mere objects of valuation' would undermine my own subjective ability to act as a source of value, and therefore my ability to treat anyone as anything. I cannot treat others *wholly* as a means to my end while allowing them to treat me wholly as a means to theirs. Indeed, I cannot *allow* a person to treat me *wholly* as a means *period*, since the notion of allowing involves the idea that I have some sort of authority over myself, which means that I am not wholly a means to an end after all. Therefore terrorism is wrong from the perspective of the first formulation of the CI. Moreover, this is just as much as to say that we have a duty, when we recognise persons as persons, not to treat them wholly as a means to our own end. Since the terrorist does this, his action cannot help but violate the second formulation of the CI, which demands that we treat all persons as ends in themselves.[33] Either way, 'terrorism is permissible' cannot be accepted as true; therefore terrorism, thought through aright, is correctly described as wrong.

At first glance, though, this does not help us all that much. For one of the considerations that I raised in Chapter 1 was that the moves that we might make to condemn terrorism might equally well be corrosive of the moral acceptability of civil society. For example, when one enters civil society, there *is* a sense in which one is attempting to use others as a means. On the other hand, civil society does not imply the *necessary* treatment of others *wholly* as a means to an end, and terrorism does; civil society's broadly consensual nature militates against it treating persons *solely* as means to another's end, so it can't really be said to sanction treating others as anything but autonomous ends-in-themselves.[34] At the same time, there is reciprocity within the *polis* (since one also allows oneself to be treated as a means to an end in a demonstration of a maxim safely universalised), proving that respect for personhood is retained, even if we do not realise it. With terrorism, though, there is no reciprocity – and certainly no consent; hence it fails the universalisation test. The proposition that the *polis* is (generally) morally permissible and terrorism is not might not be *wholly* proven thus, but at least it looks as though there is here a serious moral difference between the two. (As an aside, it is also interesting to note that Kant proposes a similar argument concerning consensual sex: granted, we might seek enjoyment from it and from our partner, but neither partner treats the other wholly as a means to that end.[35] This idea could be translated to the *polis*: Émile Henry was

---

32 Cf. Walker, 1989, p. 62.

33 Kant, 1993, Ak IV, 429.

34 Of course, there remain problems with the practice of consensual politics – how one might *refuse* to consent, for example – but these are not pressing in the context of the present argument.

35 Kant, 1998, Ak VI, 278.

in the wrong because, although he *appeared* to be playing the same moral game as *poleis*, he turns out to have been forcing himself on the citizenry.)

Nevertheless, even if this notional defence of the *polis* here does not collapse, this is because it has not *yet* collapsed– not because it never will. There are problems, for example, in the form of the argument from Hume, which I aired in the last chapter, about being shanghaied into the crew of the ship of State: Kant's point seems to work only for consensual *poleis* and, unless we're willing to believe that legitimising consent can be given retrospectively, it won't account for our initial induction into the political community.

But, having said all this, it is wise to go back to the main argument – not to concentrate so much on Kant as a political thinker, but rather on his more general exemplification of a brand of II theory. In this picture, practical reason implies universalisation, and universalisation rules out conditionality. Hence in choosing a maxim for action, my choice is not predicated on what appears good or is good for me or on the circumstances in which I settle on that maxim, but on what must be thought of and willed as good in itself.

Lest I give the impression that II and Kantianism are essentially the same thing, it is worth iterating that non-Kantian II theorists could happily enough keep hold of the idea that reason allows us to make judgements about the truth of an evaluative statement, but relinquish the idea that the will is practical reason and the presumption that morality just *is* (more or less) applied reason. Such theorists would therefore still have to offer an account of why one should be moral and of what it is that legitimises the ascription of moral epithets (since rationality would not imply permissibility, nor irrationality impermissibility). What counts in all cases, though, is the idea that the moral characteristics of an act, class of act, or actor are not so much related to a fact about it or him, so much as to the way in which it or he is represented to us – that is, the way in which we understand matters when we understand them aright. Thus it might, as yet, be a moot point between II theorists concerning whether, in relation to the moral value *v* of act *A*, which of the statements '*A* is *v*', '*A* is ~*v*', or '~*A* is *v*' is true. However, settling the matter will have nothing to do with picking out characteristics of terrorism that it simply *has*; moral characteristics are functions of our thinking, and the truth of a moral statement is comprehensible in terms of the coherence of the thought behind it.

Nevertheless, there remain a number of problems. To show what they are, I shall not move far from Kant's own famous example of the murderer at the door, in which a man knocks at my door asking to know the whereabouts of a certain person. I know where this person is, but am also reasonably certain that the stranger at the door wants the information so that he can murder him.[36] Kant is concerned with the question of whether I could lie, thus breaking an imperative of truthfulness, or tell the truth, thus almost certainly contributing to the untimely demise of another person, famously arguing that the demand to tell the truth is overriding, even though

---

36 *On a Supposed Right to Lie because of Philanthropic Concerns* in Kant, 1993, Ak VIII, 425 ff.

it entails knowingly endangering another's life. I want to focus here on a different aspect of the problem.

I shall assume, for the sake of the argument, that, whatever their methodologies, all II theorists would agree that lying in this case is wrong. The actual content of any given II moral scheme is beside the point here: I am pretending that they are all as one to clear as much space as possible for my argument. The point that I want to make is that, even if an II theorist is correct to insist to think that there is a way in which we are constrained to think about or evaluate a particular action *in abstracto*, he may find it difficult to apply this formal reasoning unless he can establish with certainty what the maxim that best describes a particular action *is*. In other words, a will to deceive might be impermissible – but there is likely to be a range of arguments at the disposal of an agent that will allow him to deny that his will was framed around a maxim of deceit. Hence even if the truth of a statement such as 'deceit is impermissible' can be established – and I am not sure that it can, for reasons that I will outline in a moment – that of ' … and *this* is an instance of deceit' is much less certain. This is a problem that I shall call the Problem of Formalism. In addition, I will argue later that there are serious questions that we can ask about reason's place in moral thought: these questions can wait, though.

The Problem of Formalism

Hegel accuses Kant of 'empty formalism', the idea is that the Categorical Imperative presupposes social institutions. For example, the injunction against theft only functions in societies that have private property as an institution; without such a background, taking things at will would not undermine itself as a maxim.[37] The point being made is that, there is no way in which the citizens of a society in which the institution of private property does not exist would give assent to a claim that theft is wrong. Hegel's argument is a powerful rebuttal of Kant's attempts at normativity, and I have mentioned it here because I also want to accuse II generally of a kind of empty formalism, though what I have in mind is different from what Hegel had in mind, and I have mentioned him as a distancing strategy.

Let us stick with the problem of the murderer at the door. In order to be able to tell me that I ought not to say to the murderer what I am saying, it is necessary to show that deceit is wrong, but, before that, to show that what I am doing is deceitful. It is far from clear to me that he would be able to show that 'deceit' really does capture definitively what is going on, though. And so it is not clear to me that it can be shown that 'what I am doing is permissible' would be false.

The idealist seems to be trading on the idea that deceit is deceit, and that all instances thereof have their moral value by virtue of belonging to that genus. So, in the example, 'lying to potential murderers' is wrong because it belongs to the genus 'deceit', all the members of which have the same moral value. If this is the

---

37 Hegel, 1991, § 135.

case, much rests on the accurate taxonomisation of an action as belonging to a given genus; such accuracy is hard to establish. But, taken to task for lying to the man at the door, I do not see why I might not reply like this:

> You are correct to claim that deceit is impermissible, but this is of purely academic interest to me. Admittedly, what I propose *looks* like deception, but the appearance is misleading: my proposed action actually belongs to a different genus altogether that can (and should) be thought of in a different way. What I have in mind is 'quiggoting'. *To quiggot* means to engage in the sort of activity that prevents murders happening, and, while quiggoting is superficially similar to deceiving, the resemblance goes no further than the superficial. (By analogy, perhaps, I would like to remind you that a dolphin looks like a shark, and does much the same thing, but ought not to be thought of as a fish.) Similarly, while the person at the door *will be deceived*, the deception is a foreseen but unintended outcome of my quiggoting, and I therefore see no reason to accept that what I am doing is wrong.

In other words, my claim would be that the reason why Kant and his ilk think that I ought to tell the truth to putative murderers is simply that they have maltaxonomised the activity that I am considering; 'deception is permissible' may be false, but 'quiggoting is permissible' certainly is not. Or I may say that two genera of maxim are elided in the criticism: that one of these is properly thought of as deception, but the other, in a more refined language, would properly be called 'quiggoting'. Again, I might see no reason to attribute wrongness to quiggoting. Intentional deceit may be wrong, but quiggoting is not, and *that* is what I was up to.

An argument from Elizabeth Anscombe might help illustrate the point. There is, she notes, any number of ways in which the same action could be described: her example is that sawing a plank and making a squeaky noise with a saw might describe the same thing.[38] Either description could be correct, though each description leads us to understand the bare facts of what is going on in a different manner. The bare facts of what I propose to do with the murderer at the door will include things like the vibrations that my vocal chords make; however, these bare facts can sustain a number of interpretations that lead us to understand them in a different way – in one sense, deceit; in another, quiggoting. And, of course, in response to the charge that what I call 'quiggoting' is just a kind of lying, I might well respond that this opens the door to a *reductio* – if my apparently safe belief about what I was doing is vulnerable, why should anyone else's beliefs about an action be *in*vulnerable? That is: if my moral judgements are unsafe, what guarantee has anyone else that his are not? There is, then, room for dispute concerning the content of my will in relation to what was going on in the action, and the possibility of this dispute is not predicated in any sense on my trying to dig myself out of a moral hole in response to the II theorist's challenge.

Indeed, the possibility that there might be several competing accounts of what I am up to is allowed for by idealism's own account of truth. For the idealist can accept any description of events just as long as it is coherent: the idea that a correct

---

38 Anscombe, 1979, ch. 6.

description must hang on reality is, *ex hypothesi*, unsustainable. So as long as a notional description of an event – 'deceit', 'quiggoting' or pretty much anything else in this example – is coherent, then there is no reason to suppose that it is false, falsity itself being a mark that an idea is unsustainable. Now, the II theorist might have a fallback position here, which is that there is only one possible set of coherent statements. If this could be shown, there would, in principle, be a way to argue that any single heterodox statement must therefore be rejected as untenable. But, of course, this means that we have to be able to show not only that there *is*, but also that there *could only be* one such set. In the meantime, while such a point wants of proof, there is no reason to accept it, and the possibility remains open that there is more than one set of coherent statements (rather as there might be more than one way to fill in a crossword puzzle coherently – more on this in a moment).

Might there be a better defence available to the II theorist? Actually, there might be two, although they are very close cousins indeed. The first is based on a claim that, even though I might have *thought* that I was performing some sort of friend-saving activity, this is not the case: the truth of the matter is that I was willing a situation in which I did not *have* to save him. After all, telling the truth cannot cause death, and it is equally implausible that lying can save a life. Meanwhile, we might want to say that, while it is *meritorious* to protect people from murderers, it is not necessarily impermissible *not* to, and such protection cannot warrant a breach of a duty of truthfulness, which it is *always* impermissible not to fulfil.[39]

The second defence is closely related and is based on the claim that willing the end implies willing the means: Kant, of course, thinks that this is analytic.[40] If quiggoting or friend-saving implies deceit, the argument goes, this is sufficient to render such behaviour problematic at best. Even if I was willing action in accordance with an imperfect duty of protection, I was also willing that we breach a perfect duty not to deceive. Even if it *was* possible actually to *save* a life by lying, the important point would be that I would have willed a transgression of the moral law at the same time. However happy the outcome, it would be tainted by a wrong forbidden absolutely by the moral law. And for this reason, my will is incompatible with the moral law. One cannot wheedle out of matters by arguing that no lie, qua lie, was willed: such a claim is false. If willing acceptable action *B* entails unacceptable action *A*, then I have willingly *A*-ed.

The two defences are so closely related that they will stand or fall together. To begin with, I cannot see that there is much mileage in the first defence, which seems to have been foreclosed by Anscombe's argument. There is not anything incoherent or untenable about a person describing his maxim as being one of murder prevention rather than deceit and denying that a disavowed maxim of deceit is present. Hence there is no idealist reason to think that, say, 'deceive' rather than 'prevent a murder' (or, for that matter, 'quiggot') was the *true* sense of the maxim on which a person is working when the murderer was deceived. (Note that the murderer being deceived

---

39 See Kant, 1998, Ak VI, 390.
40 Kant, 1993, Ak IV, 417.

in this case does not imply anyone's willing the deceit of the murderer, any more than the fact that I am deceived into thinking that the moon is larger on the horizon than at the zenith implies that there is anyone willing my deceit. To fail to notice this is to fall prey to equivocation.) The same might go for any other proposed course of action: if the notional terrorist can coherently describe his strategy as righting an historic injustice, then he can accept many of the idealist's claims without having to admit that his claim concerning his own maxim is mistaken. Hence, even if a moral claim can be shown to be able to bear the burden of truth, it does so only in the most formal, general sense, and it does not follow that it applies all that well in *this* situation: there is no reason to suppose that a claim about any particular action should be accepted as true if that action can be described in more than one way (as, plausibly, pretty much every action may be).

There is, then, room for dispute concerning the content of my will in relation to what was going on in the action. It is plausible that what I wanted to do, or what I willed, was to tell the lie, but it is equally plausible that what I wanted to do or what I willed was to prevent a murder (and moreover, in the heat of the moment, it might never really occurred to me that my activity could be described as lying – although, admittedly, in this circumstance I might not be *willing* much at all). For as long as there are several candidate descriptions of my action, there would seem to be little ground to the supposition that what I was doing was lying *and lying as a matter of necessity*. And for as long as my intentions correlate with one candidate description but not others, and this description is morally acceptable, there is room for dispute concerning whether I intended anything *wrong* – that is to say, I might agree that action *A* is wrong, and I might agree that what I did looked like *A*-ing; but I might still deny that I *was A*-ing. One *might* insist that only one description of a given circumstance is the correct one – but *how* one would substantiate this is mysterious. To reprise the crossword analogy, we can say that one version is correct and another incorrect because we can make reference to an 'extra-puzzlar' standard – specifically, what was going on inside the head of the person setting it as expressed in the clues. Translated back to II theory, though, this seems to put us back on the high road to realism because of appeals to value-bestowing characteristics beyond what we currently think.

However, the claim that willing the end implies willing the means has not gone away, and, if it is accurate, it might mean that quiggoting is impermissible by default. If the II theorist can get me to accept as true the apparently purely formal statement that '*A*-ing is wrong', and can get me to accept that, despite my stated lack of a desire to *A*, I am still *A*-ing when I *B* because *A*-ing is the means by which I *B*, then he can force me to accept that '*B* is permissible' might be false. That is, even if I deny that I am willing deceit, if it can be shown that willing deceit is the means by which I quiggot, and if deceit is impermissible, then I might be forced to accept that 'quiggoting is permissible' is false. If it is right, then my desire to prevent murder must be evaluated in terms of the means at my disposal to achieve this end; it would not really matter how well or badly my intention correlated with a notional 'correct' description of the action, since the wrongness of my action could be established deductively. All that would matter would be that my will was to save the friend and *something* else besides. Even if the murderer example is a bad one, commonsense might still find that it has to defend itself from a claim that it ought not to countenance something like lying as a means to *any* good end. An II-theoretical moral statement, apparently possessing only formal validity, could therefore be applied to the actions of real people in the real world.

I think, however, that the II theorist who takes this line is on a hiding to nothing, because there is plenty of room to doubt that willing the end *does* imply willing the means. Basically, this is because, even if willing B implies A-ing, it is unclear that this means that it implies *willing A*. The claim that willing the end implies willing the means shapes up like this:

P$_1$ I will B
P$_2$ I know that B entails A
C   Therefore I will that A

But the argument does what it should if it is supposed to convict the liar of willingly having broken a moral rule. (We might think that it makes a difference whether or not I know that B entails A – that not knowing this makes the argument weaker. However, since I think I can knock out the stronger argument, this is a mere aside.) Even if I know that in B-ing I am A-ing, I think that I might still claim not to *will* that A, simply because the question does not revolve around what I *know*, but around what I *will*. For the reason why, consider the argument:

P$_1$ I know that Stendhal wrote *Scarlet and Black*
P$_2$ I know that Stendhal is Henri Beyle
C   Therefore I know that Henri Beyle wrote *Scarlet and Black*

Although the conclusion here is pretty easy to draw, it is not a given. While I could deduce pretty quickly that HB wrote *S&B*, the important thing is that it is something that I would *have* to deduce: the knowledge is not immediate. While concluding that HB did *not* write *S&B* would indicate an error, *not* concluding that he did so would not. Now, considering that *knowing that* and *willing that* are two entirely different attitudes, how much weaker is the argument that must be made by anyone who wants to defend the elision of means and ends! Admittedly, to wonder whether B-ing involves A-ing and to deduce that it does not would quite possibly be erroneous; but not to entertain this kind of musing would indicate no mistake.

Moreover, even if one recognised that one's will that B had something to do with the fact that A-ing took place, this would imply nothing about what was willed beyond B, unless we are supposed to believe that one should have to deduce what one wills. This is a demand that appears to stretch 'will' beyond commonsense parameters (and, for that matter, Kant's own understanding of it as a *function*, not an *object*, of reason). In other words, it does seem eminently possible that one can will B without willing A; I might deduce my *involvement* in telling the lie, but, even if I do this, I might never have to admit that this was what I willed. And if I can divorce *A* from *B* – or lying from quiggoting in the example – then there is no pressure on me to admit the falsity of the claim '*B* is permissible'.

Thus it turns out that, although application of II theory thought starts its life by appearing to be too onerous to be correct – it asks a lot of us in terms of correct reasoning about actions correctly described – it is, even in its strongest form, actually too *weak* to be plausible. First, while II theory gives a way for us to say that a general moral claim is true, what it cannot do is to provide a way to say that this truth translates into particular actions, since no coherent description of a maxim can be dismissed by the idealist as false. (By contrast, when, earlier in the chapter, I introduced the idea of the hiker and his belief about the shape of the building on the horizon, his opinion could have been coherent and false – but this is possible only because of the introduction into the debate of a free-standing reality against which we can check our claims. The same considerations apply *vis-à-vis* the coherent but incorrect solutions to a crossword puzzle.) Hence II theory can give me no reason to abandon a set of moral beliefs as false as long as I can square them with each other. As long as he can describe his actions without getting caught by logical snares, an agent need not overcome any serious worries about the truth or falsity of the moral claims that he might make.

Second, as long as one's will is restricted to (acceptable) *B*-ing, one can claim that any (unacceptable) *A*-ing was a pure accident and therefore neither a content of the will nor a matter for moral scrutiny: hence an argument along the lines of '*B* implies *A*, which is impermissible; therefore *B* is impermissible' is one the conclusion of which one is under no obligation to accept. One can concede that *A* happened, but deny that this tells us anything about the value of *B*. (When I consider Adolph Eichmann in Chapter 5, I shall argue that there *is* something ethically problematic about such a restriction. But for the moment, what counts is that, at least formally, there is little to make us suppose that a failure to deduce the *y* in every *x* is enormously different from a failure to deduce that Henri Beyle wrote *Scarlet and Black*. It shows no error.) The point is that, for any particular moral judgement that he might make, the II theorist cannot rely on certainty that his claim will be accepted as true or importantly true.

The Metaphysics of Reason and the Problem of Taxonomy

The point that I have been trying to make so far has been that II theory is unlikely to be able to show with certainty that the claims it makes about a given activity are true, simply because there is likely to be room to dispute what that activity *is*. On its own, this point should leave defenders of II theory feeling pretty queasy: I think I have shown that, while they might be able to establish the formal truth of their moral claims, they could not establish the applicability of this formal truth to the real world, just because such an application would presuppose a particular understanding of that world. Note that, although I have been concentrating on Kant, the point is broad enough to cover all II theorists, since all will need to be able to say something about how *this* concrete action is definitively a representation of *that* ideal maxim, and this is something that I can't see any of them doing. Thus II theory is, essentially, a lame duck. As if this was not enough, though, there is room to swipe whatever consolation may be offered by formal truth. II theory is not only a lame duck, but a *dead* lame duck.

Admittedly, I do not think that I can prove what I am about to argue. Part of the reason for this is that I think that the position I will describe is difficult for *anyone* to prove, and this is as a matter of principle. Still, I do not think that I have to do much in the way of proving. It is sufficient, I think, to show two things. The first of these is that idealist independentism helps itself to certain strands of theoretical support, and that its entitlement to do so is challengeable. Thus the onus is on II to show that what it attempts is legitimate. The second is that it is at least possible to deny legitimacy to this entitlement. Meanwhile, the argument that I shall put in Chapters 4 and 5 should show that an involved demonstration of legitimacy is unnecessary: I can substantiate commonsense morality comparatively simply, and therefore have an Ockhamite advantage.

The argument of the past few pages has been that the truth of a claim or statement S, which ascribes value v to act A, is open to challenge because we might simply deny that what we are doing is A. The argument that I want to suggest here concentrates on the other part of the claim: I shall suggest that there might be situations in which, in relation to the moral value v of act A, a statement like 'A is v' and its negation might have similar claims to validity. That is, although there might be a way to show that a moral statement is true, it might not be possible to show that its opposite is false. It remains to be shown that there is not more than one way in which a moral claim can be rationally assessed – either because reason might be able to give more than one answer to a moral problem or (more tentatively) because there is more than one way in which one might be rational.

My argument takes its lead from this passage in *The Metaphysics of Morals*:

> [S]ince, considered objectively, there can be only one human reason, there cannot be many philosophies; in other words, there can be only one true system of philosophy from principles, in however many different and even conflicting ways one has philosophized about one and the same proposition. So the *moralist* rightly says that there is only one virtue and one doctrine of virtue, that is, a single system that connects all duties of virtue by one principle; the *chemist*, that there is only one chemistry (Lavoisier's); the *teacher of medicine*, that there is only one principle for systematically classifying diseases (Brown's).[41]

My main focus will be on the first sentence of this quotation, which makes two major claims: first, that there can be only one human reason, and, second, that there can be only one true system of philosophy from first principles. Both of these claims seem to me to be open to challenge. I shall deal with the second claim first, and

---

41 Kant, 1998, Ak VI, 207.

shall do so by discussing the second sentence, which allows us to believe that Kant thinks that there is a conceptual thread that unites natural science with the science of virtue; rational investigation into virtue is analogous to rational investigations into chemistry or medicine. Unfortunately, this analogy is deeply misleading.

In the first place, the analogy with Lavoisier's chemistry is illegitimate. Chemistry makes a claim about things that are real (or that it believes to be real): chemicals and elements, and the molecules and atoms that constitute them. But, *ex hypothesi*, this is not true for moral characteristics, and certainly not for moral characteristics as Kant conceives them (and the second *Critique* states explicitly that 'the concepts of good and evil ... do not refer originally to objects'[42]). Even if Kant were to want to put an idealist spin on Lavoisier, such that his chemistry describes how we must think of aspects of a world that are inaccessible and noumenal, it doesn't follow that we can say the same things about morality as about chemistry: chemistry represents at least an attempt to get to grips with a world 'out there' that is (or must be) taken as a given. Morality does no such thing.

What about the analogy with Brown? This is more successful, just because it is not obvious that diseases are 'discoverable' entities. Rather, the 'disease' marks a categorisation: a certain way of organising the world. Neither disease nor virtue is sitting there waiting to be discovered (we should beware of confusing a disease with its symptoms, after all); rather, each is something that we bring to the world. Yet the analogy does not provide Kant with what he wants; it is possible to dispute the contention that disease is something that must be categorised or understood in a specific way. For example, Peter Sedgwick mentions a case study that deals with a South American Indian tribe in which 'the disease of dyschromic spyrochetosis, which is marked by the appearance of coloured spots on the skin, was so "normal" that those who did not have them were regarded as pathological and excluded from marriage'.[43] What is important here is that, although two people might agree on the empirical features of some aspect of the world, there is no necessity that they should agree that those features constitute disease. In an important sense, one person's health is another person's disease, and there need be no suggestion that the members of this tribe had made an error of reasoning that nullified their understanding of the world; probably there *can* be no such suggestion that is not, in some way, begging the question against the tribesmen.

There is no such *thing* as disease, as something to be discovered in its own right: the signs and symptoms might be discoverable – empirical matters in Kant's argot – but the *disease* (in the sense that Kant is using the word) is something formal – it is a way of talking about those symptoms. (So, for example, we do not discover that we have chicken-pox: we discover that we have itchy skin and so on, and determine that we have chicken-pox afterwards.) It is possible to make compendia of signs and symptoms, and it is possible to make compendia of diseases. But there is no reason to assume that these compendia would be congruent. Based on the formal demand

---

42   Kant, 2004a, Ak V, 65.
43   Sedgwick, 1981, p. 123.

that the truth of a statement should be primarily assessed not on the adequation of statement to world but on its coherence, statements such as 'dyschromic spyrochetosis is a disease' and 'dyschromic spyrochetosis is not a disease' could be held to be equally true by equally rational groups of people for just as long as they are coherent with other claims that they might care to make.

So far, so Kantian. But the important point is that, if ostensibly conflicting statements about disease could be made and be held to have an equal truth-status, and if there is an analogy between the science of virtue and the science of medicine, then, plausibly, in the moral context, so could '*A* is *v*' and '*A* is not-*v*'. If Brown's classification of disease is simply an expression of a particular 'episteme' – a way of ordering the world rather than the order itself[44] – then the same might be said for the 'science of virtue': within itself, it may classify all behaviours, but it is not inconceivable that there might be other competing moral epistemes that simply organise their thought differently. The empirical facts of an act or event need not tell us anything about how we are to think about that event or the facts themselves.

Thus there could be lists of 'goodnesses' without a single corresponding inescapably valid virtue category, just as there can be lists of symptoms without a corresponding inescapably valid disease category. As such, one should be wary of the claim that one can make moral claims that are correct or incorrect from an impersonal perspective. If there might be more than one way of looking at the world, then we might be entitled to think that the truth of any given moral claim is not exclusive or exhaustive. Hence there may be several moral truths: 'this is true for me, but not for you' could be less the woolly thinking of the philosophical novice than it may appear at first. The claims made by any system of philosophy can be accepted as true – in the specialised way in which an idealist must conceive of truth – for just as long as its proponents avoid logical snares. Kant's claim that there can be only one true system of philosophy from principles is inaccurate.

This point should worry *all* II theorists, not just Kantians, since it swipes from them all the means by which we might be able to separate true and false moral statements. We have to re-evaluate how we might go about judging the truth or falsity of particular moral claims. Such an argument may be unpalatable to some: I think, though, that it need not be. I need not be seen as making any positive claim in favour of conceptual relativism. All I am claiming is that a presumption of rational conceptual homogeneity is capable of being doubted, and, as such, is in need of argumentative scaffolding. As it happens, I will later be making claims that could be seen as amounting to a plea for conceptual relativism in moral matters, and this means that an attempt to construct any such argumentative scaffolding will be, in the long run, unnecessary. But to make such positive claims at this stage would be to risk getting ahead of myself.

---

44 Here I have borrowed Foucault's sense of the word 'episteme', which is the principle by which 'knowledge, envisaged apart from all criteria having reference to its rational value or to its objective forms, grounds its positivity and thereby manifests a history which is ... that of its conditions of possibility' (Foucault, 1997b, xxii).

I am, I will admit, less happy about this next line of argument than I am about the last one. The questions it raises are reflections of sceptical doubts about the claim that there can be only one human reason. Such a claim rests on the idea that, whatever the differences between people might be, 'reason' is the same in all cases. This is a point that is not confined to II theorists, of course: for example, it is one on which Aristotle relies in the opening paragraph of *On Interpretation*:

> Words spoken are symbols or signs of affectations of the soul; written words are the signs of words spoken. As writing, so also is speech not the same for all races and men. But the mental affections themselves, of which these words are primarily signs, are the same for the whole of mankind, as are also the objects of which those affections are representations or likenesses, images, copies.[45]

The contention is that what is going on 'inside the head' – thought, reason and the like – is *weltfrei*, immediate to itself, and prior to its expression (for example, through language). Any *zōon logon ekhon* will have the same mental characteristics – I think that it is legitimate to suppose that reason is here included (for example: think of the manner in which Socrates 'educates' the slave in *Meno*:[46] even an uneducated slave has a rational capability that is similar in type to anyone else and that allows him to engage in intellectual activities such as geometry). Kant subscribes to this belief; so must anyone who wants to maintain that there might be only one set of true moral claims, each of which is independent of, but accessible by, the individual agent. Have we any reason – the pun is *almost* intentional – to doubt the belief? I think that we might.

What might serve to motivate my doubt about the priority of reason? I am, I admit, almost certainly swimming against the tide, although my suspicion that the paths of reason are beaten by historical and cultural factors shares features with the thought of Hegel (which, unfortunately, I have neither the resources nor the expertise to investigate further here). My suspicions are raised by the fact that the traditional idea of the rational animal is, by and large, Greek. Even if we allow the Aristotelian contention that man is essentially *zōon logon ekhon* (though a quick glance at Plato should be sufficient to show that the idea wasn't all that innovative: the tripartite soul has reason, *logos*, as an attribute: '[w]e shall call the reflective [*logizetai*] element in the mind the rational [*logistikon*]'[47]), 'reason' is not the only possible translation of *logos*. It can also mean 'speech'[48] (and Plato himself calls thought the 'silent inner conversation of the soul with itself'[49]). Clearly there is a close relationship between language and thought, but it is not obvious which is the dominant partner.

---

45 Aristotle, 1974, 16a5–8.

46 Plato, 1981, 82b ff.

47 Plato, 1987, 439d; slightly modified.

48 Given the use that I will make of his thought later, it seems appropriate to note a point that Heidegger makes in his essay *Logos*: 'it remains incontestable that λέγειν means, predominantly if not exclusively, saying and talking' (Heidegger, 1975, pp. 60–61).

49 Plato, 1921, 263d–e.

If the II theorist wants to show that a moral statement acquires its truth courtesy of a criterion of rationality that is independent of the individual (as he must), then he has to be certain that mental activity such as reason is *not* parasitic on or mediated by a cultural factor – for example, something like language. For, if reason could be structured differently in different people, it would remain a possibility for Smith to claim that *A* is *v*, and for Jones to claim the opposite, with equal veracity: each would be speaking the truth (at least within the confines of the idealist conception of truth).

Placing such a heavy emphasis on language is not without its dangers, of course: a coincidence of words in Greek is not all that much on which to base an argument. Still, there might be something more worth saying based on a mode of thought suggested by Plato's line about thought and conversation. It is, after all, implicit in the concept of rational thought that it is meaningful. This leads naturally to the thought that reason must depend on some medium of comprehension, which is the essence of language: it is not much to suggest that someone who thinks that reason is incomprehensible has much of a chance of defending this thesis. It is not at all obvious how one might have a thought – by which I mean something deliberative, as rationality seems to demand, and so qualitatively different from intuitions and feelings – that is not mediated in some form by language.[50] Whatever we think about the basis for moral claims, just in order to think about it we still need to make use of some sort of linguistic medium.

Put another way, if reason's position in relation to language is anything other than a straightforward priority, then it (or at least its ability to make representations) might be as malleable or as variable between individuals as language; hence the idea that reason allows one to make an II-friendly moral judgement or truth-claim that has nothing to do with one's biographical particulars is one that now appears to need support. Here at least, Plato is on to something important when he talks about silent inner conversations. If reason *does* relate inseparably to something like language, and given that languages do differ from culture to culture, then there is reason to suspect that reason itself might not be universal. The onus is on the defender of the thought that reason might be universal to calm this scepticism concerning the independence of reason from language. He needs to show that language does *not* manacle reason.

Without this being done definitively, then the supposition that reason is universal is not one that can be made with impunity. Moreover, even if reason *is* dominant over language, then the point is still one that has to be *proven*: again, my intention here is not so much to make a positive claim that reason is a function of language as simply suggest that the priority of reason over language is one that I think has simply been taken for granted. For as long as, and to the extent that, the Kantian or the II theorist feels entitled to help himself to the claim that reason is reason, there is room to doubt his certainty about the truth of a moral claim.

---

50 Cf. Lovibond, 1983, p. 83.

Not least among the problems with this line of argument is that, even if there might be different 'rationalities', no one might ever be in a position to say so, since it is plausible that each of us would be intellectually confined to a 'local' reason – we would lack the transcendental entitlement to call participants in other reasons rational. And if we cannot occupy the position necessary to say that Smith and Jones have differing conceptual schemes, then we ought not to say that they might. To be able to make any kind of comment about the mental activities of another person is to presuppose that there is some sort of common ground between us, which is the same as saying that, to all intents and purposes, there is something like a transcendentally valid forum for any disputes.[51] I am more convinced of the dubiousness of the other component of the universality claim, though: that, even if there is only one reason, there is no reason to assume that it can only entertain one possible solution to any given problem (or that it must conceive of something *as* a problem). Reason could accommodate more than one way of thinking about the world. And this kind of rational polyvocality is sufficient to destabilise the II contention that there is a definitive way to discern true from false moral statements.

Reason and the Moral Will

A range of other problems might well be suggested for II theorists to get over as well. Primarily, the question is one of whether morality can properly be said to be the domain of reason – or, at least, the *exclusive* domain of reason. There is a plausible difference between the motivational psychology of rational persons and non-persons; humans are the only animals known to be persons and the only animals known to have will. (Aristotle, too, capitalises on this when he compares the human capacity for deliberation (*bouleusis*) to the more limited, animalistic capacity for choice (*proairesis*).) However, whether this is sufficient to merit a claim quite so strong as the claim that the will is *essentially* rational is a moot point. So is the claim that the truth of a moral claim can be assessed solely rationally.

The II theorist trades on the assumption that, if we are to make sense of, or try to resolve, moral disputes, then we have to conceive of them as tangles that are amenable to ironing out by reason. But there are cases when this is not so. For example, there are instances when two exclusive maxims might each be rationally tenable, and so might be expected each to have an equal claim to direct the will. Take, for example, the maxim espoused by Ed the Egoist, which runs along the lines of 'I shall show more concern for my own welfare than for that of others'. I shall allow that Ed is disinterested: it is just that he thinks that *everyone* can, or should, be an egoist. There is nothing that cannot be accepted by the II theorist here. Such a maxim is not self-refuting, since it undermines no institutions upon which it relies itself. It clashes with no formulation of the Categorical Imperative, either: it could be adopted by everyone, it is not incompatible with treating others as ends-in-

---

51 Viz. *On The Very Idea of a Conceptual Scheme* in Davidson, 2001.

themselves, and it is not incompatible with being both monarch and subject in the Kingdom of Ends. But compare this maxim with that of Alice the Altruist, which is something like 'I shall show more concern for the welfare of others than for myself'. Again, there is nothing that should be taken as problematic here. And compare both to the maxim of Indifferent Sid, who thinks that benefiting oneself and benefiting others are morally indistinguishable.

Now, Ed, Alice and Sid will all think that the others are wrong – not just in the moralistic sense, but deeply wrong, inasmuch as each will think that the others have misunderstood the basis on which moral judgements should be made. Would any be able to point out the error of reasoning made by the others, though? I do not think so. And, for this reason, it is not clear how, or *whether*, a rational argument could convince any to shift to another's position. At the same time, though, there is no reason to suspect that any would willingly relinquish the idea that he is morally 'correct'. Rather, what seems more likely is that we would be forced to agree that, when it comes to deciding whether to be egoistic, altruistic or indifferent, reason simply is *not* what makes the dispute comprehensible *as* a moral dispute.

That is one instance of the impotence of reason, and Hume could have pointed out as much. But the point that I want to make goes the other way, too. Not only is it unclear that the right thing to do or the right way to be is the rational thing to do or be: it is also unclear that to do the rational thing is to do the right thing. Without having begged the question in favour of reason, some explanation needs to be offered as to why, say, a judgement of a situation based on emotion cannot indicate something of moral import. This is a kind of objection that is often ascribed to feminist thinking; the idea that reason is the *wrong* moral tool to use can also be seen in Williams' 'one thought too many' argument.[52] At least sometimes, emotional responses may be the vanguard of moral reactions, alerting us that there is something amiss. Seen from this standpoint, II theory's opening claim that the truth of a moral statement must be something that we ascertain impersonally would be rejected. Of course, to vacate this position would be to abandon II theory – but it remains to be seen why such a dereliction would be wrong-headed.

Certainly, if we take seriously the essential identification of the will with practical reason, and if we take seriously the contention that judgements are based on what is willable, then we have a reason to sideline emotions. But the Ed, Alice and Sid example should show that judgements are based on what is willable, and it is *far* from clear why we cannot admit factors such as emotion as having at least some part to play in the determination of the will. It may be objected that emotional responses are fickle: emotion cannot play a (significant) role in moral judgement because it is inherently a personal and interested phenomenon. But this is to assume that a judgement, in order to count as a *moral* judgement, *cannot* be correspondingly fickle. In such assumptions, we may detect Platonic ghosts: it seems to be taken as read that what validates a moral judgement is an atavistic reflection of something like an unqualified Good-in-itself. And although we are used to thinking of moral

---

52 Cf. 'Persons Character and Morality' in Williams, 1993a.

judgements as being disinterested, it is not obvious that the link between morality and impartiality (hence reason) is necessary. Talking about the moral is not just a way of talking about the rational, as is demonstrated by the moral admiration we might feel for someone who goes to extraordinary lengths – irrational lengths, that is – to save a person from their burning house.

Some independentists might allow that emotional reactions play a role in judging what is right or wrong. But, granted that emotional reactions are dependent on particular individuals, in order to retain his independentist credentials, an independentist must also insist that the criteria for moral judgement are not *wholly* reducible to these reactions: he remains welded to the idea that there is a moral factor that is *not* dependent on the individual's reaction. This leaves the metaphysical question of what exactly it is that makes a judgement specifically *moral* still in need of a convincing answer. What is the moral criterion that unites all instances of right or good acts or events *as* right or good (as opposed, say, to simply *pleasing*, since 'the pleasurable' is surely uncontroversially variable across persons) with reasonable certainty? Even though a moral characteristic might not be inherent in an act or event, there is still the assumption that we are judging something *about* it.

I shall, as a Parthian shot, allow to the idealist one point of concession: idealism (of a sort) might have a better chance of understanding commonsense moral judgements and commenting on the tenability of moral claims if it is willing to devalue reason. While an understanding of the world might well depend on reason – it really is inconceivable, for example, that a box could be simultaneously cuboid and not cuboid, or that a person might be simultaneously hungry and not hungry – I suspect that an understanding of ethics will depend on no such criterion: I will elaborate on this in Chapter 5. While my suggestion a short time ago that a moral claim and its opposite might have an equal claim to truth was meant (at that stage) to destabilise II theory, I think that it is something that ethics as a line of study might be able to accommodate. Ethics needs to obey the rules of reason only if reason is prior to ethics. I have already begun to doubt the priority of reason. Later on in the study, I shall develop the idea that such a priority simply reflects a prejudice[53] and develop the idea that reason is not prior to ethics – perhaps the situation is more likely to be the other way around – and that, as a result, there is no need for ethics to make rational sense. A Kantian insistence that morality must conform to, say, the principle of non-contradiction is, I think, simply an *expression*, rather than a *condition*, of value.

---

53 Cf. Nietzsche, 1968, §407: 'Philosophers are prejudiced against appearance, change, the senses, the aimless. They believe … in the comprehensibility of human actions' (slightly modified).

Independentism and Commonsense Morality

Thus there are several reasons to be suspicious of independentism. Even if none is definitive, they ought to give us pause to wonder whether other approaches might merit consideration.

Realist independentism faces no (or few) problems arising from claims about rationality or universalisability. However, the metaphysical start-up cost of RI is enormous, and it is unlikely that it could ever really be recovered. There is, in addition, no guarantee that the application of RI would be without problems: we might ask how, for example, an irreducibly moral property could have normative power. (Plato thinks that simple knowing of the Forms is sufficient to motivate the soul, but relies on the twin claims that knowledge depends on the Forms, to which the soul is naturally attracted, and that wrongdoing implies ignorance. But this simply raises a question: is evil knowable? If it is, then it must have its own Form, and thus a soul might be attracted to evil. If it has no Form, then it falsifies the initial claim that knowledge depends on the Forms. The only alternative is implausible: that we might never be able to know that something is evil.) However, since it is implausible that a realist could ever establish convincingly what it is that makes a statement such as '*A* is *v*' true, there is no need to worry too much about why we should or should not *A*. Hence if we want independentism, it has to be some sort of idealist version. Yet the metaphysical demands here are no less onerous – albeit for different reasons. Idealism also has difficulty establishing the truth concerning the value *v* of act *A*. Once again, this means that the question never gets as far as an assessment of normativity.

Commonsense wants morality to be able to tell us reliably what the right thing to do is in all circumstances. Independentism claims to be able to meet this demand, and is initially a promising candidate for being able to provide a backing for commonsense intuitions about the moral difference between the *polis* and the terrorist organisation. But, when it is examined more closely, there is good reason to think that it cannot do what it promises. Therefore if there is anything that makes it true that terrorism is bad and *poleis* are not (as) bad, independentism is not it, and the question of independentism's normative power – its second-order characteristics, according to the rubric that I set out in Chapter 1 – is merely academic. The rather obvious next question, then, is this: is dependentism any better a candidate?

Chapter 3

Dependentism: Buying Truth and Pawning Normativity

What I have called 'independentism' contends that moral judgements have their foundation independently of the moral agent and the context in which he is operating. However, as the last chapter tried to show, there are problems with this: if the independentist wants us to think that there are self-supporting sources of morality, outside of the head of the judge, he wants us to think something that is, at best, metaphysically problematic. If what is being pushed is the belief that these sources are not self-supporting but are nonetheless 'independent' in the sense that they are perspective-free, he is expecting us to accept a system that is no less problematic – albeit for different reasons –and we are no better off.

The obvious response to independentism's inability to bulwark the kind of moral judgements that we might get from commonsense morality is to turn to what I have called 'dependentism'. At the end of Chapter 2 I asked whether dependentism is any better a metaethical theory than independentism. The concern of this chapter is to answer that question. The idea that I shall pursue is that a dependentist moral theory can do what independentism cannot; it need not fall into the metaphysical traps that sprang on independentism for the simple reason that it claims to be able to draw on a much more plausible metaphysical support: the moral picture it offers is self-sustaining and naturalistic. But I will argue that the price dependentism pays for its metaphysical security is an inability to sustain 'second-order' moral features – that is, the normative characteristics that a moral theory might need for it to count as powerful. Although dependentism thinks that it can provide normativity without independentism's metaphysical expenditure, it cannot: it must either smuggle in assumptions that are broadly those of independentism, or it must fail. Hence, in the end, it is no better than independentism at providing a secure foundation for commonsense morality.

The dependentist's strategy is to tie the applicability of a moral term to the moral judge. This can pan out in two ways. I shall call the first way 'teleological'. Its proffered account of concepts like 'good' is based around an account of what the object of moral concern is. Hence something is good for a human, and can be said truly to be good for a human, in as much as it meets a standard based on humanity; for otters, the standard of good is based on 'otterness'. The approach contrasts with a second version of dependentism, which I shall call 'Humean', and which regards moral judgements as expressive of the tastes of the judge, and the truth of a moral claim as resting on those tastes, irrespective of what this judge or the object of moral concern is. Naturally, what this judge is might determine his tastes – but the Humean sees no need to count this as relevant: what counts are the tastes themselves, not the fact that I have them because I am human. We go no further.[1]

Teleological thinking can be further divided into two subtraditions, the first of which I shall call 'eudaimonist'. Here, the truth of assessments of what would count as a good action or event are based on whether or not it is conducive to a 'good life', however that may be defined. I shall cite Aristotle as an exemplar of this strategy. What is good in this sense is whatever leads to a good life (although the goodness of good things might not be immediately obvious). So, the argument might go, it is true that x is good, and we ought to x, because it is conducive to *eudaimonia*; it is true that y is bad, and we ought not to y, because it is not.

The point might be made that this gives a fairly myopic, if not downright omphaloscopic, version of morality: it provides a way for us to talk about well-being, but provides no reason to extend the scope of our concern to others. Hence we may legitimately ask whether eudaimonism counts as a *moral* theory at all, given a strong intuition that morality has at least something to do with how one treats others. Is it possible for a broadly teleological account of morality to take a reasonable account of those others? Or must we admit that morality is self-centred? As it turns out, I shall argue that the tradition that gives rise to eudaimonism is capable of giving rise to a complementary account of morality that I shall label 'cosmological'. Under this account, moral claims can be founded not just in terms of what guarantees *eudaimonia*, but also in terms of the natural order (*kosmos*) of the world and the place therein of all beings. I shall explain this strategy in more detail later on, and once again I shall draw mainly on Aristotle, tempered by a couple of later theorists, to illustrate the argument. I do not think it implausible that, if these approaches work, they might be run together to give a teleologically-indebted 'grand unified theory' of morality that suggests, cosmologically, what I may hope for myself and must hope for others, and eudaimonistically, how I might achieve it.

I shall not bother trying to give such a unified account, though, since both the eudaimonist and cosmological approaches fail. Making judgements about *eudaimonia* upon which we can build a system of true moral statements means making too many assumptions about what it means to live a good life, and an attempt to argue cosmologically would be in vain: the cosmological approach is simply untenable. In any case, assessments based on either kind of reasoning cannot give imperatives with the non-hypothetical bite that we expect from a thorough morality. By the end of this chapter, I will have argued that one of the features of dependentism as a whole is that even those hypothetical imperatives that it *can* offer have little to recommend them on balance.

Before I get that far, I will deal with the suggestion that metaethics must be understood in terms of the more emotionally-driven approach that I have already labelled 'Humean'. This is an approach that says that the determination of 'good' is based on our emotional states: attributions of moral characteristics express approval

---

1   Hume, 1985, III, i, 2, p. 523.

or disapproval, and the truth of a moral claim must be understood as based on emotional responses. This account does have *prima facie* a reasonable chance of securing the truth in a moral statement; however, it will turn out to be metaphysically gappy when it comes to saying what it is that provokes a specifically moral reaction; moreover, it is normatively weak, and, following Jean Hampton,[2] I will argue that even when it does attempt to give norms, however restricted their scope might be, this approach is just as bad as independentism because it seems to give a place to reasoning that involves some suppositions from which, officially at least, it distances itself: suppositions that look independentist, in fact.

Naturally, insofar as both are dependentist, there is overlap between the manners of argument represented by Aristotle (in both his eudaimonist and cosmological guises) and Hume; nevertheless, there is a fairly obvious difference in their manners of operation. For the post-Aristotelian teleological traditions, the basis of moral judgements is what is being judged; for Humeans, the basis of moral judgements is the judge's mental state.[3] Even though teleologists would deny that there are inherently virtue-bestowing properties to an act or event – things are only good to the extent that they promote *eudaimonia* or accord with the *kosmos* – they can still admit that the virtue or vice of an act or event is linked to properties that it *does* have. Humeans would deny this: there is nothing about values, says the Humean, that does not have to be added by the agent.

To illustrate the difference, we can take as read that a dim view would be taken of Émile Henry's bomb-throwing by adherents to the eudaimonist, cosmological and Humean traditions; the question, to which all offer candidate answers, is one of *why* this dim view is taken. A eudaimonist would condemn Henry because bomb throwing is damaging to human flourishing – both his and, plausibly, Henry's own – perhaps inherently. He would hope to be able to say also that Henry threw the bomb because he was a bad person, in the sense that there was some vicious mole in his nature that prevented him flourishing qua person. The cosmologist would condemn Henry because persons are (at least in a loose sense) entitled not to be bombed. In contrast to both these approaches, Humeans would be far more concerned about this instance of bomb-throwing, and base their moral assessment on a reaction to that. It would only be as a spin-off from this judgement, irrespectively of why the bomb was thrown and its eventual outcomes, that he would be comfortable saying anything about Henry qua the sort of person who throws bombs or about bomb-throwing per se. Even if Humeans agree that there is something morally bad about Henry, they have still to admit that the badness is something projected by us onto him, rather than anything about Henry himself. The nature of the condemnation that each tradition can offer is slightly different: when the eudaimonist or cosmologist calls someone a good or bad person, he really means it; when Hume says the same thing, it is more synecdochial.

---

2   Hampton, 1998.
3   Hume, 1985, III, i, 1.

If You Know What's Good for You: Eudaimonism

It would be easy to think that Aristotelian moral thinking utterly rejects the Platonic starting point. Notwithstanding the distance I would draw between myself and those who think that the two were saying similar things – especially those who think that Plato was some kind of naturalist[4] – the vehemence with which Aristotle turns against his teacher is, I suspect, less than is commonly assumed (and I will have argued in a few pages' time that, although Aristotle and other eudaimonists play a different game from Plato's, it is still Plato who provides the ball). Certainly, Aristotle appears to have dismissed the idea of a Formal quality of good in the *Nichomachean Ethics*, but he does also admit that investigation of such a notion has a place in 'another branch of philosophy'[5] from that which concerns him immediately. The *Nichomachean Ethics* is not concerned with the question of whether there is just one Form of Goodness since 'clearly it cannot be realised in action or acquired by man. Yet it is precisely that sort of [realisable or acquirable] good that we are looking for now.'[6] By contrast to Plato's theoretical approach, Aristotle's remit is 'good' in its practical sense: he calls ethics a political science[7] and identifies the end of political science as 'the highest of all *practical* goods'.[8] Aristotle does think that he can refute Plato – his suggestion that 'the Good [will not] be any more good by being eternal'[9] seems to give plenty of evidence for this, for example – but it is also fair to say that his primary concern is based more on a rejection than a refutation. He is concerned by what can be done on a human scale: things beyond that scale are left untouched.

Aristotle's manifesto is built around the contention that, in these restricted and practical terms, the good at which all things aim is happiness (*eudaimonia*).[10] The extent to which something contributes to *eudaimonia*, by extension, determines whether it is the sort of thing to which we might properly apply such terms as good or bad: that is, something is good or bad 'by proxy', according to whether it contributes to or diminishes happiness. Happiness, it is worth noting, is not as simple an idea as it might appear at first: in this sense, happiness is a function of a well-lived life and denotes something like flourishing. A happy person is not (necessarily) someone with a permanent broad grin. Instead, happiness is 'rich': it encompasses such characteristics as sociability and the use of reason. After all, if to be human means to be *zōon logon ekhon politikon* – a political and rational animal – then in eschewing society and reason, one is discounting one's own humanity. But a human that discounts its humanity cannot be flourishing *as* a human, so cannot really count as happy. But this means that ascriptions of goodness and badness, if they are tied

---

4   See 'Two Sorts of Naturalism' in McDowell, 1998, or Gadamer, 1986, for example.
5   Aristotle, 1976, I, vi, 1096b31.
6   Ibid., 1096b33–35.
7   Ibid., I, ii, 1094b11.
8   Ibid., I, iv, 1095a14–17; emphasis mine.
9   Ibid., I, vi, 1096b3–5.
10 Ibid., I, iv, 1095a18.

to happiness, are not reducible to judgements about pleasure. This, as we shall see, turns out to be morally important.

One might be an adherent of the broad eudaimonistic thrust of an Aristotelian account of morality without sharing Aristotle's particular contentions. All that one has to say is that there is such a thing as human flourishing, however it might be conceived, and that some circumstances are more conducive thereto than others. Next, all that has to be claimed is that a word such as 'good' is an adjective appropriate to these circumstances: that a certain standard of well-being serves as a criterion for goodness based on the kind of being that we are. Hence understanding something about humans enables us to say something about what is good practically and thereby to flesh out the idea that a statement along the lines of 'this is good' could be true or false. One might want to introduce a Darwinian factor into the debate, too, and claim that natural selection has made us creatures who thrive in certain conditions and who have the intellectual wherewithal to understand those conditions and how best to promote them, at least in principle: what is good is whatever is good for us in terms of the way we have evolved. Our genes may be selfish – but our intellectual evolution means that we are in a position to direct this selfishness. This might even mean the recognition that human flourishing is 'holistic': tied in, that is, with the preservation of the rainforests, different cultures or whatever. Importantly for the motivation of this book, though, the upshot is that, on this basis, we can ascribe truth to a claim that such-and-such an action or *modus vivendi* is good or bad with only a little extra work.

Thus eudaimonism gives a guide to how an ascription of value might incorporate a claim to truth. And, from this, it is possible to glean some sort of insight into how this might translate in terms of the specific question of the moral difference between violence and democracy. Human well-being involves living within a political framework, for example: we need to live with others simply because of the demands and limitations of life. Largely, this is for the simple fact that humans are not seen as self-sufficient (*autarkhes*) while living alone: therefore households exist by nature, Aristotle thinks, and these households equally naturally coalesce into primitive *poleis*.[11] Famously, the contention guiding *The Politics* is that humans only achieve *eudaimonia* within a political context. 'Any one who *by his nature* and not simply by ill-luck has no state is either too bad or too good, either subhuman or superhuman', he claims.[12] Non-Aristotelian eudaimonists can make a claim that is different in detail, but still bears a recognisable structural similarity to this. The basic claim is that we call civil society good derivatively, because it is a means of achieving a teleologically-defined standard of good, but that claims to this effect need be seen as no less true for that. Membership of a *polis* or a *polis*-like institution is teleologically appropriate for humans: it is under political conditions that we come to flourish. On the other hand, people like Émile Henry disrupt the stability of the

---

11 Aristotle, 1992, I, ii.
12 Ibid.

polis, and so they are inimical to our living a good life: they threaten the way to *eudaimonia*.[13]

This, then, is how commonsense morality's take on terrorism could be fleshed out: all humans have an interest in human flourishing; as long as we are willing to annex to this the idea that political existence is the best guarantor of this, we can claim that one should refrain from activities such as terrorism: it is straightforwardly true that terrorism is inimical to the *polis*; but if being inimical to the *polis* is corrosive to *eudaimonia*, and if it is *eudaimonia* that bankrolls moral claims, it takes little to claim that we can legitimately ascribe moral claims to terrorism. In the end, 'terrorism is wrong' is true because terrorism is antagonistic to one of *eudaimonia*'s necessary conditions. Indeed, this argument can be extended to a wider point: we should refrain from antisocial activity generally – theft, drunken singing on the way home from the pub and so on – because every instance of antisocial activity removes another layer, howsoever thin, from the lacquer of human existence. Because we have a teleologically comprehensible need for existence alongside others, which pans out as political existence, alienating these others will have, ultimately, a negative impact on us. Not to put too fine a point on it: pissing people off is counterproductive, and, all else being equal, moral statements that reflect this have a claim to truth.

(Whatever the differences may be between Aristotle and Hobbes, there is a similarity between some of the political points that a eudaimonist might make and Hobbes' account of man in the State of Nature, whose life is famously 'solitary, poore, nasty, brutish and short'.[14] After all, such a life is easily classified as being anything *but* well-lived (*eudaimonikos*): what he sees as the self-evidence of the superiority of political over apolitical life is enough to convince Aristotle that political life is much better suited than apolitical life to the human *telos*. If this was not the case, would not apolitical people – non-Greeks – possibly lead lives as good as the Greeks'? What a thought![15] This is a point that any eudaimonist would understand, even if he might not *agree*.)

---

13 It is worth clarifying the point that Aristotle's picture of the *politikon zōon* contains more than someone existing within a collectivity of private individuals. Aristotle represents a tradition in which the moral individual is conceivable only within a social matrix. As MacIntyre points out, even for Plato, 'there is no way to be excellent as a man that does not involve excellence as a citizen and *vice versa*' (see MacIntyre, 2000, p. 141). And it is not completely out of place to remind ourselves of one of Socrates' arguments concerning his refusal to escape his own execution: was it not the city – indirectly at least – that made possible his very existence? (*Crito*, 50d) By taking his life, the *polis* is only *re*claiming what, in an important sense, was its own from the start. Equally, for Aristotle, the idea of a moral self makes sense only within a network of other moral selves. This casts light on how it is possible for Aristotle to promote self-sufficiency (*autarkheia*) as a virtue, but still to insist that humans are interdependent. Interdependence and submission to the *polis* is not *heterarkheia* – it is the key to *autarkheia* on the condition that the moral 'self' is only realised alongside others.

14 Hobbes, 1999, XIII, p. 89.

15 Aristotle makes the point that a 'brutish' person is rare among humans; such people are commonest among non-Greeks, although such monsters may be spawned through 'disease

However, there is a fairly obvious counterargument that can be put here. So far, all the analysis does is point out a weakness in our constitutions. It relies, ultimately, on *our* frailties: at most, we could say that one is foolish to be antisocial, but this is not a particularly compelling *moral* critique, and it does not really entitle us to say anything about Henry in a direct sense. His badness under this picture has to be filtered through us: if we were more robust – for example, if we were self-sufficient creatures with no need for *poleis* – Henry, or any terrorist, for that matter, would arguably not merit moral comment: any value-claim about terrorism would be, at best, trivially true. As things stand, in fact, there is not much basis for the thought that there is a significant moral difference between Henry and a hurricane. A stronger argument that would be more directly about Henry is also possible, though, and it would have the same sort of starting point. Someone like Henry is not bad because he is a threat to the political existence that we need (and he needs) teleologically: he is a threat because he is a bad person. Again, I will use Aristotle to demonstrate how a more generally eudaimonist argument might manifest itself.

When he talks of the asocial as too bad or too good for political existence, Aristotle is not simply being hyperbolic in his statements of disapproval and approval of people with antisocial propensities or supersocial abilities; he really does mean that such people either fall short of the 'model' of humanity, or else that they exceed it. The effect is the same: such people are not fully *human*. (A more modern spin could be put on the same point to make it less specifically Aristotle's without too much difficulty: there is something *wrong* with antisocial types just as there is something *wrong* with psychopaths: we do not have to say that they are any less human to be able to say that they are impaired in some aspect of human *functioning*.) Evidence that this is how Aristotle thinks comes from the fact that the word used for 'bad' is *phaulos*; for 'good', *khreitton*. I am not going to worry too much about those who are 'too good' for political existence: *khreitton* is a word that is used in the context of excellence, and so it can be assumed that this category of beings simply covers those who are teleologically self-sufficient; these beings are 'not a part of the state at all',[16] and nor have they need to be. I shall let these characters get on with whatever higher pursuits may take their fancy.

More interesting for present purposes are the extra-political *phauloi*. '*Phaulos*' pertains to something trivial and of no great import; that is, something that has fallen a good deal short of excellence. When he is talking about the 'bad' people in this context, Aristotle is not talking about people whom we might dub evil because their actions are contrary to (our) practical good so much as he is talking about people who are, effectively, teleological abortions (at least as far as the *telos* of a *human* is concerned), too base by nature to live in a *polis*, and unable to live a good human

---

or arrested development' as well (*Ethics*, VII, i, 1145a30–32). The clear implication must be that the prime causes of brutishness are either retardation or simply having the misfortune to be born into a non-Greek race: *eugenesis* begets *eudaimonia*. It is difficult to avoid detecting a subtext that says that Hellenes are physiologically predisposed towards certain virtues.

16 Aristotle, 1992, I, ii, 1253a27–29.

life. An example of this kind of person is the 'war-mad' (*polemou epithumetes*) extrasocial soul whom Aristotle mentions:[17] such a person's nature is skewed against political existence.

The argument, basically, is that being a *politikon zōon* is a sign that one has a personality of a certain quality – that one *truly is* a good person in a sense that describes the characteristics of the soul and its predisposition towards behaviour that promotes flourishing. Again, this is an argument that could be given a more modern, post-Darwinian twist: all we have to be able to say is that one is not 'successfully' human if one is incapable of living in a social context, because of the importance of the social context to human *eudaimonia*. A feature of the general pattern of human behaviour is a certain degree of affability and peaceableness. Even when forced to go to war, we tend to look forward to an honourable peace. From this basis we can make claims about the propensities of humans and the nature of human interrelationships. In acting antisocially, Henry is allowing us to discern something about the way he is built: he is giving away that he is a bad person (*phaulos*). Political existence simultaneously guarantees a good life and reveals a certain character of the soul that is practically good in a human context – one that is capable of a specifically human flourishing.

But what is 'the soul' for Aristotle, and how does it entitle us to talk about good and bad people? And is talk of a soul a major blunder that prevents Aristotelianism ever claiming to be free of suspect metaphysical commitments?

Souls, Naturally

Clearing up the first question will tell us how to respond to the second. Plato is clear that 'good and evil are meaningless to things that have no soul',[18] and Aristotle concurs in thinking that the soul is important in consideration of issues that might be dubbed 'moral': for him, though, the soul is not a discrete feature of a particular being – a sort of metaphysical organ – and nor is it something easily separable from *telos*. In effect, 'soul' is a metaphor for the principle underlying the 'complete', flourishing human:

> [F]or body is not something attributed to a subject; it rather acts as the underlying subject and material basis ... Soul therefore will be a perfect realisation of a body such as has been described ... [It] is the earlier perfect realisation of a natural organic body.[19]

A soul is a bit like an architect's blueprint; it tells us what a human can and *will* become according to teleology. Updating this line to the ages of Darwin and Dawkins, 'soul' might be seen as something like a basket term that covers accounts of genetic and psychosocial propensities. It is the 'soul' that makes the difference between

---

17 Ibid., 1253a6.
18 Letter VII in Plato, 1973, 334e–335a.
19 Aristotle, 1882, II, i, 412a17–412b6.

species, and determines how species behave: say, why humans and chimpanzees socialise in slightly different ways. The soul of a thing unravels as that thing reaches its 'end and perfection', and determines its development thereto: given two recently fertilised eggs, we might not be able to tell which is human and which is chimp, but as they develop we will be able to get an insight into what it is that draws each zygote down its particular developmental path. (A genetic fingerprint, perhaps, could be seen as a means of looking into the soul, especially if theories about the genetic and chromosomal basis for behaviour have much to them.)

'The living animal is at once the soul and body in connection' goes Aristotle's claim:[20] although the soul nudges its bearer towards certain things, it 'grows into itself' as the life of its bearer progresses. Accordingly, we learn about the soul, and *can* learn about the soul, only from the living animal, rather than from any a priori principle. And when we ascribe characteristics to a person, at least a part of what we are doing is stating a theory about the kind of soul they have. Hence, for example, magnanimous people '*are thought to* remember the benefits they have conferred, but not those they have received';[21] one might theorise about the magnanimity of a soul from the tendency not to take petty risks, disposal to confer benefits, to walk with a measured gait, and so on.[22] Aristotle offers a psychology or natural history of the kind of person who has certain characteristics.

This theory can deepen the picture of how to assess good or bad behaviour, in the sense of befitting or unbefitting. To call someone a 'good' person is to make an assessment, based on the kind of soul that we think he might have, of whether that soul has unravelled itself properly or is able to 'behave' according to its *telos*, and the truth of our ascription will be a function of the accuracy of that assessment. We might have reason to believe that someone has a magnanimous soul, but note also that, since that bump on the head, he has been behaving pusillanimously; from these two beliefs we might surmise that something has gone wrong. At other times, we might be able to diagnose something wrong with the way that someone is put together: if Henry was born with a propensity to antisocial behaviour, and if, nevertheless, we think that he is the possessor of a human soul, we might say that his soul has not so much *gone wrong* as *always been* bad qua human soul – that he has some sort of psychic birth defect. In just the same way, we might say that when a piece of the engine has fallen off the car due to rust, it has gone wrong, but that if the car was built without some vital component, it has always been of a low quality or defective qua car.

Accordingly, we might be able to say of someone like Henry that he is one of the *phauloi* mentioned above. (We can still hope for reform, of course: just as we can modify a vehicle that, even from the moment it left the production line, was never going to run except with this modification, it should be possible in principle to 'repair' even the *phaul*est personality defect.) Aristotle does not worry about the

---

21 Aristotle, 1976, IV, iii, 1124b12–14.
22 Ibid., 1124b6ff.

distinction between 'the disposition [and] the person who corresponds to it':[23] the moral characteristic *is* a disposition that cannot easily be separated from the person.

But what is it that is a characteristic of a *good*, in the sense of well-put-together, human? Aristotle sets great store by moderation as a mark of human virtue; this might allow a critique based on the contention that moderation is something that someone like Henry obviously lacks: he's too hot-headed, too belligerent – war-mad, maybe – and so on to count as possessing moderation. This backs up the idea that he is a bad person in the sense that he is badly put together. Someone might become immoderate, or might be immoderate from birth. If he becomes immoderate, this might be a sign of some kind of moral ill-health. But if he has always been immoderate, this person would seem simply to be badly constructed qua human: he is just unfortunate enough to have been born a bad person.

Of course, not all Aristotelian points are peripatetic enough to be adopted by other thinkers: there is, therefore, a question concerning how closely we want to be tied to Aristotle. But, even if some points are not transferable, there seems to be mileage in a claim that we can make sense of good and bad behaviour from looking at the agent: that there is a way to work out secure moral guidelines from observing the world and the way it works, and with no need for reference to Platonic or irreducibly real moral characteristics or to the machinations of a norm-creating *noûs*. If this strategy can be made to work, ethics can be naturalised. Adherence to such a claim would allow us to get an intimation of how one might defend the *polis* from the terrorist: all we have to do is refer to the manner in which (say) the *polis* is the criterion of something like human *eudaimonia*. It would be foolhardy to dismiss *ab initio* the possibility that observation might tell us that there is *no* basis for many of our moral beliefs – but even this would not be a disaster, since we would still have a secure way of judging acts and events in the world around us.

Whether the strategy works is, of course, another matter. But before I consider whether or not eudaimonism works, I want to turn my attention to the account that I have labelled cosmological, since I do not think that eudaimonism can account for *all* the expectations of commonsense morality: beings other than the agent do not get much of a look in. To fill the gaps, an account that pays some heed to cosmological concerns is appropriate and complementary. Because of the close teleological relationship between eudaimonism and cosmological accounts of morality, in the end they will stand or fall together.

Cosmology as a Moral Tool

Eudaimonism, as it stands, can offer a partial account of the things that we should bear in mind when making a moral evaluation of an act, event or person. But, at the same time, it is not inconceivable that circumstances could fall out in such as way as to make it possible for one agent to put others at his disposal in a manner that conflicts with

---

23 Ibid., 1123b1–2.

some of the precepts of commonsense morality and yet is teleologically acceptable, and there is, at present, precious little to suggest how we should respond to this. For example, it might be that I have good reason to believe that my flourishing would be hastened by enslaving my neighbour. To claim that social cooperation is more conducive than unaided nature to well-being is one thing, but it is compatible with this to suggest that setting out to make my neighbour my slave is more conducive to *eudaimonia* – to mine, at least – than either. Tricking someone into becoming my household skivvy would allow me to become a man of leisure – a scholar in the strict sense. Is the undertone here that antisocial behaviour is wrong (and a statement to that effect true) only if it turns out to be counterproductive? That it might be practically *right* to enslave him as long as I can get away with it? Might Aristotle wear Machiavellian garb? If eudaimonist conceptions of goodness are restricted to the practical, might we decide, like Milton's Satan, that evil is our good?[24]

The problem is one that Plato faced in the story of Gyges and his ring;[25] his picture of the soul and the Forms suggest that bad behaviour is that which is over-concerned or bogged down by the physical, and that there is a good reason to forgo bad behaviour even if one is invisible. Idealists have their own versions of an immutable *ought*. Teleologists have no such ballast. Nevertheless, there is room for them to suppose that some moral guides *can* be found, and that these guides can be derived cosmologically – that is, in terms of an account (*logos*) of the order (*kosmos*[26]) of the world. If successful, this second, cosmological, approach would allow dependentism to plant its flag on the moral pole reasonably securely (though, in the end, the claim will fail, for reasons that I will suggest in a while). As before, much will come from Aristotle, although something broadly similar might be said by others – briefly, I will suggest who some of these others might be.

The starting point for the argument lies in the familiar idea that there is a serious moral difference between humans and non-humans. What makes the human soul *human* is possession of *logos*; in turn, this is what allows humans to be moral creatures. The reason for this offered in the *Politics* is that in having *logos*, man is alone among animals in having the capacity to 'deliberate concerning good and evil':[27] put simply, it is only humans for whom moral concepts are meaningful – and we do not have to be Aristotelians to admit that it does seem uniquely to be humans that can understand moral epithets. However, the ability to understand moral epithets is not enough to tell us about how we should treat others, especially when there is a potential conflict between *my* well-being and yours. A cosmological analysis of *logos*, though, can help.

---

24 Milton, 2000, IV, l 110.

25 Plato, 1987, 359c ff.

26 'Κόσμος' also means 'good order, good behaviour, decency' according to Liddell and Scott. There would therefore seem to be reason to think that morality, in a sense, *just is* a branch of cosmology.

27 Aristotle, 1992, I, ii, 1253a15.

Several causative factors might drive the motions of entities in the Aristotelian universe. Some things do what they do because of luck (*tukhe*), as when a coin lands 'heads'. Others behave in the way they do because of necessity (*ananke*); this is the factor that causes billiard balls to ricochet around the table in the way they do. It is also what causes ploughs to plough. A third causal principle is nature (*phusis*); for example, a plant's growth can be explained according to (its) nature. The final cause is human agency – the power that humans have to determine their own actions.[28] And, Aristotle thinks, the deliberative power that is uniquely human is underpinned by *logos*.

Aristotle denies that one deliberates concerning what is not in one's power – '[t]he effects about which we deliberate are those which are *produced* by our agency'[29] – and what is not undetermined:[30] he distinguishes between matters of choice (*proairesis*) and of deliberation (*bouleusis*) and suggests that to *choose* is to select one from a range of given options, while to *deliberate* is to be able to generate one's own options. Therefore deliberation is a sign that human agency can be a kind of behavioural prime mover. Implicitly, too, creatures without *logos* cannot be self-determining. In other words, the human power of *deliberation* is taken by Aristotle to be evidence of the power of human agency to act as an *arkhe* – a first link in a particular causal chain. It is only that which is a matter of deliberation to which Aristotle is willing to apply moral consideration.

To illustrate what Aristotle means about deliberation and how it is different from choice, consider this example: we might choose between picking up the apple or the orange on the table, these being things that are already 'givens'. By contrast, in relation to good and evil, where there is nothing set out before us, we would deliberate: we have to start the decision-making process from scratch. (We would also deliberate over whether apples or oranges are preferable.) By 'choice', Aristotle here seems to mean something roughly in line with the Hobbesian idea of liberty, insofar as Hobbes thinks that '*Liberty* and *Necessity* are consistent; as in the water, that hath not only *liberty*, but a *necessity* of descending by the Channel'.[31] I think that it would not be asking too much to say that this could be put into Aristotelian parlance fairly easily if we think that the water might 'choose' to run down the channel, one of several potential routes down the hill, but not deliberate about its route.

There are certain traits that can be seen in creatures with *logos*, then, that are untraceable back to other factors. There is something teleologically 'right' about humans forming their own paths because man is the *zōon logon ekhon*. For the sake of the argument, I shall link *logos* to a category of causation that I shall call 'personal', since it makes the difference between a person and a thing and allows humans to be considered the only beings that are (known to be) self-directed. This

---

28 Aristotle, 1976, III, iii, 1112a18 ff.
29 Ibid., 1112b2-4; emphasis mine.
30 Ibid., 1113a2–4.
31 Hobbes, 1999, XXI, p. 146.

ensures a special place for humans in comparison to the rest of the world, just insofar as humans are self-moving.

Teleologically speaking, the good man will be the man who is making full play of the fact that he is *zōon logon ekhon*, and not (wholly) determined by the more 'impersonal' causes such as necessity and nature. In the *Politics*, Aristotle is clear that he thinks it right for reason (*logos*) to rule over emotion because anything else would be 'fatal all round'[32] – note the wholly befitting, albeit perhaps overplayed, appeal to practical concerns rather than a priori ordering. Now, if a part of what it means to be a human *zōon logon ekhon* is to be self-directing, there is a mode of behaviour which is teleologically appropriate for humans and therefore something which allows the Aristotelian to claim that certain behaviours might be open to criticism: it is wrong – in the sense of cosmologically inappropriate or unbefitting – to subordinate me, a human, to causes that are not personal – not, that is, my 'own'. Accordingly, what is wrong about the bomb-throwing terrorist is that he ignores this. In using coercive intimidation, he is forcing people to act in a manner that is not their 'own'. As such, he acts in a way that is at odds with the greater cosmological scheme of the world. Examination of the human *telos* will reveal that he is *zōon logon ekhon*; subsequent cosmological analysis of the *zōon logon ekhon* will show, naturalistically and practically, how he should be treated – what good treatment is.

Admittedly, a strong wind or hunger might force us to do things that we otherwise would not. But, of course, possessing *logos* is an extra that means that we *can* do things deliberately: natural forces cannot. This is the difference between Henry and a hurricane: hurricanes do not have *logos*. What grants terrorism its *moral* aspect is that it is the product of deliberation and that it seeks to intimidate people into behaving in a certain way, not simply that it operates contrary to their place as human and self-determining. Deliberation is what makes an action an action, and an action is open to moral criticism if it is inappropriate and plaudits if it is appropriate. When I am considering whether to enslave my neighbour, I should bear in mind that he is human, and so self-directing. And on this basis, he would be able to claim that there is a simple fact about the world that means that it is unbefitting that he should be enslaved. This fact about the world would not rely on a priori moral rules, but would give me an insight into befitting behaviour.

It is interesting to note, of course, how this relates to Aristotle's support for slavery. If it is unbefitting their status that humans be enslaved – that is, treated as tools, with impersonal causes substituted for personal ones – how come he still allows some humans to be slaves?

The simple answer is that he does not. This is for two reasons. The first is that having overcome the enemy in battle and enslaved him is taken as a demonstration that the Greek has the cosmological edge over the non-Greek. He has shown his superiority, and therefore his entitlement to dominate. Slavery is the naturally appropriate resolution of a state of war (though it is worth noting the contrast here with Locke, who defends slavery when it represents 'the state of war *continued* between

---

32 Aristotle, 1992, 1, v, 1254b6–9.

a lawful conqueror and captive'[33]). It is right, muses Aristotle, that, as the poets say, Greeks should rule non-Greeks,[34] because Greeks are simply and demonstrably fit to rule, and *hoi barbaroi* fit to be ruled. Just as the elements have their own strata, so that air will always float on water, earth will always sink and fire will always be in the topmost stratum, the same applies to humans in their different types.

The second reason why slavery is unproblematic is related to this, but goes further. More or less, it is that, while all men are humans, some are more human than others. A slave is a slave 'by nature'.[35] He is a tool, not a self-directing *zōon logon ekhon*; he might give the impression of being an animal with *logos*, but this is a false impression.[36] A slave is a human of sorts, but he is something of a second-division human – perhaps the fact that he has been enslaved may be seen as hinting as much – and to leave a slave-human to his own devices would be as teleologically inept as trying to *impose* devices on a *zōon logon ekhon*: a slave is not something that is fitted to rule – it is in fact in his teleological interest to *be* ruled, roughly as it is in the Greeks' practical interest to rule him.[37] Not only is it not inappropriate to rule the slave: it might actually be befitting.

Consider, as an analogy, an axe: the thing that makes it an *axe* rather than just a thing, 'would constitute its essential nature or reality and thus, so to speak, its soul';[38] and the thing that makes an axe an *axe* is just that it is fit to be used for chopping. By this token, not to use an axe as an axe or to wait for it to direct itself is to misunderstand what 'axeness' or 'axish' flourishing is all about. One *could* use it as an oar, but this would be to miss the point of what makes an axe an *axe* and different *from* an oar. Similarly, not to use a being that is a slave by nature *as* a slave is to misunderstand what *he* is all about, just as to think of (Greek) humans without *logos* is to misunderstand (Greek) humans. It stands to reason, then, that one is not treating him unbefittingly by imposing *ananke* on him. A slave's alogical nature ties him to a heterarchy that would be impossible for the (Greek) *zōon logon ekhon* with whom he does not share teleological entitlements. To think that the slave is being mistreated in his slavery is to have missed the point: by the same token, 'wrong' is a word that does not apply to slavery.

One does not have to agree with Aristotle wholesale to admit that the strategy we might adopt as Aristotelians is similar to that which we might adopt as members of other traditions. The point is that, simply from an analysis of the sort of creatures that humans are (or axes, or anything else), we can build up a picture of the place that they rightfully occupy in the cosmos, and, indirectly, of 'entitlements' that they might have as functions of what is befitting. We do not have to accept the defence

---

33 Locke, 1967, IV, § 24. There is a separate question to be asked here concerning what basis Locke has for calling anyone captive or conqueror in a state of *continued* war.

34 Aristotle, 1992, I, ii, 1252b8.

35 Ibid., I, ii, 1253b32 ff.; vii, 1255b16 ff.; III, iv, 1278b34.

36 Ibid., I, ii, 1254b22 ff.

37 Ibid., 1252a24-34.

38 Aristotle, 1882, II, i, 412b12–13.

of slavery to take on board the claim that there is some standard of treatment that a human can claim *simply by virtue of being human*, without the need for a priori moral rules – all that a given human needs to be able to do is to point out that he belongs *here* rather than *there* in the scheme of things. *Logos* is pretty special and marks a difference between persons and non-persons; correspondingly, persons can demand a different treatment from that afforded to non-persons.

We might see a trace of this kind of thinking in human rights-speak: the claim is made that, simply by virtue of being persons, certain creatures have basic yet morally weighty entitlements. Apparently, there need be no recourse to the rather baroque norms that the independentist wants to provide. We might cite someone like Tom Paine as belonging to this kind of tradition: 'there can be but one element of human power; *and that element is man himself*'.[39] Paine is making a plea against the division of humanity into king and subject, ruler and ruled, but backing it up with nothing more than the power of the concept of a person, which is sufficient to delegitimise arbitrary power of one person over another. Moreover, by adopting the tradition of translating *zōon logon ekhon* as 'rational animal', it is possible to read Mary Wollstonecraft as putting the same point:

> In what does man's pre-eminence over the brute creation consist? The answer is clear as that a half is less than the whole, *in Reason* … Consequently the *perfection of our nature and capability of happiness must be estimated by the degree of reason*, virtue and knowledge that distinguish the individual … and that from the exercise of reason, knowledge and virtue naturally flow, is equally undeniable, if mankind be viewed collectively.[40]

From a slightly different angle, the Marx of the 1844 *Manuscripts* could be interpreted as sharing concerns about the teleology of the industrial worker, in this case understood as a member of the species *homo faber*, and thence addressing how he should be treated,[41] again without reference to a priori norms.

We can draw the line in any number of places, of course: instead of making personhood or rationality a criterion, we might just as well claim that sentience is sufficient to give morally weighty entitlements, so that simply by virtue of being sentient, there is some sort of entitlement to a certain standard of treatment (allowing a very loose sense to 'teleology'). Nevertheless, the overall point is that, if we have some action in mind, the rightness or wrongness thereof is influenced by the nature of whatever it is on which we seek to act. There is a place for teleological-cosmological analysis, or something appreciably similar, in the solution of a moral dilemma, since an appeal to cosmology could found a claim about the 'entitlements' of the object of our attention. Naturally, things are not always straightforward. It is not immediately clear how acknowledging that someone is self-determining could explain what is wrong with theft, for example – except that it might be pointed out that to steal something from someone is tantamount to enslaving them, and this

---

39 Paine, 1985, p. 142; emphasis mine.
40 Wollstonecraft, 1992, p. 91; emphasis mine.
41 Marx, *Economic and Philosophic Manuscripts of 1844*, in Marx and Engels, 1975.

would be teleologically inappropriate: perhaps the argument would be that they have had to earn the money for this item, and by depriving them of it you are effectively appropriating their labour, and thereby treating them as a tool in a manner that runs contrary to the way in which the world is ordered.

Hence an approach that draws on teleology or on something very like it can, it is claimed, begin to provide us with a backing for commonsense morality on two grounds. Eudaimonistically, I can look towards my own flourishing as being something that can provide a basis for understanding things as good or evil: they are matters which, respectively, encourage or hinder my *eudaimonia*. Cosmologically, I can look towards the nature of others to provide me with a behavioural guideline or boundary (depending on the nature of the question). Each of these modes of argument claims to be safely natural, and yet not to be reducible to facts that are entirely dependent on the passing opinions of a moral judge: there would seem to be *some* kind of fact of the matter that informs moral judgements and provides a way for them to be *true*. Granted that there is a need for security for the sake of flourishing, and that this is best served when one is behaving in an appropriate manner towards one's fellow citizens, we are in a position to make a claim about good behaviour. With the appropriate development, it is apparently possible that this might be an approach that can be developed into a workable and complete moral theory.

In Defence of Politics

If the approach outlined is right, it should be able to provide at least a nascent truth-criterion for moral judgements, including that concerning the difference between democracy and violence. At first glance, things look promising: as I have just argued, there is a range of reasons that might be cited to substantiate the idea that a statement about the moral values of civil society and political violence could be true. First, the *polis* is a nurturing environment for human *telos*, whereas the terrorist disrupts this environment – a bad thing. Second, the terrorist reveals himself as a 'lower-quality' or 'faulty' person, thus giving us a reason to suspect that the activities that characterise him *as* a terrorist are in some sense unworthy of emulation or admiration. Third, insofar as the terrorist relies on forcing people to behave in certain ways, he is treating his targets inappropriately and in a manner constitutive of badness. Hence the terrorist is open to moral critique from a eudaimonist position in a way that the *polis* is not. How convincing is the argument? It is in this section that I shall begin to test the account. If it fails to tell us anything convincing about the terrorism problem, it cannot be adequate to commonsense morality generally, since a compelling and successful metaethic must be applicable in all circumstances.

One thing that is worth bearing in mind is the leeway that the defender of the *polis* can claim thanks to the dissociation of *good* from more immediate happiness. This sanctions the implementation of rules that are not conducive to immediate happiness – or are even contrary to it – in the name of future flourishing. In a moral defence of the *polis* from the terrorist, the *polis* can come to be seen as a sort of nursery for the *zōon logon ekhon* – and a good nurseryman will be willing from time to time to do things that might *appear* to be harmful to his plants. For example, he might deprive them of water to force them to develop deeper roots; he might cut whole branches off a tree so that the following year it will grow more vigorously. The nurseryman knows, though, that his regime is for the plants' own good, and it is *true* that he is acting in their interests. Similarly, imposing laws that *appear* to restrict the happiness or self-determination of the *zōon logon ekhon* may turn out to be a condition of his flourishing in the longer term – it might even be a condition of his gaining the intellectual wherewithal to complain in the first place. Making a law is a method of bringing on growth in human 'saplings': it is Solonic irrigation.

Hence there is nothing that need be morally problematic about the role of the *polis* and some of the apparently coercive tendencies that I noted in Chapter 1. States impose laws, but these should be thought of as a means of ensuring *eudaimonia*, not as hardships. By contrast, regardless of any claim they might make about future justice, what is indisputable is that terrorists disrupt present stability. This disruption leaves the way clear for a Hobbesian argument that it is better to live under the Leviathan, no matter how onerous his demands, than it is to live in a State of Nature, since a State of Nature is antithetical to any form of flourishing. At least a Leviathan can impose rules around which people can arrange their lives: however unpleasant life in Afghanistan was under the Taliban, they did at least make the streets safe.[42] As long as humans show a disposition to prefer safety to risk, peace to war, it cannot be right to bring war to a *polis*. Peace being a condition of flourishing, whatever gives peace and so nurtures is good and its promotion is just. The terrorist disrupts peace, and is therefore unjust.

Yet the nurseryman argument is not powerful, largely because it rests on an appeal to future *eudaimonia*, and there is no obvious reason why the terrorist can not claim something that is all but identical. He might (claim to) know, for example, that the conditions necessary for maximising human happiness can only be achieved by violence – which becomes thereby practically good. The state's imposition of taxes (he might continue), backed by the threat of prison, is not paradigmatically different from his own coercive intimidation: it is extortion with menaces; arguably, this is violent. But since it is the violence of terrorism that contributes to the problem that we have with it in the first place, an ability to show that the state is comparatively violent will diminish the state's moral advantage. The *polis* is not peaceful after all: the difference is that its structural violence is insidious. Thus, initially at least, it would appear that, even if teleological arguments can provide a criterion of truth for moral statements, they may have little normative power.

In effect, the only strong argument that is available to the theorist who wants to protect the *polis* from the terrorist is that the terrorist has simply got things wrong. Either he is wrong in thinking that the sort of change he wants will be (as) conducive to human flourishing as he hopes, or he is wrong to think that his chosen method

---

42 A story from the BBC shortly after the fall of Kabul makes this point: crime rose when the Taliban left: see http://news.bbc.co.uk/1/hi/world/south_asia/1754821.stm for details.

– violence – is the correct one. However, neither of these versions of the argument is *morally* powerful, and, as we have just seen, only the first version offers a particularly robust defence of the *polis*. And, of course, it remains a logical possibility that some terrorists might turn out, in fact, to have the moral *advantage* over the *polis*. This means that the argument enables us to say that *this* terrorist may be in the wrong – but it does not allow us to say anything about terrorism in general: only about the comparative merits of *poleis* through history. Since commonsense draws a general moral distinction (it *is* intuitively attractive to say that terrorism *is* morally worse than civil society, after all), albeit one to which there might be exceptions, and it is this distinction that I am pursuing, I am still not satisfied.

In principle, the same problem – that general guidelines are more difficult to derive than defenders of the approach adopted to this point might like to admit – could apply to any other issue with which moral thinking might concern itself. Even if an appeal to teleology can provide the metaethical scaffolding for commonsense moral judgements in *some* cases, we would be left with a fairly raggedy moral theory that would not reliably foreclose the possibility of problematic exceptions, and that would have to be supplemented by other theories if we wanted to cover all cases while still keeping hold of commonsense moral judgements. If it cannot sustain these distinctions, then eudaimonist accounts simply *cannot* be what founds them: commonsense must have got its expectations from somewhere else. A critical normative test seems to have been failed. Admittedly, this might only be criticism for as long as I want to keep the content of commonsense moral judgements: it might be that I simply have to change my morality to fit the theory. I am reluctant to do this, though, and in Chapter 4 I will explain why I do not have to. More immediately, the argument that I am about to venture is that changing the morality to fit the theory would not do much good in this case anyway, because the theory is unsound in the first place. This normative problem is just one among others, as I shall explain now.

Eudaimonism, Cosmology and Essentialism

It might not be a problem that the moral difference between the democrat and the terrorist is not as clear as commonsense may have hoped: maybe a clear-headed study of humans and the human good would force us to admit that the difference has to be re-evaluated. What would be left would still be a means of determining the moral status of acts and events: that the outcome is unexpected does not count against the method. But there are still big obstacles to the acceptance of a moral theory that bases moral evaluations on an analysis of something like teleologically determined eudaimonistic good or cosmological fitness. I will deal first with eudaimonism.

The first problem here is that, while eudaimonism claims to be naturalistic and so metaphysically secure in a way that is not true of independentism, its claim is not compelling: in making a claim about what constitutes human good, non-naturalism has been smuggled into the eudaimonist argument. We can say easily enough what makes an artefact like a clock a good clock – clocks are made to some design, and it is on this basis that we can say whether they are working well, being treated well, and so on, according to their 'soul' or *telos*. We can say, for example, that they are a tool for telling the time and not a weapon (irrespective of how useful they might be in this capacity); their perfection comes in striking the hour and not in striking me. We can even talk about the characteristics that would be possessed and behaviours that would be displayed by a good doctor, lawyer, milkman or whatever (slave?), insofar as the agent who performs a role has made a kind of artefact of himself.

But there is no reason to think that there is a teleological template when it comes to non-artefacts like people. For this reason, it is not easy to argue for a particular picture of what a well-lived (good) human life is without quietly ignoring the essential question concerning just what the standard is to which we should be looking. We cannot take for granted that there is a 'final form' for humans in the same way as there is for artefacts such as clocks.[43] Without such a final form we cannot be sure what is meant by 'flourishing'. There is no basis to think that there is any robust difference at all between *eudaimonia* and bog-standard hedonism: it begins to look ambitious to say that there is something right for humans qua humans rather than simply qua animals complex enough to distinguish between pleasure and pain.

Surely, though, there are certain things that are good for certain species simply by virtue of their membership of this species? This being the case, there is room to talk about *human* 'goods' and *otter* 'goods' and the possibility that they might be different. Certainly, otters may well have proclivities that are not generally shared by humans. But why do we stop looking for the practical good at the species level, rather than carrying on all the way down to the individual? Why do we think that differences at this level are unimportant? This is not a silly question.

For example, men and women belong to the same species, but differences have been noted in the neuroanatomy of the sexes, and it is suggested that this might have something to do with explaining (some) behavioural differences.[44] Other differences have been found between homosexuals' and heterosexuals' brains, even though they belong to the same species – Allen et al. note that homosexual men and heterosexual women have larger anterior commisures than heterosexual men, for example.[45] Given that there seems to be a noteworthy physiological difference, it might seem fair enough to say that there is a different *telos*: that the 'souls' of men, women, gay and straight people manifest themselves in such differences. Intuitively, these differences in how someone is built make a difference in terms of what might be deemed 'good' for him, and so what is practically right. If my brain is put together in such-and-such a manner, any sexual *mores* that I might display are something that I can claim as being right or good *for me*.

The alternative is to suggest that there is something that would allow us to say that brain *x* deviates from a particular norm in some manner. But what establishes this norm? Things look as though we're assuming that there is an *ur*-brain that sets

---

43 Cf. Hume, 1998, esp. III, VII.
44 Allen and Gorski, 1990, 1991; Allen et al., 1991; also Gorski, 2000.
45 Allen and Gorski, 1992, p. 7201.

the standard – which seems to be perilously close to Platonic essentialism about what it means to be a human brain and which needs to deal with the possibility that each brain might be a manifestation its *own* ideal anyway. Or perhaps we could talk in terms of the majority of brains, so that deviation is considered in terms of frequency and infrequency. But from where do we get the rule saying that the archetype is whatever is common? Again, we have veered off into independentist territory.

Going down this path opens the way for an argument to the effect that, everyone being slightly different in some way, 'right' will be correspondingly different because what counts as *my* eudaimonia need not be the same as anyone else's. (Shaw's 'golden rule' from *Man and Superman* stands consideration here: 'Do not do unto others as you would that they should do unto you. Their tastes may not be the same'.[46]) At least in principle, there seems to be no particular reason why we cannot draw such teleological distinctions for almost any difference that one may suggest. In other words, while we might still have a sort of teleological criterion of truth for moral claims, we might not be able to say with certainty that x is good for *humanity* without steamrollering certain teleological differences between humans. And this makes it difficult to sustain the idea that there can be much of a moral plumb-line that tells us in any practical sense about the rightness of any behaviour. Unless we can come up with some way to nail evaluative terms into place, 'right' and 'wrong' could have an indefinitely wide range of plausible applications – which means, in effect, no useful evaluative aspect at all.

Why not suggest that someone like Émile Henry *just was* the kind of creature for whom bomb-throwing was good, therefore (in practical terms) right? The only reason why this might not be a valid move is to suppose that, while there might be a range of characteristics that can be accommodated by the idea of a 'good' human, being an *apolitikon zōon* is not one of them. But this sort of move is one that has just been ruled out on the basis of its inclination towards *a priori*ty about the sort of thing that a human, and hence a 'good' human, can be. Quite aside from the problems of Platonic essentialism, it certainly sits queasily in what is notionally a dependentist account of the moral. Even a broadly teleological critique of someone like Henry is impossible unless we can say that he is not fulfilling his *own*, personally defined, *telos*. And what on Earth would allow us to say something like that?

So the problem that confronts anyone who wants to define good in such practical terms is that norms only look particularly compelling if we can be absolutely sure that there is one particular standard at which these norms should be aiming. But if there is such a standard, then we have given too much away already: without warrant, we have helped ourselves to a norm, the establishment of which is independent of the characteristics of the actors in question. Dependentism of this sort only seems to avoid running up independentism's metaphysical bills by becoming a shoplifter. And even if we can somehow secure a normative system that can tell us how to behave qua humans, there is still a difficulty in establishing that this is the whole story – that

---

46 *Maxims for Revolutionists* in Shaw, 1946, p. 251.

satisfying our human *telē* is just the same as satisfying *everything* that is right for us.

A version of the objection is mounted neatly by Nietzsche, who writes in *Twilight of the Idols* that:

> To call the taming of an animal its 'improvement' is in our ears almost a joke. Whoever knows what goes on in menageries is doubtful whether the beasts in them are 'improved'. They are weakened, they are made less harmful, they become *sickly* beasts through the depressive emotion of fear, through pain, through injuries, through hunger. – It is no different with the tamed human being ...[47]

What counts as 'improvement' – being brought closer to some standard of excellence – alters from context to context. We want certain characteristics in our zoological specimens – good plumage, for example – but this might be at the expense of some other characteristic. It is perfectly coherent to think that standards of excellence are variable according to point of view: what counts as an excellence depends on that for which one is looking. It might be that the *politikon zōon* is more 'excellent' than the 'war-mad' *apolitikon zōon* only from the point of view of another *politikon zōon* and only because he represents a benefit rather than a threat – and even this might not always be true: the old Norse berserkers were simultaneously war-mad *and* practically good from time to time.[48] So it might be with eudaimonian excellences: perhaps the 'war-madness' of the *apolitikon zōon* is not a sign of depravity, but of adaptation. For this reason, the idea that there can be a set of norms that is anything but barely instrumental is not a live possibility.

If one accepts this kind of point, then one is conceding that the root of moral evaluations is how appealing a certain characteristic is. This is fair enough: but it rather swipes the ground from a position based on the claim that there is something about humans qua humans that means that a mode of behaviour (such as peaceful political existence) has anything to recommend it generally. What remains is a proto-Humean argument along the lines that what I might recognise as an excellence – that is, as something praiseworthy – depends ultimately on my propensities. And, as I will show in a moment, for the eudaimonist to swallow his pride and defect to the Humean camp is not likely to leave him much better off.

For the moment, though, it is worth pointing out that, even if an account such as eudaimonism *can* be rescued metaphysically so that we can say with a reasonable degree of certainty that action *A does* imply value *v*, the authority of its norms is still questionable. The cosmological basis for norms is no basis at all. Let us assume that I decide to treat someone like a slave, even though the fact that I will thereby undermine the good opinion that others have of me gives me a good reason not to do so. The cosmological argument is meant to defuse this: the kind of creature that he is tells me that I am still doing something unbefitting. But I might not care.

---

47 *Twilight of the Idols*, 'The 'Improvers' of Mankind', § 2 in Nietzsche, 1990b, pp. 66–7.

48 See Prins, 1990, for discussion.

Unless some cosmological norm can be offered that has the force of a categorical imperative, there does not seem to be much scope for critique. Foreshadowing Hampton's curmudgeon,[49] to whom I will turn my attention soon, a categorical behavioural guideline to the effect that I really should pay heed to cosmological fit is not forthcoming without non-naturalistic support. As things stand, what I have has no more moral power than the washing instructions on a sweater: it might be bad if I boil-wash it, both for the sweater (it will shrink) and for me (I will become sweaterless). But this is not a *moral* guide. If *telos* is to be powerfully normative, the kind of dependentism with which I have concerned myself up until now must give ground to the independentist. If it is not, all it does is offer recommendations and leave unclear why we should pay heed to them.

Teleologically-inspired accounts of morality, whether eudaimonistic or cosmological, are unconvincing both metaphysically and normatively. To meet the commonsense expectation that morality is able to offer a critique of action, it has to embrace independentism: this is the only way that we could call an action right or wrong convincingly. The alternatives are that it should abandon the idea of being able to offer a strong moral critique – which seems to amount to the suicide of dependentism as a moral theory – or it must admit that moral evaluations are simply ways of talking about the sort of standards that a moral judge would *like* to see – which seems to be an equally suicidal concession. In other words, eudaimonists have to decide: at heart, are they independentists or Humeans?

Having said all this, there is something that can be salvaged from the wreckage that I will develop in the next two chapters. Aristotle seems to have thought that the moral capacities of human beings tend not to come to fruition outside the *polis*, and that therefore the *polis* is a precondition of moral existence. I am sympathetic to the second clause of this – that the *polis* is a precondition of moral existence, and I will be arguing in Chapter 4 (in the section titled 'Problems with the Account') that one is a *zōon logon ekhon* thanks only to membership of a *polis*-like institution. But I would deny that it has anything to do with a standard of fruition, although I am going to keep the reasons why this is to myself for now.

Moral Feelings

If teleology cannot provide a convincing morality without selling itself into independentism, perhaps we should accept a picture in which the basis for moral judgements and the truth of moral statements boils down to nothing more than the proclivities of a given individual. What counts as good, bad or evil is entirely a function of the feelings that a moral observer might have about a particular act or event. A moral statement such as 'act A has value v' is true to the extent that the speaker *feels* that A has v. There is no other standard that might provide a moral

---

49 Hampton, 1998, p. 143 and *passim.*

benchmark. At least at first glance, Hume is a fairly obvious example of someone who is willing to bite this bullet:

> Take any action allow'd to be vicious: Wilful murder, for instance. Examine it in all lights, and see if you can find that matter of fact, or real existence, which you call *vice* ... You never can find it, till you turn your reflection into your own breast and find a sentiment of disapprobation, which arises in you, towards this action. Here is a matter of fact; but 'tis the object of feeling, not of reason.[50]

Moral questions reveal themselves as being nothing more than matters of approval and disapproval: we call 'good' whatever makes us feel good, and 'evil' whatever produces an unpleasant feeling in us.

Admittedly, the inclusion of sympathy means that Hume's account is a little more sophisticated than this caricature would suggest. I shall probe sympathy more deeply in a while. But even at this stage, I can point out that Hume does not feel any need to refrain from moralising. For example, he is more than willing to advocate certain standards of behaviour despite the fact that we might have adverse passions. There are times when, examining 'all the questions, that come before any tribunal of Justice, we shall find, that, considering each case apart, it wou'd as often be an instance of humanity to decide contrary to the laws of justice as comfortable to them'.[51] For example, it might seem absurd that a poor man might be punished for stealing bread. However, having satisfied himself that '[s]ociety is absolutely necessary for the well being of man',[52] and given that it is difficult to see how well-being could fail to give a sense of pleasure, it is possible for him to argue that the general advantages of a system that punishes all instances of bread-theft equally is advantageous to the interests of the members of society.

In other words, Hume encourages us to take the long view in deciding virtue and vice, and feels equipped thereby to demand the steadfast application of some principles that might appear occasionally to run contrary to the direction suggested at first glance by a moral system that is rooted in feelings of immediate pleasure and pain. Turned back to the problem of terrorism, a Humean argument might point out that, despite the apparent unfairness of civil society, its general tendency is to the good;[53] political violence, on the other hand, displays an anti-social tendency. Therefore there is something that morality can say to resist terrorism. Similarly,

---

50 Hume, 1985, III, i, 1, p. 520.

51 Ibid., III, iii, 1, p. 630.

52 Ibid., III, ii, 6, p. 578.

53 It might be thought that there is an inconsistency in Hume's thought here in comparison to the argument that I cited in Chapter 1 about being Shanghaied into a social contract. I do not think that the charge is serious, though: Hume is simply asking us to bear in mind that, given the choice between obeying and disobeying moral rules (and the political rules that instantiate them), we are better off obeying. The Shanghai argument debunks the idea of a social contract; this does not preclude Hume from making a wider point about the relative merits of a life lived in accordance with established moral rules.

we can offer moral critiques of any course of action based on an appeal to wider interests.

This is something that Hume seems to have bequeathed to later generations. Gibbard, for example, argues that normativity is effectively the result of negotiations and accommodations between agents living alongside one another, and that we ought to train our feelings in order that they grease the wheels of cooperation, which will turn out to be of benefit to us in the future.[54] The power of the *ought* here comes from a sophisticated Humeanism that relies on a certain picture of human interactions to draw up a guideline for what counts as welfare-maximising behaviour: and for as long as we are human, it is rational to tailor our feelings and judgements in such and such a manner to negotiated norms. How convincing it is for either Gibbard or Hume to argue that one ought to curtail one's short-term desires if they might conflict with longer-term or wider goods *without* making a tacitly independentist claim is something that I will question later when I consider how we might decide what relative weights to give immediate and longer-term desires that are potentially conflicting.

Before going this far, though, it is worth uncovering the mechanics of the Humean account of moral values. The Humean approach reverses a theme that was common to independentism and teleologically-inspired dependentist theories: for theorists in these traditions, there is a standard of good or bad of some sort, and it is this that prompts us to have a certain feeling. For the eudaimonist, for example, 'good' might change, but the standard by which it is applied does not. Under Humean dependentism, by contrast, the standard for good and evil is nothing but the feeling that we might have in a certain situation. In this sense, Hume owes a great deal to Hobbes, for whom:

> whatsoever is the object of any mans Appetite or Desire; that is it, which he for his part calleth *Good*: And the object of his Hate, and Aversion, *Evill*; and his Contempt, *Vile* and *Inconsiderable*. For these words of Good, Evill, and Contemptible, are ever used with relation to the person that useth them: There being nothing simply and absolutely so.[55]

Instead of objects of attention having characteristics that are good or bad, productive or counterproductive of a good life, any moral attributes that we may detect in the world are projected by us, qua moral individuals, into a world that is, in itself, *wertfrei*. When we call something good or bad, we cannot be making a claim to the truth of the matter; the most we can claim is that a given act or event appears good or bad to us (although the fact that something appears good or bad to us will be in some measure influenced by the sympathy – fellow-feeling – that we have in our make-up qua humans, suggesting that, *ceteris paribus*, all humans will make the same moral claims). In effect, whereas for the other thinkers I have used, moral evaluations are a matter for debate, in this picture they are not, except perhaps in terms of whether or not a particular act is conducive to long-term benefit – again, one might cite

---

54 Gibbard, 1990.
55 Hobbes, 1999, VI, p. 39.

Gibbard in this context. There *are* real moral debates – but their scope is limited to questions about how we ought to organise our preferences and how to satisfy them Pareto-optimally.

One of the attractive parts about this way of thinking is that, after the eudaimonist false start, it promises a method of grounding values and norms that appears to be purged of extravagant metaphysics. We do not have to worry about Forms, universalisation or *telē*: all we need to worry about is the impact that a given act or event has on us. Much dead wood can be cut from moral philosophy on this basis. When we want to come to a conclusion about the moral comparison of the terrorist and civil society, all we need to say is that we prefer *poleis* to bombs. The moral buck stops before it ever had much of a chance to get started. Although it may well be determined by sympathetic fellow-feeling for those harmed, the reason for our moral preference is not something about which we have to worry particularly. 'The very *feeling* constitutes our praise or admiration,' Hume suggests. 'We go no farther.'[56]

In addition, we have a simple account of motivation: it is simply a function of various emotions. Nothing more needs to be involved. Allowing that '[r]eason,' for example, 'is, and ought only to be the slave of the passions'[57] allows us to sidestep some of the problems that faced the Kantian account of rational morality. It is the 'passions' that tell a person what is good and bad, and it is the passions, therefore, that direct our actions. Famously,

> 'Tis not contrary to reason to prefer the destruction of the whole world to the scratching of my finger. 'Tis not contrary to reason for me to chuse my total ruin, to prevent the least uneasiness of an *Indian* or person wholly unknown to me. 'Tis as little contrary to reason to prefer even my own acknowledg'd lesser good to my greater, and have a more ardent affection for the former than the latter.[58]

What *is* open to criticism on rational grounds is the strategy that an agent might use to meet his ends; but in the choice of those ends, reason plays no part except as a means of attaining Pareto-optimality in an imperfect world. Referring back to Aristotle's terminology, in which deliberation is morally crucial and springs from the motivational power of reason, Hume would seem to be coming out on behalf of choice.

An immediate response to this is that Hume is curtailing moral freedom. After all, *animals* are slaves to their passions, and it is humanity's unique capacity as

---

56 Hume, 1985, III, i, 2, p. 523.

57 Ibid., II, iii, 3, p. 462.

58 Ibid., p. 463. In this passage, it seems to be important to note that we should read 'good' eudaimonistically. Failure to do so will bring this passage into direct conflict with the idea that to call something 'good' is simply to express approval, or else it will amount to the incoherent claim that it is not contrary to reason to prefer that which I like less over that which I like more. This ambiguity in the term 'good', I venture to suggest, is what allows Hume to moralise, but it would not be appropriate to get carried away with an investigation of the implications of this point at the moment.

logon ekhein that makes the difference qua moral creatures. By denying the role of reason, he is either reducing human agency to a basic animalistic level, or else elevating animals to human standards of behaviour. Either way, though, something is wrong with this elision. But this is not Hume's point after all. All he is suggesting is that reason is the tool that allows us to *arrange* our 'goods'. Perhaps deliberation *is* eclipsed by choice (in Aristotelian parlance), but this is not really too big a problem. Indeed, if the point of Aristotle's distinction is that we can deliberate concerning what should *count* as good, Hume's in a considerably stronger position than his rivals, precisely because he gives us a simple criterion of what is good that does not involve spurious recourse to *telē*, *noumena* or Forms. What counts is this: reason allows us to prioritise the passions, to work out which passions are compatible with others, which have the bigger pull, and so on. We still *can* be morally different from animals (if, in a fit of anthropic pride, establishing that difference is important to us): we can recognise situations in which acting on one maxim might transgress a second maxim and we can form programmes of action to accommodate this in a way that an animal, perhaps being easy to distract, cannot.

However, another immediate problem with this approach, which I do not think *is* the result of a misunderstanding, is that it seems to suggest that we can only ever have a moral opinion about that which we have experienced. Still, the problem is easily overcome. The fact of our having noted the 'constant conjunction' between one thing and another is enough to give us the notion of cause and effect;[59] the same could be said fairly easily of moral facts and phenomena: our having been repulsed by something in enough instances leads us to avoid similar situations in future. Further, by marrying together ideas, I can come to a conclusion about things I have never experienced and never will experience directly: I can have, as it were, virtual experiences. I can therefore be repulsed by or admire mere suggestions. Never having been mugged, for example, I do not know what it is like; but I can marry together things I *do* know about what I believe to be features of being mugged – fear, pain, and so on – to formulate an attitude to it. In addition, sympathy ensures that putting myself in the place of the mugged is not something that I *ought* to do; it is something that I will find myself doing *anyway*. The point stands that *all* moral dicta are, at root, claims about preservation of welfare, either mine or, courtesy of sympathy, anyone else's (inasmuch as sympathy means that I will share the comfort or discomfort of others). If the idea I have in mind is attractive, I call it good; if not, I call it bad or evil – and that is all that there is to a true moral statement.

Some problems are not so easy to get around, though. Whatever advantages Humeanism might have in establishing the means by which we could say of a moral statement that it is true, it has none when it comes to questions of normativity. Humeanism cannot meet the commonsense expectation that there is such a thing as compelling moral critique nearly as easily as Humeans seem to think. Suppose, for example, that I am doing something that other people find offensive. Without recourse to external standards of right and wrong, the most compelling critique of

---

59 Hume, 1985, I, iii, 4; also I, iii, 14.

this activity that is likely to have an effect on me is to have it pointed out that I am acting against my own acknowledged interests: it is foreseen that I will not find happiness in whatever it is I am doing: maybe continuing with my present activity will anger everyone else so much that eventually they will lynch me. But I might not believe these arguments; and as long as I do not believe them, there is no guarantee that the critique will work – and I cannot be thought of as morally lacking simply on the basis that I do not believe a predictive statement about my future well-being.

Or supposing I *do* believe them: so what? The critic's expectation is that sooner rather than later my moral sentiments will alter (or be altered) in some way. Hopefully, this would direct my self-serving desires away from antisocial behaviour. But there are a couple of problems here. First, such an expectation reduces morality to a battle of wits: the picture here is that whoever shows the most endurance de facto becomes the moral arbiter. If I change my behaviour, I will do so not because I have come to see the world in a different light, but because I have come to be aware that my welfare is under threat. This strategy does not point to resolution of moral disputes: it points to their suppression. I may have altered my behaviour, but I will not have done so for the right reason, and the reason why I changed my behaviour is morally important. Second, the criticism is powerless anyway: as long as it is not irrational to prefer my acknowledged lesser good to my greater, there does not seem a lot to be said when I carry on as before.

But perhaps this argument is rendered superfluous when we bear in mind that critique can draw on an appeal to sympathy. I can see that what I am doing is creating fear, pain, misery, or whatever, and, having an idea of what these are like and how repulsive they are, I should recognise their moral value, and come to recognise the wrongness in my action: sympathy means, in fact, that I *will* experience this kind of recognition. Unfortunately, this kind of appeal may often represent a false start. Even if, from time to time, there might be a powerful appeal made to sympathy, the fact that at other times there might not be is enough to suggest that a Humean approach to moral critique is intolerably gappy. Sympathy is more difficult a normative tool than Hume seems to allow for, and a moral theory without normative bite does not convince as a moral theory.

The first gap in the theory lies in the possibility that the pleasure that I get from my offensive activity could be so vast that other people's misery is discounted; Hume himself admits that 'sympathy … is much fainter than our concern for ourselves'.[60] I could claim this and still claim to be a sympathetic person: my claim would amount to no more than that other people's miserable feelings are simply at the lighter end of the moral balance. It would be difficult to argue conclusively for or against this, since it is unclear just how one might quantify and compare sentiments. Still, if I carried off the argument successfully, it would seem to suggest that I should carry on with my activities as before. This argument runs into one that I shall moot as a third problem with sympathy in a moment.

---

60 Hume, 1994, V, p. 64.

Second, I might point out that, while others are sympathetic and so care about others' misery, I am simply *not* sympathetic. I am just 'wired' differently: perhaps I am a psychopath or autistic in some way and therefore I do not have the sympathy that Hume assumes to be built into human nature. It might be the case that *anyone* who is not obviously sympathetic is developmentally abnormal: that anyone who does not display this characteristic thereby reveals himself to be psychopathic or autistic. (Of course, there need be nothing pejorative about saying that psychopaths and autistics are developmentally abnormal – the statement is simply a matter of statistics.) But when we say that such a person *should* have developed differently, we are not using a moral *should*, any more than we are offering a moral critique when we say that babies should not to be born with spina bifida.

Anyway, it does not follow automatically that there is something *morally* lacking in Smith if he is left cold by something that animates Jones any more than there is something morally lacking in those who cannot see the attraction of gardening. Any reasonably complex account of the psychology of reasonably scrutable humans would surely have to account for the possibility that there is a range of human propensities and that different things might therefore excite the sympathies of different people. A *difference* in sympathy does not necessarily mean a *lack* of sympathy. If someone appears to lack sympathy, we can legitimately ask: so what? We might want to avoid such a person (he might be a threat), but this is no moral critique. Or we might just have to admit that *de sympathis non est disputandum*.

Other people, on the other hand, we might imagine as being developmentally normal, having similar sympathetic responses, but suppressing sympathy all the same and not letting it get in the way of a cause that they have adopted. These people – who are much more interesting than psychopaths from the point of view of a study that began with a comparison of terrorism and civil society – I shall call zealots, and they present the third problem for Humeanism. Zealots differ from the people who gave Hume his first problem, since a zealot might have to work hard to suppress his sympathy. I shall allow the ideas that a zealot might have to be fairly wide-ranging. Someone like Émile Henry could have been a zealot, inasmuch as he had certain social ideas and discounted the suffering that he might cause in the short term and in the pursuit thereof; an animal liberationist or 'pro-lifer' willing to kill research scientists might also be a zealot if he is distressed by the details of his actions but not so distressed that he is incapable of mortgaging these feelings against his chosen end. The judge who sentences the poor bread thief might also count as a zealot; if my argument is sound, it would mean, ironically, that Hume championed the wrong person. Finally, someone might have an inflated view of his own importance, and be willing to tread on others in the pursuit of self-interest. This person, too, I shall allow to be a zealot, since his idea or cause is himself.

What might we say in a moral critique of zealotry? *Any* argument that tries to resist zealotry seems to be making a demand that one *ought not* to be a zealot or that one *ought* to let sympathies play a bigger part in determining action. Officially, such a demand can do no more than express feelings. To suppose that it does any more than this seems to make an appeal to a higher-order norm unrelated to feeling for substantiation: exactly the kind of norm that Humeans would dismiss as spurious. In saying that one *ought* to be moved more by sympathy, I would be claiming effectively that I would prefer it if one was moved by sympathy. This would amount to an expression of a preference that people have other preferences. And to this, the zealot could very well respond with nothing more than a blank look.

Someone like Henry might be plentifully happy with his bomb-throwing and, all told, he might prefer to throw bombs than not, even though he foresees an encounter with the guillotine that is clearly a 'lesser good'. As things stand, if Hume's theory is what underpins commonsense morality, and if, at bottom, feeling *is* all that there is to solving moral problems, then, as far as I am concerned, it might be true that terrorism is wrong. But there does not seem to be much basis for the thought that my having found something wrong with throwing bombs will have any authority over the bomb-thrower (and ditto for any other form of morally dubious activity and its practitioners) without smuggling in an a priori norm.

Independentism's strength is that it can offer a moral fulcrum to provide us with a moral push against zealots and their ilk; dependentism having rejected independentism's metaphysics, this fulcrum is lost. If a Humean approach is the right approach, then the most potent critique that commonsense might offer of the bomber would concern technique. Sympathy amounts to a devastatingly weak position from which to launch a moral argument. Even if we allow that reason might allow us – or even force us – to arrange our sympathies (for example, our realisation that we ought to punish the bread thief presumably has at least something to do with the resolution of a conflict between our sympathies for individuals and for the community at large), this is not the same as there being any way to determine what the right sympathies are to have in the first place. Punishing the bread thief does not mean that we are unsympathetic to his plight; it just means that other things are vying for our sympathy with which the bread thief cannot compete.

One last point is that a Humean sympathy argument can be turned around by the zealot anyway; even if it was not inert, it would be an unreliable moral tool. The Humean critic is suggesting that the zealot ought to have different preferences or sympathies. But the zealot could volley this shot and demand that it is his critics who ought to revise their sympathies. Might it not be that, supposing he was a zealot, Henry was sympathetic to the suffering of the proletariat in a way that we are not? And if this is so, might not he make some kind of claim to be *even more* morally sensitive than the average person? A similar argument might be put by the animal liberationist: that his sympathy extends beyond the human to all living things. Even if we think that unsympathetic people are more likely than the rest of us to throw bombs, we are not committed to thinking that people throw bombs *only* because they are less sympathetic than the rest of us. In other words, while some people might repudiate the idea that they are zealots, others might deny that their zealotry is a sign of an unsympathetic temperament.

To suppose that someone might be *too* sympathetic looks arbitrary without presupposing some prior guiding norm – and, anyway, if it is sympathy that provokes moral feelings, such a supposition leads towards the thought that someone might be too morally sensitive, which is surely absurd. Aristotle thought that it might be possible to instil in people the 'right kind' of moral feelings[61] – a point that presumably would extend to having the right sympathies. But the rightness of those right sympathies still has to be accounted for. If someone is unsympathetic, or has the 'wrong' sympathies, however defined – if he sympathises more strongly with the bread thief than with the society that he might even acknowledge as representing his 'greater good' – Humeanism has to stop dead.

Instrumentalism and the a priori

Let us allow the Humean to dig in his heels and insist that moral judgements *are* just expressions of pleasure or displeasure, and that we are being oversentimental – or *under*sentimental – to think otherwise. There would remain scope for moral debate: granted that everyone wants to maximise his own welfare, we can criticise some behaviours as being less efficient than others as means of securing this. As I have already stated, Hume argues for the long view, and insofar as he does this, argues for a 'delayed-pleasure' principle. He can hold to the moral judgements that we make concerning terrorism – all he says in addition is that the *why* of these arguments is not what we thought it was: exposed to the heat of inquiry, the a priori moral aspects of judgements evaporate, and are replaced by judgements concerning the instrumental efficiency of a strategy of welfare maximisation. However, in an argument that owes much to Jean Hampton,[62] I am going to suggest that someone who wants to argue in this way – and, more importantly, to use this kind of argument to underpin a critique of action – cannot do so without admitting an a priori principle of evaluation on the sly. The argument has two stages.

Instrumental reasoning is hypothetical in character: it says that, if we want to be good or happy, we ought to do *x*. For Humeans, this is notionally as far as the *ought* goes. It does not refer to any external moral standard; it just tells us about the pragmatic business of achieving whatever it is that we want to achieve, and that rational behaviour consists solely of doing that which furthers some end. When we say that someone ought to do something, we are commending a strategy and nothing more. The first stage of the Hampton-based argument is that, although instrumental reasoning is assumed to be more scientifically respectable than non-instrumental reasoning – that is, 'categorical' reasoning – because it avoids questionable a prioris, this assumption is not sustainable.

An appeal to strategies does not always do the trick in motivating action, and we can show this through consideration of a curmudgeon – a person who resolves to do only that action which is prompted by the strongest occurrent motive[63] – who has a desire for healthy teeth, but has no desire for the correspondingly necessary visit to the dentist. Clearly, we could issue a kind of hypothetical imperative that, in effect,

---

61 Aristotle, 1976, II, iii.
62 Hampton, 1998.
63 Ibid., p. 143.

describes the facts of the matter: that if he wants *this*, he must do *that*. But this will not work against the curmudgeon: he might *know* that in order to get healthy teeth he must visit the dentist – but since, at this time, he has no particular desire to go to the dentist that stands comparison to his other current desires (or, more powerfully, he has a disinclination to go to the dentist), this is too bad. If we wanted anything more from the situation, we would have to make a case along the lines that he is *wrong* not to frame a desire to go to the dentist that is strong enough to outweigh any other desires he might have.[64] But if this is the case, we must be making an appeal along the lines that there is some objective standard according to which he ought to frame his instrumental imperatives: we seem to be supposing that there is what Hampton calls an Instrumental Norm along the lines of 'Act so as to perform the most effective means to a desired end'.[65] In other words, when a person has two competing and exclusive predispositions (as surely we all have from time to time), there is no standard according to which we can assess this person's behaviour. We either have to give up on the idea of criticism – even instrumental criticism – or we have to admit an action-guiding principle that applies *regardless of the individual's current desires* – that is: independently. To have normative power, instrumental reasoning must rely, at some stage, on a factor that lends it authority over curmudgeonly desires and over sloth. To avoid a *regressus*, we have to accept that this factor is not just another instrumental reason for action. (This is a point that can be carried back to the Humean and Gibbardian assumption that 'wide perspective' desires such as a desire for healthy teeth or a peaceful life trump 'narrower perspective' desires such as that to avoid dentists or perform antisocial actions: what is the foundation to such an assumption? Hampton gives reason to think that we have to admit that it belongs to the tradition that I have called independentist.)

The upshot is this: naturalism supposes that criticism of action can only be built on instrumental ground; but this turns out simply not to be the case. Criticism needs non-instrumental grounds if it is not to be forced to throw in the towel. And if we are willing to accept that there might be an normatively compelling standard according to which we can assess a person's (notionally) instrumental behaviour, then there seems to be no good reason at all why there might not be a similar standard according to which we can assess their behaviour *period*. So either we can accept that moral reasoning of an un-Humean kind has a reasonably secure claim to legitimacy, or we can drop the idea of ever being able to criticise any behaviour, either in moral terms or – more importantly for a naturalising tradition – in terms of the practical effectiveness of scientifically-acceptable instrumentalism.

Hampton takes her point further, into a second stage, suggesting that the instrumental reasoning that we might think we can claim is not even instrumental after all.[66] Admittedly, I am not sure about her categorical confidence along these lines – but it is enough for her to be able to argue that *at least one* 'instrumental'

---

64 Ibid., p. 143 ff.
65 Ibid., p. 144.
66 Ibid., § 5.

reason *is not* instrumental for her to have rescued the legitimacy of non-instrumental normativity wholesale, and so to have weakened the argument of avowed naturalists such as Humean dependentists against non-naturalists such as independentists. In a very rough-and-ready state, the argument is that we need some way to organise our conceptions of 'good', and this lets in a priori normativity *ab initio*. The starting point in the argument is that, whatever our conceptions of the 'good' at time *t*, we might expect these to have changed by *t*+1. For example, we might have a desire to read this evening and we might also have a desire for a beer with dinner. We know, though, that having a beer will implant a desire for a second beer, which will take us to the point where reading is not a viable option – we will fall asleep. Should we refuse the first beer?[67]

On a simple interpretation, we should: we know that it is counterproductive to our desires. However, given that having the first beer is not contrary to the literary plans we have, the reasoning behind this must be that we do not think that our present desires should change, or that we should knowingly put ourselves in a position in which we fully expect those desires to change. In effect, we're discounting some desires and potential desires in relation to others. But why would we do this? The only conceivable answer is that we think that some desires are 'better' – more worth having – than others. We can fill in any number of things that might give us reason to think this that would give us an instrumental reason to avoid the beer. But the thought eventually brings us up to the same issue: we have decided in this case that pragmatism is more important than the beer consumption and that this should stay the case. The point is that instrumental reason alone cannot tell us that a pragmatic desire is more important than a bibendary one and why, as a result, desires at *t* are more 'legitimate' than desires at *t*+1. After a beer, my desires will have changed: reading will no longer seem as important as it did at *t*. Instrumentalism cannot tell me why I should not just go along with this: why some desires trump others.[68] Such a claim requires arguments of a different kind: straightforward normative arguments. (A Millian distinction between higher and lower pleasures has the same presuppositions: what is the ladder up which poetry is higher than pushpin? It is not that of instrumental reason.)

Hampton's many variants of the argument all boil down to the same point. Even instrumental reasoning has at least a non-instrumentalist kernel to it – there is an implicit critique here of instrumentalism of both the Humean and the Utilitarian sorts. If it was not for this, deliberations concerning good and bad would never get off the ground. (Note that eudaimonists do not face this problem: they have an idea of what the good is that is not predicated on desire. That their picture is metaphysically shaky should not be too much of a worry in this context: shakiness is beginning to

---

67 Ibid., p. 183.

68 This point obviously can be carried back to the Humean insistence that we can justify moral norms by an appeal to general sources of pain and pleasure: why should we prefer the general as opposed to opting for present desires and taking our chances with the future?

look unavoidable. This is not a retreat to Aristotle: that eudaimonism is the best of a bad lot is not much of a recommendation.)

Morality and the Snark

As with independentism, there are subtraditions of dependentism. Those that owe most to Aristotle, eudaimonist and cosmological approaches, argue differently, but share the claim that the considerations that lead us to be able to call something 'good' accurately are related to the nature of the kind of being that concerns us. In the second type of dependentism, the Humean, all bets are off: an accurate ascription of goodness is dependent on nothing more than the agent's own notion of what is attractive or unattractive. Eudaimonist and cosmological approaches claim to be able to offer norms as powerful as independentism's, but without the cost. Humeanism makes more modest normative claims, but still insists that it can provide a means to evaluate and criticise acts and events. It, too, claims not to rely on extravagant metaphysics.

However, there are problems with both views. Arguments based on *telos* suffer from the presumption that there really *is* a *telos* that serves as a template for 'the good'. Eudaimonism *does* seem to imply – although, admittedly, it is no more than an implication – that there is a Form of Humanity; and if this *is* what is meant and what we should use to mould our ideas of what is practically good, it faces exactly the same problems as Platonism. On the other hand, a softer reading of eudaimonism would have to allow a teleological leeway such that each individual can have his own template of 'the good'. However, what we lose by following this line is the notion of normative power; it is susceptible to the charge that it is nothing more than 'Diet Plato': it tastes of Plato, but does not give enough moral calories to achieve anything.

And even if we can tolerate the idea that creatures might have a *telos* that might have a specific place *vis-à-vis* other beings, there is still a question to be asked about what normative significance it has without recourse to exactly the independent norms that we are supposed to be avoiding. The moral cosmologist might have recourse to an argument that it is counter to our *telos* as *politikon zōon* to treat ourselves or others inappropriately, but in order to avoid a curmudgeonly comeback or a Humean barb about deriving an *ought* from a taxonomical *is*, he must rely at some point on a source of normativity that is not teleological. It is bad enough that no such source is immediately forthcoming, notwithstanding the internal difficulty that even if there was, it would undermine exactly the purported naturalism of the notion that it was supposed to be supplementing.

The Humean strategy does not suffer from Platonism – but because of this it lacks many of the normative characteristics of a moral theory that are expected by commonsense morality. Hume's approach rejects the idea that there is *any* external standard of behaviour whatsoever. All action is motivated by the sentiments, and an attempt to go further is posturing. But if all there is to morality is sentiment, moral critique is in trouble. We cannot praise or blame anything according to any standard except that it accords or discords with our particular preferences. And if this is so, moral philosophy is hobbled. If we want to keep a reasonably strong picture of what morality involves, we either have to revert to eudaimonism's insistence that there is a naturalisable standard of good that has nothing to do with an individual human, or else admit that there is an independent standard of good after all.

Both of these moves are dubious. The outcome would appear to be that we are offered a dilemma: either we can have morality, or we can climb out of metaphysical and metaethical holes. It is not really plausible that we can do both at the same time. Dependentism's claim to provide morality at off-the-back-of-a-lorry metaphysical prices is therefore something to be treated with suspicion. Even if dependentism can be self-supporting *once it gets going*, Hampton's argument against the unacceptability of queerness and the revelation of eudaimonism's suppressed assumptions show that there has to be a *primum mobile* at some point. And so the programme of finding something to back up commonsense morality would appear to be in trouble.

In trying to give an account of what might base moral judgements, I have looked at four traditions: realism, idealism, teleology (which embraces eudaimonism and moral cosmology) and Humeanism. The four can be put into a matrix according to whether they are dependentist or independentist, and according to whether the standard of evaluation is internal or external to the agent:

	External standard of evaluation	Internal standard of evaluation
Independentist	Realist independentism	Idealist independentism
Dependentist	Teleology	Humeanism

So, for example, *what* is good in the teleologist's view is not independent of whom or what we are considering, although the framework that we use in moral deliberation is external to the agent. Clearly, there are no spaces in the matrix: all the permutations of traditional metaethics seem to have been taken. Is there any way in which the metaphysical security of dependentism can be combined with the moral robustness of independentism? Not easily: the strongest points of each view are those with which the other is likely to have the biggest problems – metaphysical extravagance on one hand, threadbare normativity on the other. At this point, commonsense morality looks to be in mortal danger. Either we have to be internalist or externalist, dependentist or independentist: there does not seem to be much scope for a middle way.

Is there any way that the situation can be resolved and commonsense morality substantiated?

Lewis Carroll suggests to his band of hunters that 'the Snark's a peculiar creature, that will not be caught in a commonplace way'.[69] Commonsense morality is a Snark. When trying to find out what it is that could allow us to call a moral judgement accurate or inaccurate, true or false, I will not be able to proceed in a commonplace way. Instead, I will face the possibility that commonsense morality cannot ever be justified. But I will argue that this does not matter at all. It is just that we have to discuss moral judgements and their metaethics in a different way. Instead of having to find a way to found and evaluate the notions of commonsense morality, we should just accept it as a given, and deal with it from that perspective. In the next two chapters, I will argue that we just are born into a world with a certain moral weighting, and that there need not be anything particularly to guarantee its coherence, before I open up the question of what this might mean in terms of making a moral evaluation.

Allow me to explain myself.

---

69 Carroll, 1995, p. 68.

Chapter 4

The Reality of Values: Heidegger and Moral Thought

Morality and Commonsense

I began this investigation by posing a question: given that we want a moral claim to be both true and normatively powerful, are our desires likely to be met? I used the example of terrorism to illustrate the implications of the question: commonsense wants to be able to say to the putative terrorist that there is a moral reason not to do what he does, and that therefore he ought to stop it. However, as the last couple of chapters have shown, it is not easy to show how moral statements can be true and normatively powerful at the same time. Those that stand a chance of being compelling – the independentist theories – are too metaphysically demanding to be able to provide believable moral claims, because they either rely on there being intrinsically and irreducibly moral characteristics that would endure in a universe denuded of sentient life, or else on the supposition that all agents think in the same way and do so necessarily. Neither of these suppositions is without its problems. On the other hand, dependentist theories are better at providing truth for their moral claims, but lose normative power in the process. As things stand, commonsense morality looks to be lacking in foundation. Roughly speaking, while each theory can provide a little of what we want from morality on a commonsense level, none is able to do enough.

It is unlikely that a middle way might be found between independentism and dependentism. If there was such a way, it would have to be *very* finely balanced indeed; but given the antagonism between independentism and dependentism, I doubt that it would be possible except as an indication of the null point at which the two poles cancel each other out. This is not the making of a theory that can be trusted to tell us anything about the provenance of moral distinctions that we might draw except by accident. So another response might be suggested: that we admit that commonsense lacks foundation, and radically re-evaluate what – if anything – we are entitled to ask from morality. If it becomes clear that the expectations we have of morality are unsupportable, there is no indignity in admitting that they have had their day, and moving on to something else. Maybe the claims of commonsense morality have had their day: they cannot stand up without crutches – and intellectual honesty demands that we swipe these.

However, there is no reason why we should jump to a conclusion like this so hastily. Over the course of this chapter, I shall outline an account of the provenance of commonsense moral claims in which it does not matter whether or not we can find some underpinning for them. It is enough that we discern a difference between (say) terrorism and civil society for there to be such a difference. Indeed, while I do not want to say that we ought not to delve into the provenance of such claims, I want to suggest at the same time that there is at least a reason simply to accept them as givens. I will argue that the boundaries of common sense mark out the territory within which metaethical thought must work, but that we can abandon the idea that any particular theory provides a necessary or sufficient bedrock criterion for commonsense morality.

Basically, the strategy will be something like this: when traditional metaethics – with one important exception – has been trying to locate the origin of moral claims, it has wondered how such claims might adhere to reality. So, for example, if we allow φ to stand for an evaluation of some sort, when we think that φ, realist independentism wants to say that the accuracy of our thought is bankrolled by some aspect of mind-independent moral reality. For Aristotelians, the picture is roughly similar, except that the φ-ishness of the world is not irreducibly *moral* in character. In both these accounts, mistakes are possible: it is possible that the world is not as φ-ish as we thought; however, in both these cases, the problem is not with the world, but with that thought. Humeans, by contrast, claim that the perceived φ-ishness of the world is simply a function of our thought; in making this claim, they must relinquish the idea that φ-ishness figures in reality, but they keep hold of the idea that the provenance of φ-ishness can be traced back to an aspect of the world – in this case, a psychological fact.

The important exception to this pattern is Kant. For him, it is not the case that moral evaluations are accurate if they pick up on some aspect of moral or psychological reality. Rather, he is willing to redefine reality in terms of the necessary operations of the intellect. So it is not that there is some aspect of the world either inside or outside of our heads that obliges us to think φ, so much as it is the case that we cannot help but to think that φ, and that therefore the world must conform to this on pain of inconceivability. And, though I put the boot into Kant in Chapter 2, I think that his strategy is, if not correct, at least able to provide an important clue as to the correct way to proceed in matters metaethical. Much of the argument that I want to put owes its ancestry to the work of Martin Heidegger, but it also echoes Kant. I want to argue for the position that moral distinctions are built into the world in which we live; the difference between my position and the RI theorist's lies in my willingness to question what a word like 'reality' indicates: all the same, I shall be fighting shy of a belief in irreducibly and intrinsically moral properties. Having proposed a model for the provenance of values, I think that I will be able to explain how norms work – my proposed account of norms follows on naturally from my account of values. Hopefully, by the end of this chapter, I will have made a case for *dissolving* rather than *solving* the problems of traditional metaethics.

Before I get going, though, given that my strategy owes much to a reading of Heidegger, I need to clear up a couple of other issues.

Heidegger versus Morality?

First, given that I am going to be drawing on Heidegger, I am aware that some would be suspicious of his introduction into *any* area of philosophical inquiry. Certainly within the predominantly anglophone 'analytic' tradition of philosophy, Heidegger's work has a reputation for being not just difficult, but senseless; one might also accuse it of trying to wring too much from philology. I shall assume that Heidegger *does* have something valuable to say – although this is not the place to argue the point – and allow that, *if* Heidegger is right, even if only in certain respects, his thought might suggest *these* interesting (and, hopefully, valuable) moral consequences. We all have to stand somewhere.

Second, and more seriously, Heidegger is not an obvious player in what is ostensibly a piece of *moral* philosophising. He is not often thought of as having anything to do with moral philosophy. Joanna Hodge points out that Heidegger 'writes very little about ethics, and then only to state that ethical questions are not his concern'.[1] Certainly, ethics as an area of study gets only a cough-and-spit appearance in *Being and Time*,[2] and even this brief engagement with the subject is dismissive. Within *Being and Time*, it would be a mistake to read the passages on guilt (*Schuld*) and being-guilty (*Schuldsein*) as if they were passages on moral philosophy (although they will play a part in the next chapter). Ethical themes are touched on in *The Essence of Human Freedom*, but it is only the lightest of touches.[3] Along similar lines, Heidegger deals with *dikē*, a word commonly translated as 'justice', in the essay *The Anaximander Fragment*[4] – but this is not *dikē* in any sense recognisable as moral-philosophical. 'Ethics' does make a more substantial appearance in the *Letter on 'Humanism'*,[5] but here, too, it is treated in an unexpected manner; at least at first glance, there is reason to think that if this *is* Heidegger's attempt to engage with ethics as an area of study, it is unlikely to succeed.

There is another very good reason to treat with suspicion any link between Heidegger and ethics. Heidegger was a man who was a member of the Nazi party from 1933 until it ceased to exist in 1945[6] and who between 1933 and 1934 was vocal in his support for Hitler; who, in his 1935 *Introduction to Metaphysics*, lamented the National Socialists' infidelity to the 'inner truth and greatness' of their own movement,[7] and who never seems entirely to have disowned this talk.[8] It would appear plain that he failed to grasp the moral import of the Third Reich even after its end, as well: in an unpublished lecture from the 1949 series *Insight into That Which Is*, he made this astonishing claim:

---

1 Hodge, 1995, p. 1.
2 Heidegger, 1999a, H 16.
3 Heidegger, 2002a, *passim.*
4 In Heidegger, 1975; translated as *Anaximander's Word* in Heidegger, 2002b.
5 *Letter on 'Humanism'* in Heidegger, 1999b, H 184 ff.; 1999c, pp. 256 ff.
6 Ettinger, 1995, p. 10.
7 Heidegger, 2000, H152.
8 Cf. 'Only a God can Save Us' in Wolin, 1998.

Agriculture is today a motorised food industry, in essence the same as the manufacture of corpses in gas chambers and extermination camps, the same as the blockade and starvation of countries, the same as the manufacture of atomic bombs.[9]

It is not without reason that one might condemn Heidegger as a moral pariah. And this sort of consideration might not be wholly as *ad hominem*. Inasmuch as a person writes about, say, metaphysics, we might think that we can put certain features of their biography to one side. When it comes to framing an ethical argument, though, we might be reticent about enlisting to our aid someone whose behaviour seems so at odds with basic moral demands. Admittedly, not every ethicist matches the highest ideals of virtue, and this fact may not disqualify him from ethical debate – one may be a bioethicist and an adulterer, for example – but there are some moral failings that are, we might think, so large that they bring the legitimacy of a thinker's inclusion in a moral debate into question from the start.

It is not only Heidegger's involvement with National Socialism that might lead us to think that he has nothing – or nothing worthwhile – to contribute to ethics, either. He hinted, for example, that he trusted Sophocles as an ethical thinker more than Aristotle.[10] This is mild in comparison to Nazism, but it still feeds a powerful intuition that an attempt to link Heidegger to any kind of moral thinking is on a hiding to nothing – he simply had no inkling of what the subject was about. Richard Wolin takes a much stronger view: he thinks that Heideggerian philosophy is consistent with – indeed, *contributive to* – Nazism, and that, as such, his thought is singularly *unable* to provide any worthwhile comment on moral philosophy. Heidegger's claims about truth – that, for example, '[t]ruth is un-truth'[11] – and his insistence that truth can be divorced from correctness[12] lead him, in Wolin's opinion, to 'extreme judgmental incapacities',[13] further, 'by radically privileging *ontology* over *ethics* ... the amoralism to which Heideggerianism succumbs seems theoretically preordained'.[14] Nevertheless, I disagree with Wolin's critique, and shall explain why in the next chapter. Certainly Nazis could find consolation in Heidegger; but they could also have found consolation in Rousseau if they had looked in the 'right' places, and this does not necessarily tell us anything about Rousseau. Certainly Heidegger behaved fairly reprehensibly, notably towards Husserl and the chemist Staudinger,[15] and, as Ott points out, in deliberately obscuring his record after the war;[16] but there is a difference between 'Heidegger', the intellectual precipitate of *Being and Time*

---

9   Cited *inter alia* in Wolin, 1990, p. 168; Lacoue-Labarthe, 1990, p. 34; and Lyotard, 1990, p. 85.

10   *Letter on "Humanism"* in Heidegger, 1999b, H 184 ff.; 1999c, pp. 256 ff.

11   *The Origin of the Work of Art* in Heidegger, 1999c, p. 185.

12   See *Plato's Doctrine of Truth* in Heidegger, 1999b, and *On the Essence of Truth*, in Heidegger, 1999b and 1999c, *passim*.

13   Wolin, 1990, p. 123.

14   Ibid., p. 149.

15   See Ettinger, 1995, §7.

16   Cited in ibid., p. 63.

and *The Question Concerning Technology*, and Heidegger, the man with a certain biography. The line of thought that I want to outline in this and the next chapter will take its lead, and look for support from, 'Heidegger', and henceforward – unless I make an obviously biographical point, when I use the name – it will have to be read as if it was written between invisible scare-quotes. The context should make it clear to whom I am referring.

In effect, I will be treating Heidegger as someone whose thought lends itself to ethics more or less despite itself. Hodge's claim about the poverty of ethics in Heidegger's work is a rhetorical trope: 'the question of ethics is,' she continues, 'the definitive, if unstated problem of his thinking'.[17] *Definitive* is probably too strong a word; however, it is true that a text such as the *Letter on 'Humanism'* could be taken as having features to which ethicists – especially ethicists working in the analytic tradition – would do well to pay attention. Correlatively, texts such as *Being and Time* contain elements that have serious ethical implications. Heidegger's thought has a component that has serious ethical import. Uncovering this component will concern me throughout most of the remainder of this study.

Having claimed that Heidegger's thought has an ethically important dimension, it is worth conceding that it is obviously not the case that it confronts issues of morality or normativity. My explanation of *why* Heideggerian thought can be thought of in ethical terms will have to be built up over the next two chapters. As a preliminary explanation, though, I ought to make clear that I am not trying to spell out a Heideggerian moral philosophy; what I *am* doing is trying to is to elucidate an approach to understanding morality and ethics that is suggested by Heideggerian elements: '[a] proper commentary ... never understands the text better than its author understood it, though it certainly understands it differently':[18] that certain problems in moral philosophy might be amenable to a solution that comes from Heidegger's work (which is what I want to suggest) does not imply that any of Heidegger's work constitutes moral philosophy. It is on this basis that I will consider myself entitled to choose some Heideggerian ideas and ignore others. My own thought will owe much to Heideggerian *thought*, which is ethical in a sense that I hope will become clear in what follows, not to Heideggerian *ethics*, which are simply not there.

Attempts to identify any useful themes in Heideggerian thought are complicated by the 'turn' in Heidegger's thought that took place in the mid-1930s: *Being and Time* focuses on Dasein, whereas later work relegates Dasein's importance. Although the strategy is risky, I shall weave between pre- and post-turn work: again, even allowing that I might not understand Heidegger's work better than (or as well as) Heidegger himself, I can still claim to understand it differently – and this difference means that I do not necessarily have to follow the paths through the forest that Heidegger himself may have beaten.

Drawing on earlier and later aspects of Heidegger's thought, this chapter will concentrate on how evaluative and normative thought can be elucidated by

---

17 Hodge, 1995, p. 1.
18 *Nietzsche's Word: 'God is Dead'* in Heidegger, 2002b, p. 160.

consideration of the way that the world is revealed to Dasein.[19] There will be two main aspects to the argument. In the first, I will be seeking to show how moral values can be found in the world. Making use of a strategy suggested by Heidegger, it is possible that Mackie's worries about 'queerness' need not be insurmountable. Indeed, the phenomenology of things such as values need not suffer from queerness any more than do a good number of other things – 'proper', three-dimensional things, that is. In what I hope will be a nice demonstration of the possibility of reconciling 'analytic' and 'Continental' philosophical approaches, I shall rope in John McDowell as support here.

One of the impressions that the argument is likely to give is that there is nothing at all that could limit caprice in morality; the second aspect of the argument is to show how this is not the case. The thought that I shall pursue appropriates certain themes from Putnam and the later Wittgenstein. If my limitation of the flexibility of morality is successful, the problem that I will then have to face is one of having gone too far in the other direction. I do not think that there will be much scope for a middle ground between caprice and moral inflexibility: the argument I will use against caprice will suggest that there is not much *auto* in *nomoi*. So the possibility of moral critique looks to be endangered. I will illustrate the problem with reference to the relationship between Heidegger and 'Heidegger'. All I can do in this chapter is outline the problem; in Chapter 5, which will be concerned with another aspect of the relations between the putative moral agent and the world and will focus on how ontology might impact on moral thought, I hope to be able to propose a solution.

Truth and Reality in Moral Statements

I want to start off with quite a bold claim: the reason why something like RI gets itself tied up in metaphysical knots trying to provide irreducibly moral characteristics of the world is because its account of reality is lacking. There are irreducibly moral characteristics about the world after all, though we do not have to think of them as enduring in a sentience-free universe in order for them to figure in reality.

Remember that the basic claim of realist independentism was that our apprehension of moral values is apprehension of *something*, and, correspondingly, that our moral claims are accurate to the extent that they pick up on an irreducibly moral characteristic of enduring reality – that is, of the world as it exists outside of the head. The argument from queerness is a classic example of an argument that calls RI's bluff: its retort is that, since these purported moral characteristics are too *odd* to be intellectually respectable, we are not entitled to talk as if there were any such thing. And, for this reason, there is no such thing as an objective moral value; even if it is possible somehow for moral statements and evaluations to be *accurate*, it is not because they reflect any particular aspect of the world qua world.

---

19 'Dasein' is a term that has a claim to explanation, but since the concept will be considered in its own right in Chapter 5, I do not think it necessary to spend time discussing the meaning of the term here.

Nevertheless, it pays us to note that both RI and its sceptical rebuttals such as the argument from queerness draw from the same metaphysical well. Both accounts can agree that moral appearances *could* be objective if they were capable of being referred back to some objective and irreducibly moral part of enduring reality. RI theorists think that they can trace this referral; members of the opposing camp think that they cannot. But the dispute is not one about methodology: it is simply about the likelihood that the method will meet with success. RI theorists think that it will; people like Mackie think that it will not.

Put another way, RI theorists have one ontology, their opponents another. Now, a difference in ontology is one thing; all the same, each camp in the dispute is committed to the same metaphysic. In attempting to act as a bulwark against what can be cast as Platonic profligacy in RI, strategies such as the argument from queerness still draw on Platonism of another sort. In itself, this is not a problem – Plato, after all, cannot be dismissed out of hand, and strategies like the argument from queerness do have their place. However, this place is within a particular account of reality – that (something like) the argument from queerness, or my own argument against RI in Chapter 2, is fine as a means of combating Platonism if we assume a certain account of what reality is. But this account also owes its provenance to Plato, and it is open to question. If there is anything to this challenge, a way remains open to provide an ontology of values that allows them to be built into reality.

Traditional metaethics – and here I am not restricting myself to RI: my challenge could be laid at the door of Aristotelianism and Humeanism, too – understands terms such as 'reality' or 'objectivity' as indicating that which I have labelled 'enduring reality'. The claim is that, if characteristic x is not a part of enduring reality, then x-ness is not really or objectively there in that thing. At most, x is quasi-real. And this presupposition, I think, is Platonistic.

But Platonistic in what sense? The clue comes from Heidegger's work on truth. For Heidegger, the history of philosophy maps closely onto the history of metaphysics, and the history of metaphysics itself maps onto the history of a particular understanding of truth; his position is spelled out in essays such as *What is Metaphysics?* and *On the Essence of Truth*.[20] Before Plato, the story goes, truth was a feature of the phenomenal world and lay in appearance – the world having been revealed in a certain way – rather than in the agreement of a statement with a state of affairs. Indeed, the Greek word for *truth – aletheia –* is a matter of uncovering, revealing, or bringing-to-presence by wresting from (indicated by the *alpha*-privative *a-*) oblivion (*lēthē*). With Plato, though, a shift begins; henceforward, the relationship between truth and appearance is one in which 'the true' is understood to mean something residing and enduring *behind* appearance rather than that appearance. This move, Heidegger alleges, opens the way for a 'metaphysical' account of reality – that is, one in which 'the real' or 'the true' is understood exclusively as something *meta ta physika*, or beyond that which shows itself (*'physis'* derives from the same

---

20 Both reprinted in Heidegger, 1999b and 1999c; cf. Heidegger, 2004.

root as '*phuein*', to shine). Once made, the move divorces what something *is* from its appearance. And this means that we can disregard appearance.

Following this route, the mere fact that there is an observed moral value to (let us say) terrorism would not necessarily tell us anything about the reality of affairs; at most, it would provide us with a clue. And, depending on the way that we solve the clue, we might come to the conclusion that moral appearances *do* refer to irreducibly moral characteristics; but we might equally well come to the conclusion that those moral appearances refer 'in reality' to conduciveness to promote flourishing, or to our own predilections; or we might conclude that they refer to nothing at all. Correlatively, if a statement such as 'terrorism is wrong' is *true*, it might only be true courtesy of those other considerations. We can think about matters by drawing on a non-moral example: a thing might appear blue, and a statement like 'this item is blue' might be true, but the provenance of blueness could arise from a number of sources: an irreducible property of blueness, surface characteristics and the frequency of electromagnetic waves reflected from that surface, or some feature of the eye that gives everything a blue cast. In all three accounts, though, the 'reality' of the matter, and the guarantor of statements concerning blueness, would lie 'beyond' the appearance.

But why should we deny that appearance can be the backstop of reality? Thinkers such as Nietzsche have provided diagnoses of why this tendency should be, though it would be a distraction to investigate them here.[21] However, what I can do is to ask whether there is any reason *not* to look beyond appearances to bankroll reality. And, quite possibly, there is. Should there be anything to this line of thought, the implication would be that it need not matter if we could find nothing outside of a moral statement to make it true. Rather – with an important qualification that is particularly important *vis-à-vis* the normativity of a putatively true moral statement and that I shall spend most of the next chapter outlining – the mere fact that there appears to be a difference between (say) terrorism and civil society is sufficient for there really to be such a thing.

How to Philosophise (with) a Hammer

The position that I want to adopt is that values are quite unremarkable and that they can be slotted into reality without difficulty and without having to think too hard at all. However, wading in with talk about values too quickly might be foolhardy, so I will begin by exploiting an example that Heidegger gives in *Being and Time*: that of a hammer.

Uncontroversially, hammers have a place in reality; they are unremarkable features of the world that we inhabit, and we accept them as such fairly unthinkingly. And it is odd to ask questions about *how* a hammer features in reality – even the grammar of the question is disconcerting. Still, forced to provide an answer to a

---

21   Viz. 'How the Real World at Last became an Illusion' in Nietzsche, 1990b.

question like this, we might frame our response along the lines that every object in the universe is made up of atoms held together and pushed apart by forces, or that the fabric of the universe is like the vibration on a cosmic 'string', or some such. Whatever the account, the point remains that we would still be saying that the world, at root, is made of *this* kind of thing behaving in *this* kind of way. At the same time, our experience of reality is explicable in terms of there being a stimulus of a certain sort on our optic nerve (or whatever); put another way, all that there *is* to an encounter with something like a hammer is a transaction between two entities and a subsequent chain of neuroelectric impulses and responses. The process is unidirectional: the hammer – or, more properly, the agglomeration-of-atoms-held-together-by-forces – reflects light, and the eye receives this light in the form of colour; something roughly similar goes on for the other senses (the hammer 'has' mass, and my toe 'receives' this mass in the form of weight when I drop said hammer). And this sort of story, we might think, would account for the fact that there is a hammer in front of us.

Still, it sometimes pays us to adopt a *faux-naïf* position in philosophy, and, having done so, we might echo Magda King's example[22] and express puzzlement at the account just given. For none of it really seems to capture the 'hammerness' of the hammer. Certainly, we have an account of what the hammer is made from. But the account still does not describe reality recognisably. Framed in an appropriate manner, it would be just the kind of thing that could be processed by a computer – *and that is exactly what is wrong with it*. What it fails to capture is what the difference is between a h a m m e r[23] and a collection of undetached hammer parts. Whatever the merits of the account in terms of *correctness* in respect of what is going on when we encounter a hammer, its scrutiny of the hammer is so close that the object of its attention falls out of consideration entirely. And, as such, an account like this fails to tell us how the hammer figures in reality.

In effect, this account fails to account for the reality of *things*, qua objects that we might encounter. Those things appear as, at most, addenda to enduring reality. So what there truly *is* for metaphysics is a collection of atoms held together by certain forces. Yet, as it provides this account, the 'metaphysical' account tells us a story about a world that we do not inhabit, and about a version of reality with which we have no contact, and to which we could ascribe queerness just as accurately as we could to Plato's Formal domain (of which it is a descendant, of course). Here, 'reality' is taken to mean 'enduring reality'; but enduring reality is not necessarily the same as the lived reality with which we have our primary encounters.

---

22 King, 2001, p. 6.

23 I have spaced certain words in this way in an attempt to avoid their being taken for granted. My point here is that the hammer as a whole should be taken as phenomenologically more important than the bits that comprise it. It is the 'hammerness' of the thing lying in front of us that we notice first: anything we might say about its component parts only follows on from this. Later, I will be spacing the various forms of the verb 'to be': in this case, I want a similarly emphatic effect. The verb in these cases will play a part greater than simply holding a sentence together.

In places in *Being and Time*, the difference between enduring reality and lived reality is characterised as the difference between 'the real' and 'reality';[24] elsewhere, the distinction is framed in terms of the difference between the ontic and the ontological. It is also what sustains – indirectly – the distinction between the ready-to-hand, under which aspect something like a hammer is available for use, and the present-at-hand, under which aspect the hammer loses its 'hammerness'. In adopting too analytical an approach to the hammer – that is, though prioritising the metaphysical account of truth as correctness over the non-metaphysical account of truth as the way in which a thing is revealed and thereby attending to its presence-at-hand – it falls from our intellectual grip. Hence:

> The kind of Being which equipment possesses – in which it manifests itself in its own right – we call 'readiness-to-hand' … If we look at Things just 'theoretically', we can get along without understanding readiness-to-hand. But when we deal with them by using them and manipulating them, this activity is not a blind one; it has its own kind of sight, by which our manipulation is guided and from which it acquires its specific Thingly character.

By contrast:

> [W]here something is put to use, our concern subordinates itself to the 'in-order-to' *which is constitutive for the equipment we are employing at the time*; the less we just stare at the hammer-Thing, the more we seize hold of it and use it, the more primordial does our relation with it become, *and the more unveiledly is it encountered as that which it is – as equipment.*[25]

So, then, the reductionist, present-at-hand worldview might try to grasp the hammer, but the paradox of the issue is that the tighter the scientific grasp, the more easily the h a m m e r slips out of its hand.

The position amounts to this: that an attempt to burrow behind appearance, motivated by the insistence that 'reality' must be something that endures behind that appearance, is to look at the world backwards and to lose sight of it: it is only by virtue of apparent, graspable hammer, in fact, that we are able to talk about the present-at-hand undetached hammer-parts in the first place:

> To lay bare what is just present-at-hand and no more, cognition must first penetrate what is *beyond* what is ready-to-hand in our concern. *Readiness-to-hand is the way in which entities as they are 'in themselves' are defined ontologico-categorically.* Yet only by reason of something present-at-hand 'is there' anything ready-to-hand. Does it follow, however, granting this thesis for the nonce, that readiness-to-hand is ontologically founded upon presence-at-hand?[26]

---

24 Heidegger, 1999a, H 212.
25 Ibid., H 69; emphasis mine.
26 Ibid., H 71; emphasis in original.

Obviously Heidegger thinks the answer is 'no' – hence the rhetorical confession that he is only entertaining the thesis 'for the nonce'. Without doubt, the bits that make up a hammer are, qua present-at-hand material stuff, parts of enduring reality; but this is only secondary to the non-present-at-hand 'lived' reality. Ontologically, we need to have h a m m e r s before we can start talking about undetached hammer-parts. (It might be supposed that this is an epistemological point rather than an ontological one. However, given my claim that the reality in which we live is constituted formed by objects such as h a m m e r s, there is a close relationship between our understanding of the world around us, and our understanding of what it means for something to b e in the first place. This allows Heidegger to make a claim to ontology where others might settle for epistemology. This issue is perhaps peripheral to the metaethical argument that I want to put across, and is not one that I can afford to confront directly here, although it is implicit in a good deal of the argument of Chapter 5.) These h a m m e r s are not just things in the world, though: they are built into the world that we inhabit. More: they are in-the-world.[27]

A useful development of the example is offered by Mark Platts. He points out that the face in the newspaper photograph is only there to be seen because the dot-arrangement is as it is, but he points out that, notwithstanding this,

> We do not *see* the face by *attending* to that dot-arrangement, where that arrangement is characterised in terms free of picture and face-vocabulary – say, by a mathematical grid system. Indeed, the more we so attend, the less likely we are to see the face that is there pictured.[28]

Platts' suggestion is that we do not see the face on the basis of judgements concerning the dots, but that the judgements that we *do* make – 'That's a face' – are primary (although not literally true). As it happens, I think that Heidegger would have had problems with the idea of individual judgements playing a role at all here, especially in the period roughly from the *Nietzsche* lectures onwards;[29] he would have disputed Platts' suggestion that the judgement is not true from even earlier in his career. But this does not impact on the general utility of the example (and, indeed, much of what I argue in this chapter could happily share page-space with significant chunks of *Ways of Meaning*; I hope that this is a matter of iteration rather than repetition). The photo would not be recognisable as such if we admitted that there was nothing more to it than dots on newsprint; Platts' having taken the thought beyond equipment, to which Heidegger limits himself, has an importance that will become apparent later.

What I hope to have provided in this section is the outline for a claim to the effect that we can spend the rest of eternity studying the ontic present-at-hand – the hammer qua physical object made up of *these* atoms or with *these* surface qualities

---

27 There is a serious difference between being in the world and being in-the-world (or even being-in-the-world); it is not a difference that I think I need to explore too deeply here, but it is one that will get more attention in the next chapter.

28 Platts, 1979, p. 244.

29 Viz. Heidegger, 1991c, *passim*.

– but we will never, in so doing, deal with the hammer qua h a m m e r. The upshot is that it is quite possible for the world to have more about it than can be accounted for by brute classical science. To insist that talk about the world in these terms still reduces – or collapses – to more 'respectable' language is to miss the important point that things like hammers *just do not* present themselves to consciousness as collections of sense-data, and that this is not attributable to any epistemological infelicity or mistake that we make in our interpretations of sensory knowledge of the world: it is built into the way that we live in the world qua human beings rather than walking spectrometers. Sometimes, in McDowell's words, it pays to 'exorcise the idea that what it is for a quality to figure in experience is for experience to have a certain intrinsic feature',[30] the thing has the quality of hammerness, even though hammerness is not the kind of feature that would figure in enduring reality.

Whatever the problems raised with this sort of account, the basic vision is about right (although some of the supporting argument will have to wait until later); for example, we would be puzzled by someone who said that he could see the effects of electromagnetic waves of varying frequencies but cannot, for all that, see the colour, for he seems not to relate to the world after all. What is provided by the Heideggerian account is a disruption of the idea that all that there is to reality is *enduring* reality. Moreover, if there is anything to the account, it makes it fairly easy to vault our way to providing a similar analysis for values. For as long as we are reasonably happy that things can be a legitimate object of experience without having any 'ontical' backing, we do not have to worry about the provenance of the perceived difference between (say) terrorism and civil society. It may not be scientistically respectable, but the guiding thought here is that there is, nevertheless, such a thing as moral perception, involving sensitivity to an aspect of the world.[31]

Appearance and Values

If an account of reality need not be reducible to the barest, most stripped-down facts to be true, and if talk about the hammer (properly and recognisably understood) is not simply a way of talking about undetached hammer-parts and is neither a metaphor nor a record of a misperception, then value-talk need not be inescapably simply a way of talking about the present-at-hand components of value (whatever they might be); neither must it be a metaphor nor a record of a category error.

Values are parts of reality. The fact that we can distinguish clearly between terrorism and civil society, even though, when we scratch the surface, there is no clear delineation to be found, is ample evidence of this. We are not wrong in our initial evaluation, and it does not matter whether that evaluation can be cashed out in terms of RI, or any other theory; nor does it matter what difficulty we might meet in trying so to do. It does not matter at all if we are unable to provide something that would be recognised as a sufficient ground for our moral beliefs by traditional

---

30 *Values and Secondary Qualities* in McDowell, 1998, p. 138.
31 Ibid., p. 131.

moral thought. Indeed, we have a reason not to go searching for the underlying distinction too hard, for in doing so, we risk unweaving the rainbow; at best we will dull its vibrancy. Lived reality does not have to be reducible to enduring reality; if we are unhappy with the claim that values can be built into lived reality as objects of experience, then we ought also to be unhappy with the idea that hammers can be built into reality as objects of experience. Further, I think that it does not take too much to claim that things like values can be said to figure in lived reality *objectively*.

There are two senses in which this claim might be understood. What I have in mind here is the idea that a value, while not an object or entity in its own right, might nonetheless be something with which we find ourselves 'confronted' – that is, the idea that a value might be something that we come up against 'in the world'. To the extent that the world is presented to us as a 'given' – that is, as constituted by objects with the characteristic of, say, hammerness or (I claim) goodness – this means that a value might also be something objective in the more everyday sense of being 'impersonal'. And this is as much as to say that anyone who inhabits the same world as me ought to be sensitive to the same values as those to which *I* am sensitive. Having said this, I still want to fight shy of the idea that objectivity means 'intrinsic to enduring reality', and I shall investigate the implications of my desire to divorce objectivity from intrinsicness as I go along.

The problem that remains is that of accounting for how a value-property or value-characteristic might be something that we encounter, given the *ex hypothesi* idea that it need not be anything intrinsically built into enduring reality. While not seeking to deny that this is a problem, one point that can be made fairly quickly is that the problem applies equally well to a host of other things that are not values. For example, I have claimed that the characteristic of hammerness that the hammer possesses is not reducible to the bare constituent undetached hammer-parts of the thing. There is therefore a problem concerning how to deal with hammerness. (As it happens, Heidegger's thought seems to suggest that there is a more radical problem of accounting for the very 'thingness' of things or 'objectness' of objects once we place too much emphasis on truth as correctness rather than truth as revealing.[32] Whatever the merits of this line, I do not think that I have to be quite so radical to make my point.) But once we can give some account of how hammerness gets into the world, it takes only a very small extra step to be able to offer an account of how something like moral goodness gets into the world as well.

Categorisation and Apophansis

The question here is this: if the hammerness of hammers does not have to be bankrolled by a more basic enduring reality behind the appearance, how come it has any validity at all? What is the difference between recognising a hammer and being a passive recipient of the undifferentiated raw data that (scientistically) hit

---

32 Cf., *passim* and *inter alia*, 'The Question Concerning Technology' in Heidegger, 1999c and 'The Thing' in Heidegger, 2001.

our retina? The idea that we arrange gathered raw data from the world around us and that it is in this way that we get h a m m e r s from undetached hammer-parts is clearly a non-starter: not only does such an idea go against the grain of the argument that I have just sketched – that is, that our primary encounter is with the hammer – but it would also presuppose that we have some sort of category of 'hammerness' that can govern any such arrangement and, which would itself require explanation. Heidegger's explanation for how hammerness gets added to the raw data, though, is still heavily reliant on the idea of categorisation.

In his account, it is not that we arrange the entities that we encounter in the world into categorical good order: rather, it is the categorical ordering of the world that *sustains* encounters. He suggests that 'categories are special ways of addressing things – *kategoriai* in an emphatic sense – for they sustain all our habitual ways of addressing things; they *underlie* those everyday ways of addressing things, which in turn get developed into assertions, "judgements"'.[33] In other words, addressing something in an everyday sense is reliant on its *already* belonging to a category:

> Κατὰ-ἀγορεύειν means: to accuse someone to his face in the ἀγορά … From this comes the broader meaning: to address something as this or that, so that, in and through our addressing it, the thing is put forth into the public view, into the open, as manifest. Κατηγορία is the naming of what something is: house, tree, sky, sea, hard, red, healthy.[34]

It is this *kata-agoreuein* that gives something the 'standing-on-its-own' quality of 'thinghood'. The accusation across the *agora* picks out the accused from the undifferentiated mass of people: it makes him unique and independent. Correlatively, picking things out is what grants the standing-on-its-own quality that guarantees the being of beings.[35] (There is scope to add to this the example of learning a language: to begin with, speech is one long flow of sounds; yet we 'hear' distinct gaps between the syllables that are not in the sound wave, but which are phenomenologically 'added' courtesy of familiarity with the language being spoken – courtesy, that is, of the way that familiarity with a language involves familiarity with a method of picking out the words from the sounds.[36]) It is at this point that we hear echoes of the Kantian contention that the world fits to thought rather than *vice versa*.

But has this not just shunted the problem back a level? What, after all, is the provenance of the categories that supposedly pick things out from the mass of *stuff*? For Kant, the categorical framework around which the world is built were rational in essence; although Kant clearly resounds in Heidegger's account, the latter's allows

---

33 *On the Essence and Concept of* φύσις *in Aristotle's* Physics B, *i*, in Heidegger, 1999b, H 323; emphasis mine.

34 Ibid., H 322; see also Heidegger, 1999a, H 44–5.

35 Heidegger, 1999b, H 322–3; see also the discussion of *Lichtung* in *The End of Philosophy and the Task of Thinking* in Heidegger, 1999c.

36 Derrida quips that, because the inaudible difference between two phonemes is what allows them to be recognised as phonemes in their own right, 'there is no purely phonetic *phonē*' (*Différace* in Derrida, 1982).

very little – if any – input from any transcendentally rational agent. For Heidegger, what provides the backstop here is language or discourse. Even earlier work such as *Being and Time* argues that *logos*, here meaning *discourse* rather than the traditional *reason*, has 'the function of ... letting something be seen by pointing it out',[37] and it is this point that marks the difference between Kantian and Heideggerian categories. In essence, something's having come to prominence depends on the apophantic function of discourse:[38] that is, it is thanks to discourse that *kategoriai* have the power to address it and so have given it a public identity *as* a thing. When we confront the world, we confront it ready-made; the making is done by the discourse in which we participate.

A close reading of a short passage from Saint Augustine's *Confessions* provides support for at least the general direction of Heidegger's thought:

> When they named any thing, and as they spoke turned towards it, I saw and remembered that they called what they would point out by the name they uttered.[39]

For 'they named', Augustine uses '*appelabant*'. The verb '*appelare*' has a sense of appeal (as is easily visible and unsurprising). When one calls (*vocat*) something by a name, one is using its name to appeal to it – that is, to call it forth as what it is. Things take on their discrete characteristics and qualities on the basis of an appeal; things reveal themselves according to what, and how, they are called. What underpins Augustine's language is a tradition in which calling something '*x*' is simply to call it into awareness as a discrete thing *by* '*x*'. To call (*vocare*) is to appeal (*appelare*) to something to come forth. As Gillian Clark points out in her commentary to Augustine, there is a preponderance of 'will'-words (*vellum, voluntati, volebam*) in the paragraph from which the quotation is taken.[40] What is called forth depends on the will of the caller, not the thing called; the call is 'anticipatory',[41] having priority over the called – although, of course, this does not mean that all calls will be heeded.

Now, while I think that there are good reasons to relegate the importance of the will of the caller that I shall look at in a while, the idea that things are 'called forth' by language ties in well with Heidegger's claim in the *Letter on 'Humanism'* that language 'is the house of the truth of being',[42] this is a claim that appears in the later essays *The Way to Language*[43] and, slightly modified, *What are Poets For?*[44]

---

37 Heidegger, 1999a, H 33.

38 In *Being and Time*, apophansis has the sense of 'pointing out'. Hence at H 33, Heidegger writes that 'discursive communication, in what it says, makes manifest what it is talking about, and thus makes this accessible to the other party. This is the structure of the *logos* as *apophansis*'.

39 Augustine, 1898, 1, viii.

40 In Augustine, 1995, p. 98.

41 *What Calls for Thinking* in Heidegger, 1999c, p. 386.

42 *Letter on 'Humanism'* in Heidegger, 1999b, H 150; 1999c p. 223.

43 In Heidegger, 1999c, p. 424.

44 In Heidegger, 2001, p. 132; translated as *Why Poets?* in Heidegger, 2002b.

What does this odd claim mean? Bear in mind that Heidegger's 'truth' is the Greek '*aletheia*'. So the 'truth' of being is its 'unveiledness'; and this unveiledness can only take place within language.

To return to the hammer example, that there is a collection of matter that can be described in a given way is perhaps attributable to the classical laws of physics; but that there is a h a m m e r is dependent, Heidegger thinks, on the fact that that there is a concept or category of 'hammer': that there a r e things called hammers is secondary to the fact that there are things called *by* 'hammer'. At risk of overplaying a point that I made earlier, we should note that this does not amount to a denial that the h a m m e r is something objectively there: it is, and it must be, there objectively if our primary encounter with is with the hammer rather than the undetached hammer-parts. In fact, its very objectivity – the fact that it is a discrete object – is guaranteed by the discourse that shapes the world. What there is not is anything intrinsically or enduringly 'hammer-ish' *about* those undetached hammer-parts; in a world without sentient beings, there would be no h a m m e r; again: the hammer is a feature of 'lived reality', despite not figuring in *enduring* reality. For this reason, there is a difference to be drawn between the *objective* and the *intrinsic* features of a thing.

Whatever their differences, on this point Heidegger and Sartre seem to be broadly consonant, for Sartre has a similar thought about the dependence of the world on categorical structures imposed on an undifferentiated mass of being. Recall that, in *Nausea*, Anton Roquentin feels that '[t]hings have broken free of their names': something like a seat is a seat only for as long as it is so categorised, and once the power to address something as 'seat' is lost, what it *is* is up for grabs:

> I murmur: 'It is a seat,' rather like an exorcism. But the word remains on my lips, it refuses to settle on the thing ... [It] is not a seat. It could just as well be a dead donkey, for example ... [Things] are there, grotesque, stubborn, gigantic, and it seems ridiculous to call them seats or say anything at all about them: I am in the midst of Things, which cannot be given names.[45]

There is a difference between Sartre and Heidegger here to the extent that the former seems to think of language as a way of ordering unruly things and holding the world back, whereas the latter conceives of it as being that which allows there to be things and something recognisably like a world in the first place. But what is held in common between the two is the idea that world is different from *stuff*, and that it is language that marks this difference. Moreover, it is not obvious that all species have the ability to carve up the world in a neat way (or, indeed, all humans: think of the way that young children's divisions of the world might be less determined than those of a normal adult); there is reason to suppose that my cat will encounter various things, but none of them will be a t r e e, because he does not have the relevant conceptual apparatus. Put in a slightly different way, the limits of my language mean the limits of my world;[46] things without a language do not *have* a recognisable world.

---

45 Sartre, 1965, p. 180.
46 Wittgenstein, 1997, 5.6.

Participation in, and facility with, discourse – or language, in the broadest sense – provides the categorisation that underpins the world in all its richness; it is within the confines of discourse that undetached hammer-parts and dots of pigment on cellulose become h a m m e r s and p h o t o g r a p h s. In the same way, it is within these confines that we see an activity such as m u r d e r rather than as a sequence of bomb-throwing movements. When attempting to give an account of how the world comes to appear as it is, the strategy recommended is to treat the world as a given – we can investigate its metaphysical roots if we want, but ought not to forget that the world that we encounter is, as it were, the origin rather than the object of our intellectual travels. The characteristics of a given experience can be wholly *divorced* from its present-at-hand characteristics.

Still – granted that it means something to talk about bomb-throwing in terms richer than those that describe the bare facts concerning the movement of brute objects, this still will not account for values. But it can be made to do so easily enough. From the point of view of an enquiry about the provenance of values, it is worth noting that in the quotation above, in which Heidegger claims that '*kategoria* is the naming of what something is: house, tree, sky, sea, hard, red, healthy',[47] he is equally happy to place nouns and adjectives side-by-side in the list. In effect, there is no reason why calling something 'good' or 'bad' – that is, calling it forth *as* or pointing it out *as* 'good' or 'bad' – is too radical a departure from calling it anything else. Phenomenologically, an action's 'rightness' or 'wrongness' is embedded in that action just as a hammer's 'hammerness' is embedded in that h a m m e r – that is, objectively, but not intrinsically. And to miss either the goodness or hammerness is seriously to misapprehend an aspect of the world. Indeed, it seems fair to say that someone who reports an act of cruelty robotically, with no indication that he has any sense of conviction or even of deep understanding of the term, is not sensitive to an aspect of the world and that his relationship with the world is comparable (and comparably mysterious) to that of someone who says that his retina is responding to the electromagnetism but that he is still at a loss to find the colour.

The sensitivity to the world that figures in moral judgements does not, on this basis, imply that there must be a present-at-hand quality of goodness, badness, or whatever any more than sensitivity to the reality of a hammer implies that there is a present-at-hand 'essence of hammerness'. Rather, because the world as manifested to humans is not the pared-down world of the spectroscope, we should be wary of attempting to separate the thing from the qualities that it manifests. The robotic reporter has not failed to *deduce* that the act was cruel: he has failed to notice its cruelty altogether. The quality is not stapled onto the thing we encounter *ex post facto*; it 'haunts' the world and the recognition of a quality is one of the conditions that underpins a recognisably rich encounter in the first place. When we encounter a good or evil event, and want to excavate *what* is good or evil about it, my extension of the Heideggerian stance is that we are following the wrong track. Encountering it *as* good or evil is part of having encountered it *at all*. The 'good' characteristic of

---

47 Ibid.

a thing haunts the perception thereof insofar as it is a *part* of the thing perceived. (Only slightly out of context, it is possible to cite Derrida: 'To haunt does not mean to be present, *and it is necessary to introduce haunting into the very construction of a concept*'.[48])

All that is necessary for an act or event to be valuationally load-bearing is that the discursive context that determines *how* it is 'unveiled' is right. As a result, the sting seems to have been taken out of arguments such as Mackie's argument from queerness. Correct it may be; relevant it is not. Moral characteristics do not have to be cashed out in any scientifically 'respectable' way – say, by describing the features of the thing or the psychology of the observer. Rather, they are a factical feature of the world, picked out by the apophansis of a discourse that houses the truth – unveiledness – of their being. There are more things in heaven and Earth than are dreamt of in Mackie's philosophy.

Now, given that Heidegger seems willing to provide an account of how things become things, one might think that he is slipping into the traditional way of thinking from which he ostensibly wants to distance himself in *Being and Time*: is there not a serious inconsistency between the denial that reality is founded on the present-at-hand, and a claim that it grows from something as suspiciously present-at-hand as discourse? I do not think so. We can allow that, *sans* discourse, the world would be unworlded for us without having at the same time to allow that concentrating on discourse provides us with a superior understanding of that world, since clearly it no more does that than concentrating on atoms provides us with a superior understanding of atoms. Discourse might underpin h a m m e r s in a manner comparable to that in which atoms underpin undetached hammer-parts, but it is still hammers with which we have our primary encounter. It is the phenomenologically rich world that provides our starting point, do with it what we will. There are hammers, and we could say more – but we do not have to, and the expanded account will not necessarily improve on the first impression.

Problems with the Account

It is worth pausing at this point to make a brief clarification and to forestall a few objections. Although the hammer example in *Being and Time* provides a fruitful disruption of the traditional account of reality and does so by distinguishing the present-at-hand from the ready-to-hand, the mere fact that something is not present-at-hand should not be taken to indicate that it is *ipso facto* ready-to-hand. With respect of values, this would be a serious error. For readiness-to-hand presupposes a project; but projects presuppose values. Thus, even if values are not present-at-hand, neither can we think of them as ready-to-hand; it looks as though Heidegger's division of the world into these two 'modes' is insufficient. Moreover, there is a second problem, in that, regardless of whether the division of the world into the present-at-hand and

---

48 Derrida, 1994, p. 161; emphasis mine.

the ready-to-hand is sufficient, it is still never claimed to refer to anything more than entities.[49] This means that, unless one is willing to think of a value as an entity, the division does not fit particularly well.

Magda King's reading of Heidegger, especially of *Being and Time*, skirts around this problem but does appear to identify a close relationship between values and the ready-to-hand, inasmuch as what is valuable is handy for something;[50] she appears also to commit herself to the claim that a value is an entity. Such a stance is either mistaken or trading on an unorthodox understanding of 'entity'.

Still, a response to both these problems is available; it comes from the idea that King's is not the only possible (or even the best) interpretation of Heidegger. For, although *Being and Time* does give the impression that the division of the world into present-at-hand and the ready-to-hand is exhaustive, it does not claim this *explicitly*. There is no reason why an understanding of the world may not go further than Heidegger takes it in *Being and Time* while still belonging to the broad Heideggerian programme. So there might be a third or *n*th way in which things could present themselves. Alternatively, we might point out that there is no reason to restrict the ambit of the term 'ready-to-hand' to equipment, and so we could simply expand the concept beyond instrumentality. Either way, what matters is the mere fact that the introduction of readiness-to-hand and presence-at-hand can be seen as a demonstration that the world is not simply present-at-hand or wholly captured by an account that leaves out the non-present-at-hand; indeed, to attempt to understand the world in this way is to denude it of its recognisably worldly qualities. It is in the context of this point that Platts' example of the face in the newspaper is germane, since it does seem to step outside the simple dichotomy of the ready-to-hand and present-at-hand: a picture's 'pictureness' is not obviously predicated on the observer's having a project in which it serves as equipment.

Similarly, although Heidegger's work does seem to refer exclusively to entities, I do not think that we have to take this too strongly. Again, the disruption of the idea that reality reduces to enduring reality should be enough to bankroll the idea that the everyday riches of the world do not have to be mortgaged by enduring reality in order to feature *in* reality. What matters is the manner in which entities are revealed; value can be a feature *of* an entity without being an entity in its own right; and if values cannot be keyed into the world, this may be the fault of our account of values, but it may also be the fault of our account of the world. It is this disruption of too comfortable an account of reality that I want to exploit here; the details of what shape this disruption takes need not worry me too much.

One slight shadow remains. A lurking danger of attempting such an understanding of Heidegger is suggested in his own later work: in *Letter on 'Humanism'*, Heidegger admits that he has been understood as speaking or thinking 'against values',[51] and he does not deny this understanding. This would seem to count against the possibility

---

49 Viz. Heidegger, 1999a, H 71–72.

50 King, 2001, p. 74.

51 *Letter on 'Humanism'* in Heidegger, 1999b, H 177 ff.; 1999c, pp. 249 ff.

of incorporating values into the world while still claiming adherence to a broadly Heideggerian tradition. Fortunately, this danger is not as great as it seems. The explanation offered of what 'speaking against values' means is instructive. Contrary to appearances, Heidegger maintains that his 'speaking against values' does not represent willingness 'to beat the drum for the valuelessness and nullity of beings'.[52] Rather, it simply represents a refusal of a mania for *valuation*: valuation is, for Heidegger, a matter of making things subordinate objects of human estimation. Yet his suspicion of this tendency does not mean that he thinks that the values to which we may or may not be sensitive are *bogus*. It is possible to acknowledge that values are a built into the world factically while maintaining a distrust of them and the discourse that sustains them – a distrust that finds expression in his thinking upon the 'enframing' tendencies of technology.[53] It is this that I read into his 'speaking against values': it is possible within a Heideggerian tradition to admit that values are a part of the world properly encountered and to admit that they are a creation of human discourse (though not of any particular human), but, if one is so minded, to add to these considerations an existential argument against such creations.

Of course, these problems are trivial compared to the obvious objection to the thesis that I am beginning to build, which is that the Heideggerian line I am exploiting is unreliable, and that, even if it is sustainable, there is no reason why a metaphysical thesis about the way that *things* feature in the world should have much bearing on metaethical concerns. To put the same objection more positively: Heidegger's way of thinking about the world is simply *wrong*. For one thing, the sceptic might insist, it relies on a bogus ontology. The 'truth of things' – whatever that means – is *not* dependent on categories and apophansis or anything like that. Even if Heidegger's reconstruction of the pre-Socratic account of being is *accurate*, this does not make it *correct*. And if it is wrong, the idea of using the account to explain ethics is mistaken.

Having said this, I think that a comment I made a moment ago neutralises the objection effectively enough. Even if the Heideggerian account of ontology *vis-à-vis* entities *is* mistaken, it could still stand as an ethical theory, and it could do so for exactly the reasons that might make us think twice about jumping from metaphysics to metaethics. It could stand as a metaethical thesis just because, if we are tempted to think that there are such things as value-things, the arguments against RI theory in Chapter 2 should give us pause. We can happily ignore Heidegger as a metaphysical thinker if we are so inclined – this is 'metaphysical' understood in the common-or-garden way, not in Heidegger's, philologically acute as he may be – but this does not necessarily negate our ability to take his thought on board qua metaethics.

Moreover, Heidegger's account is revealed as resilient if we remember that ethics as we know it was invented by the Greeks. It is a variation on a Greek theme. If their way of thinking is wrong, then so be it. But since it was this way of thinking that bequeathed us ethics as we know it, it means that the whole of ethics is in

---

52 Ibid., H 179; p. 251.
53 Cf., obviously, *The Question Concerning Technology* in Heidegger, 1999c.

trouble, not just a Heideggerian version of the subject. And again, I can afford to be generous to the critic here. It might be that Heidegger's reconstruction of the birth of philosophy is false. This is something for the philologists and historians of ideas to investigate. Even at its weakest, though, my claim is that *if* Heidegger is on to something, *then* there are these consequences. As it happens, I think that Heidegger *is* on to something; all I am doing at the moment is tracking the consequences that his thought either has or, at the very least, *would* have.

According to the topology that I suggested at the start of the chapter, all that has gone so far belongs to the first stage of my argument. But the stage now has two elements. The first deals with, and dismisses, the suggestion that moral terms need to refer to anything 'really there' – for which we can read 'anything that figures in enduring reality'. A word such as 'good' need not refer to an enduring presence-at-hand: the world is phenomenologically richer than is allowed for by honestly parsimonious scientism. As I have suggested, Heidegger's example of the hammer disrupts the idea of the world having to be cashed out in terms of the present-at-hand, and (although I do not think that Heidegger takes his thesis far enough often enough) suggests that this is how things like values could be seen as 'haunting' acts, events and objects.

I have suggested further that the phenomenological richness of the world is granted by discourse: it is the categories factored into the way that a mode of discourse such as language works that underpin the world and – of particular concern here – its *moral* phenomena. Hence moral terms express the prevailing values within a discourse and do, in Hume's phrase, 'raise in a manner a new creation' insofar as they are parts of that discourse; but, to pre-empt a point that I will bulwark in a while, this creation is not 'borrowed from internal sentiment'.[54] In a roundabout kind of a way, the position that I am adopting is one that agrees with the projectivist account in as much as moral values have a reality that is not to be found intrinsically 'in' entities in their barely 'natural state' – but it disagrees with the idea that values actually are projected by the thinking agent. Rather, this agent is receptive to something genuinely built into the world. At this point, we could, I suppose, give free rein to any projectivist tendencies that we have and claim that moral aspects do not have to be pasted to the world because the world *in toto* is a projection. But one of the things that I want to do in the remainder of the chapter is to reject this line of argument.

Once this principle has been established, then the focus of the debate has shifted to a point at which it has to be shown that things *are not* like this for moral adjectives: why they *do* have to refer to something present-at-hand. And it is an argument built along these lines that I want to meet in the next section.

---

54 Hume, 1994, appendix I, p. 135.

Truth and the Possibility of Moral Error

A plausibly strong position could be taken against my embryonic argument based on the idea that it has an apparent difficulty in accounting for instances of moral error. Moral terms can be misapplied. Commonsense would demand that to say that terrorism is good is to make a false claim.[55] The difficulty that my account faces lies in explaining *why* this is in a way that does not smuggle in something to act as surety for values. Why is it that we say that some moral claims are false rather than admitting that they have simply unveiled a hitherto unheeded aspect of the world? Does a desire to avoid moral anaemia not commit me to the idea that there is an extra-discursive standard against which we can rate a speaker's values?

The motivation behind this section is to show that those statements that cohere with the broad thrust of a current discourse have apophantic power and are therefore called true – remember that truth is not a mark of *correctness* but of apophansis – while those that do not cohere with current discourse have little or no apophantic power, and therefore cannot have truth attributed to them. In other words, an attempt to call terrorism *right* will fall flat because it will fail to call forth the rightness of terrorism; the reason for this is that, within current discourse, a statement such as 'terrorism is permissible' has no place, therefore no apophantic power. Correlatively, the propriety of a moral claim is guaranteed by the discourse of which it is (putatively) a part rather than by any extra-discursive feature of the enduring world.

In effect, one does not have to know *what* makes a moral term appropriate – merely *that* it is appropriate. And because the truth of a moral claim reaches no further than whether it is well or ill made, it is spurious to suppose that there *must* be anything *at all* to perform this function. Such an argument strips that of my notional opponent of its merit. With this in mind, I am now going to edge into the next part of my argument. I shall not discuss moral terms right from the beginning, though: I shall begin by taking my lead from Hilary Putnam and considering the term 'water'.

For users of standard English, 'water' names the stuff that falls from the sky when it rains, that fills the oceans, and so on. Yet 'water' *means* H_2O; whenever a speaker of standard English points to something and correctly calls it 'water', this is because the stuff at which he points *is* H_2O. However, there should be no problem with accepting the possibility that he might not know this, and might lack the means to know it. Yet it would still make sense to suppose that he could use the word correctly or incorrectly; this means that my ability to use 'water' correctly does not have to involve knowing what *makes* my use correct – that is, that 'water' means H_2O. It just involves being a reasonably competent language-user.

The word has a place in the language and is *subsequently* identified as having a particular extension – in this case, H_2O: '[m]eaning determines extension – by

---

55 Even terrorists need not assent to a claim that terrorism is permissible: remember that in Chapter 1 I pointed out that one weapon in the terroristic arsenal is the ability to cause outrage. Some terrorist actions might be chosen *just because* there is something impermissible about them.

construction, so to speak',[56] as Putnam puts it. Someone who is a reasonably competent speaker of standard English *has* to mean the stuff that scientific examination will show to be H_2O in his use of 'water'. Putnam's suggestion is that there is a public meaning to words that guarantees that they can be used by anyone familiar with a particular language, even though only a few know much about the extension of the word. Thus:

> the way of recognising possessed by these 'expert' speakers is also, through them, possessed by the collective linguistic body, even though it is not possessed by each individual member of the body, *and in this way the most recherché fact about water may become part of the social meaning of the word while being unknown to almost all speakers who acquire the word.*[57]

What is going on in *my* head at any given time at which I am talking or thinking about water need have nothing to do with the extension of the term. By the same token, I do not have to know what the notional extension of a moral term is in order to be able to apply it correctly and use it meaningfully.

At first glance, the water argument does not look as though it helps my case. I have claimed that there does not have to be anything to act as surety for an accurate moral claim; but this example seems to count against me. The case with 'water' seems to be that its accurate use is *guaranteed* by the presence-at-hand of two atoms of hydrogen and one of oxygen, even if I do not know that the guarantee is available. How is this any help to me at all? Would not the analogy suggest that the accurate use of a moral term must be similarly guaranteed by the presence-at-hand of some virtue- or vice-bestowing characteristic of the world, whatever it might turn out to be?

Of course not: Putnam's mention of expert speakers obscures the important point, which is that it is possible for *no one* to have an (accurate) idea of the extension of a given term; this would have no necessary impact at all on the possibility of correct use of the word. During the seventeenth century, *no one* knew that water is H_2O. It was still possible to inculcate in people rules governing correct application of the word, though. People could identify water without having to know what made it water; there is no reason to think that anyone living before the components of water were analysed would have had any difficulty in applying the term accurately or any doubts about whether the word was meaningful.

So we can have a world without experts, and thereby a word in which no one knows the extension of a meaningful word – again: just because no one knows that water is H_2O, it does not follow that meaningful and correct use is impossible. We might imagine that 'water' had currency, but that one day someone discovered that the word had been used to describe a range of different chemicals. As it happens,

---

56 Putnam, 2001, p. 270.
57 Ibid., p. 228; emphasis mine.

this did not happen in our world.[58] But no one was to know this until comparatively recently: granted that meaning determines extension, it does not seem implausible to suppose that a term can have a life of its own, unanchored to an extension.

Now, if terms such as 'water' might be meaningful and capable of correct and incorrect application quite irrespective of the state of our knowledge of their extension, might the same be as true of moral terms such as 'good'? On the face of it, there is no good reason why not. Just as we could identify a substance as water without being able to put our finger on what *made* it water, so we could identify an act or event as good without being able to finger what made it good. The argument allows us to say that when someone uses a word like 'good' or 'bad', they do not have to be able to give a substantial account of the theoretical underpinnings of the word. In just the same way that we can say 'this is water' without knowing its chemical characteristics, so we could say 'Terrorism is wrong' without particularly having to be able to point to the extensionally *bad* characteristics of terrorism. We do not have to know why discourse unveils something as g o o d or b a d: it's enough that it *does*. (This is a point that Platts makes explicitly: 'A speaker can know, have a grasp of, the truth-conditions of a moral sentence even if those truth-conditions are beyond his (present) recognitional abilities'.[59])

On the basis of this sort of argument we can interpret Kant as having presented one possible extension of the meaningful (but as yet extensionally indeterminate) word 'good', and Hume another, just as one person might suggest H_2O and a second might suggest *XYZ* as the extension of 'water'. More important, though, is the possibility that, in trying to pin down a determinate extension for value terms, the thinkers engaged in the debates of traditional metaethics could be on a wild goose chase. When we are chasing a meaning for 'water', we have to be asking a question along lines such as 'What *is* this stuff that falls from the sky, boils at *this* temperature at *this* air-pressure, has a density of $1g/cm^3$?' But, with 'good', things are different unless we have presupposed certain conditions on what 'good' might mean; and there is no reason to think that there might be any such conditions. For one thing, there is a difference of meaning between the use of 'good' of Kant and Mr Kipling;[60] if meaning precedes extension, though, and both use the word meaningfully (as seems to be the case), and if goodness is supported only by discourse, then nothing could settle any dispute between them over which use is correct. If meaning determines extension, we can have meaning without ever having to have nailed the conditions by which extension could be determined. On the other hand, because 'good' is not a word that fits alongside 'terrorism' in standard English, there *is* a basis for saying that it has been misapplied.

---

58 I leave aside consideration of such terms as 'aqua vitae', 'aqua fortis' and 'aqua regis', largely for the sake of simplicity – I do not think that I need to complicate my basic point with them.

59 Platts, 1979, p. 245.

60 For the benefit of non-UK readers, Mr Kipling is a brand of confectionery advertised under the slogan ' Mr Kipling bakes exceedingly good cakes'.

And it is easy enough to push this thesis even further to relate it back to the argument of the last few sections: for as long as the extension of 'water' is indeterminate and no one knows the conditions for accurate use, there might as well not *be* any. It might turn out that certain words have no extension. Of course, this generates a pressure for them to be exorcised from discourse. There was a time when 'phlogiston' had currency, but when it turned out that the word was extensionless, it dropped out of use; it did not become *meaningless*, though. It was just that it no longer had a place in a discourse that sought to describe the present-at-hand characteristics of the world.

With moral terms, we might similarly find that there is no extension. This would generate a pressure to exorcise them from discourse. But I do not think that it would be a crushing pressure: the hammer argument above was specifically designed to demonstrate that the present-at-hand does not exhaust the world in which we live. Nor do I think that moral terms would be exposed as meaningless. Phlogiston remained a part of the lived-in world until well after Priestley's discovery of oxygen and despite not existing because the prevailing discourse was geared towards it; indeed, we might well still use the word in a poetic or rhetorical sense. Analogously, it is not implausible to suppose that a moral term such as 'good' can have a meaning and signify something about the lived-in world for as long as we are participants in a discourse that imparts values. Perhaps, one day, the prevailing discourse will change and any part that is not related to the present-at-hand will be exorcised. Moral terms will then disappear. But this is not the world in which *we* live, and so is not a world to which I need to pay too much attention.

Hence I think I can claim by now to have gone a good way, if not all the way, towards knocking out the idea that my argument is no better than its rivals. I think that what I have been able to show is that it is possible for a moral term to be load-bearing without there having to be any underpinning to it – real, ideal, aesthetic, or whatever else. All that determines the propriety of use for a moral term is the vertigo associated with stepping outside of prevailing meaning;[61] the propriety of a moral term is ensured primarily by linguistic rather than moral rules. More importantly, my rivals presume a prioritisation of extension over meaning – traditionally, something is *good* if and only if it satisfies criterion C – and this is a presumption that need not stand. My position allows me to say that something is g o o d, and only then do I have to decide *why* this might be. This is, I think, a hefty piece of evidence that even if I am not on *exactly* the right track, I am at least in the right vicinity and moving in the right direction.

However, there is still a fair amount that needs to be said. I have not forgotten that there is a question of authority to be settled: how 'bad' can have normativity built in so that to describe something as bad is qualitatively different from describing it as vermilion. And although my solution to the problem of why terrorism is bad and civil society good should be becoming fairly clear, there is a related problem

---

61 Cf., *per analogiam*, McDowell's reference to Cavell and his 'vertigo' argument in *Virtue and Reason* and *Non-Cognitivism and Rule-Following*, both in McDowell, 1998, pp. 60–61, 206–11.

of the stability of this distinction, given that I have apparently spent the last couple of sections hacking away at the idea that there might be any definitive extension to moral terms. I will turn to these problems now.

The Embeddedness of Norms

I am going to begin with the question of authority. Even allowing that we can recognise that something has goodness or badness built into it and that 'good' or 'bad' would be, therefore, an appropriate descriptive adjective, I still have to face the question of how moral valuations get their authority. As well as having apophantic properties, an adjective like 'bad' has a normative power that is utterly beyond that which we may ascribe to an adjective such as 'vermilion' in normal discourse, even though ostensibly the terms share a grammatical box. 'Bad' might *mean* any number of things – un-universalisable or undesirable, for example – or no thing; but it still has to be explained how this is to have any authority that can stop Henry throwing his bombs.

It is plain that this is a point that demands a response. We might shrug nonchalantly at something's having been described as vermilion, but a similar reaction to something's having been described as bad or wrong is not what commonsense wants – even though commonsense morality's demands at this point seem to transgress the boundary between an *is* and an *ought*. I think that I am able to go the extra step to normativity reasonably easily, though: some words – specifically, valuational adjectives – have an authority built into their meaning in such a way that not to recognise this authority is not to have understood the word (or so I will argue). Part of the meaning of a moral term is imperative, and this meaning is a part of everyday discourse. This discourse unveils the world; in just the same way that it unveils the world as being replete with values, so it does more or less the same thing with norms. Both are built into the world; and a failure to recognise a norm is just as indicative of a certain insensitivity as is a failure to recognise a value.

Simply by virtue of the discursive parts played by moral terms, they do more than simply indicate a value: they also have a normative impact of their own. Granting the point that it is courtesy of discourse that a murder is a m u r d e r, the same could be said of actions of this sort: 'to-be-avoidedness' is built in. When we hear a word like 'murder' or recognise something about the world *as* m u r d e r, we also 'hear' – silently – or recognise an injunction to the effect that this is something one must not do.[62] 'To-be-avoidedness' is a built-in characteristic. Accordingly, if we were to say to Henry that bomb-throwing is bad, and he was (apparently) to believe us

---

62 It is interesting to compare Hume on this matter: 'The merit of delivering true general precepts in ethics is indeed very small. Whoever recommends any moral virtues, really does no more than is implied in the terms themselves. That people who invented the word *charity*, and used it in a good sense, inculcated more clearly, and much more efficaciously, the precept, *Be charitable*, than any pretended legislator or prophet, who should insert such a *maxim* in his writings' (Hume, 1965, p. 5).

without modifying his behaviour, we would have a good basis for claiming that he was insensitive to an aspect of the world.[63] The word brings with it a normative tone that is not something that (*à la* Kant) we add to it ourselves after a process of deliberation.

Hence it is preposterous to wonder whether *A* should murder *B*. We *could* go through a process of universalisation to decide the matter, but it is somewhat superfluous and its result inevitable. We will get moral disapproval at the end of the process not because murder violates some universal and rationally available standard of morality, but simply because of the meaning of the word 'murder'. On the other hand, there is room for ambiguity. Should *A kill B*? It is still too early to say. *B* might be a child; so the question becomes 'Should *A* kill a child?', which we might think would settle the matter. But even this will not do. What if the killing is euthanasia, for example? There might still be a normative loading to the question, but it is unlikely to be as *obvious* as it would be in the example with the word 'murder': the word brooks dispute. Indeed, if *B* is not a person but a cancer cell, killing it would almost certainly be *good*, and equally, 'kill' would have a *positive* normative spin to it. However, the difference between 'euthanise', 'kill' and 'murder' is less to do with universal standards than because of the simple flexibility of the meaning of the word 'kill' and the context in which it is used. This does not do any harm to the case that I am presenting: that the way in which language is used imports norms and that we do not have to check things up against a moral standard. As long as we understand what a word means, its normative value is apparently waiting for us. As long as we recognise an action as an *action* – a recognition that is underpinned by participation in a discourse – the norm can be just another characteristic of the action.[64]

Meanwhile, this insight allows us to approach what it means to be in a moral dilemma. Dilemmas occur when the language is equivocal – when the meaning of statement 1 provokes the same reaction as that of statement 2 because it has

---

63 This point satisfies Dancy's (surely accurate) intuition that 'there is something odd about saying "This is wrong but I do not see it as relevant to my course of action" ... because normally to see something as wrong is (intrinsically) to be motivated not to do it' (Dancy, 1993, p. 26). McDowell agrees, with the proviso that Dancy thinks that imperatives can be outweighed by other considerations – a thought that solves the problem of accidie (amorality having been pretty much dismissed as a realistic possibility). McDowell argues that 'the dictates of virtue ... are not weighed with other reasons at all, not even on a scale that always tips on their side' (*Are Moral Requirements Hypothetical Imperatives?* p. 90). On this, I think that Dancy has the advantage: McDowell seems to be in need of some pretty baroque reasoning to support his point.

Of course, this point can work in reverse. I have already noted that some people – terrorists, situationists, Dadaists – might work into their strategies the idea that by appearing to be as evil as possible, they might disrupt faith in the *status quo*. But these people are, of course, still trading on the 'to-be-avoidedness' of bad things: they are banking on 'badness' being the sort of thing that one is supposed to avoid.

64 On this point, see Dancy, 1993, p. 32: 'What motivates is the matter of fact believed, not the believing of it.'

something like an equal and opposite normative loading. Consider a version of Williams' problem of whether to take a well-paid job in a chemical weapons lab.[65] There are advantages to the position, but also something queasy-making about the nature of the work. According to my account, the dilemma arises not because of the result of a process of rational universalisations of several maxims for action, or because of my moral feelings. Rather, it arises simply because chemical weapons and the harm that I can do with them are unveiled as having one value and set of normative associations; the prospect of regular income and the good that I can do with it another. These two are run together. But the moral dimension is not of our making: it is just built into having got to grips with the world as unveiled. The dilemma arises because the situation is described in such a way as to make competing moral dimensions apparent at the same time. We do not need to make extra normative claims about the permissibility of the maxims in play: it can just be taken as read that, as long as we understand the description of the situation, we will be aware of its normative tone. It is the awareness of moral dissonance that contains the dilemma.

Getting to grips with this is of no help in solving the dilemma, of course – but it would be a mistake to expect otherwise. The point is that the genesis of the dilemma comes from the fact that the same action can be looked at from more than one moral perspective, and this makes a difference to the way that its moral characteristics are revealed. Which perspective is 'better' is a different question entirely, and quite possibly one that has no meaningful answer.

Along the same lines, the account offered does not preclude the possibility that two people engaged in a moral dispute might simply be talking at cross-purposes, simply because they're unwittingly engaged in discourses that draw on different contexts. Sometimes the contexts can be radically different, although intuition suggests that a dispute is more likely when the difference is subtle enough for disputants not to notice that there are differences. This is an especially live problem, in fact, when there is nothing present-at-hand that could be used to settle matters, as is the case for discourses with moral overtones. But the possibility of disputes and dilemmas is not a point against my account: rather, it is a sign that my account coheres with recognisable moral situations.

Take, for example, this passage from *The Odyssey*:

> Athene now appeared before Odysseus, Laertes' son, and urged him to go round collecting scraps from the Suitors and so learn to distinguish the good from the bad, though this did not mean that in the end she was to save a single one from destruction.[66]

prima facie, it would seem that Homer has blundered in his moral characterisation in passages like this. Athene appears unjust in that she does not discriminate between the deserving and the undeserving – a problematic characteristic in a god of her stature. But we should not be so quick to leap to this conclusion. The possibility should not be ignored that the parameters of moral discourse were different for

---

65 In Smart and Williams, 1993.
66 Homer, 1991, XVII, ll. 360–364.

someone living at the thick end of three thousand years ago from those within which we work today. Bearing in mind the argument that it is courtesy of *logos* and the categories that it imparts that we get the values and norms built into the apparent world, there could be a difference in what is apparent between Homer and us. The passage is an illustration that Homer was engaged in a different discourse, and so was playing a different moral 'game'. What *we* expect from gods and justice might not match Homeric expectations, but if the meaning of moral terms does not rely on any present-at-hand guarantor, there is no reason why this should be a surprise.

There is room to think that, even by the time of Plato, the rules of the moral game had changed: that this is what underpins Platonic suspicion of Homer and other poets as moral teachers. Plato simply does not understand what is going on – there is a different moral discourse, with which he is unfamiliar. The misunderstanding is compounded by the Platonic insistence on an unalterable backing for moral statements. Such an insistence precludes hermeneutic modifications.[67] Plato reads Homer in moral terms rather as we might read Chaucer in literary terms if we did not realise that English had shifted in the meantime and believed that such a shift was impossible. Individual words might make sense, but they are used in an unfamiliar way; they are strange, although this does not make them any *less* English. (Similarly, we might point to the use that Descartes makes of the words 'subjective' and 'objective' – his meaning is substantially different from what we expect, but this does not mean that he was *mistaken* in his use.) Both Homer and Plato speak 'Moral'; but they do so differently – in different dialects, for the sake of the analogy – and the associations and chains of meaning are different for each.

Pace Davidson,[68] Putnam,[69] and so on, I am not suggesting that Homer used a moral scheme radically different from the familiar one. However, I am suggesting that he might have been using a scheme that was *significantly* different. Davidson's point, summed up by Putnam, is that 'a consistent relativist should not treat others as speakers (or thinkers) at all'.[70] Of course I can see that Homer is a speaker and that matters of justice arise in his language: this is enough to demonstrate that his moral discourse is not *radically* different from mine. But I still think that we should be aware of the possibility of recognising a different discourse and yet not ever being able to live under its rules,[71] unless we could somehow translate our moral thought into Homeric by forgetting all alterations in moral discourse since Homer like a moral version of Borges's quixotic Pierre Menard.

Might we be able – or forced – to say something similar in respect of Henry and our reaction to him: that we should refrain from judgement for hermeneutic reasons?

---

67 This is a belief from which Aristotle does not escape, either – his insistence that the contents of the mind are the same for all humans extends as a belief that the meaning of 'justice' cannot change from epoch to epoch.

68 *On The Very Idea of a Conceptual Scheme* in Davidson, 2001.

69 Putnam, 1998, esp. pp. 114 f.

70 Ibid., p. 124.

71 Cf. *Relativism and Reflection* in Williams, 1993c.

Probably not. Admittedly, there is something prejudicial about the word 'terrorist' that is not always found in words such as 'freedom fighter' or 'guerrilla', and so we might be doing Henry a disservice by labelling him thus. But what is more important is that, as I argued in Chapter 1, making a claim such as 'There are no innocents', with all its implied rules about innocents, the guilty, punishment, retribution and so on, and its according normative implications, is evidence that he was participating in a familiar moral discourse. He is playing it badly, though. Whereas there is no reason to think that the passage from Homer is at odds from what people were thinking at the time, this is not the case with Henry. Homer's discourse is historically exotic; Henry's is not.

The Problem of Caprice

But if there is no determinate extension to moral terms, what is to stop someone like Henry deciding that, henceforward, 'good' *can* accommodate acts of terrorism? If this is a bit implausible, it does not take much to ameliorate matters: what is to stop the modification of discourse or the introduction of a new term into discourse that will have an apophantic function that can ameliorate the negative moral overtones of 'terrorism'? If there is nothing that can limit the introduction of a new element or feature of moral discourse, it looks as though anyone might be able to come up with a moral backing (of sorts) for anything. With this point in mind, I am led to look at why I have rejected the claim that moral values and norms, albeit new creations of a sort, are not borrowed from internal sentiment. I want to defend the position that the dependence of values and norms on discourse means that they *cannot* be borrowed from internal sentiment because discourse itself is public. As a consequence, one would have serious trouble in sustaining the introduction of a new term into an existing discourse or in forging a new discourse entirely.

It is plain that trying to get a new apophansis *would* require a new discourse or, at the very least, the introduction of new components to a discourse. Introducing new components (granting, at least provisionally, that such a move would be possible) would leave the old ones intact, of course, possibly leading to dilemmas – but at least the old certainties would be shaken. By contrast, in trying to introduce a new apophantic capacity into existing discourse *without* introducing new components, one would be trying to find a way to unveil something as *right* that had previously been unveiled as *wrong*. Admittedly, such a reversal is not as extreme as it would be if I was to attempt to introduce a sense of 'square' that could accommodate three-sided shapes, but we are dealing with something that is at least comparable. The attempt to redefine terms such as 'permissible' or 'good' to accommodate (say) bomb-throwing looks like an act of spectacular bad faith: to engage in such a programme, one would have to admit that there was something *prima facie* wrong about whatever deed one had in mind, which raises questions of coherence – and of what kind of cussedness would be necessary in a person who would want to change matters.

In relation to the terrorist who uses his acts as a means to bring about a 'good' end, we might offer a related critique. If a justification is to be offered, it seems to be capitalising on a certain moral vocabulary. '*Some* innocents had to be bombed because ...' is a claim that aims recognisably at the moral. But it is one that cannot escape its own critique: implicitly it admits that bombing innocents is wrong – if it did not, justification in these terms would be superfluous. Whereas the undeserving apparently *might* be smitten by divine wrath in Homer's world despite their innocence, this will not wash as a justification in *this* world, according to the rules of *this* discourse – and, we might note, Homer does not presume to *justify* the ways of gods to man anyway. An attempt to *justify* a terrorist act is bordering on the incoherent: either one must accept that one is operating outside the parameters of extant morality, or one must play by the moral rules on pain of being *evil*.

I will admit that the terrorist might be a participant in a different discourse, or playing a different moral language-game, with correlatively different apophantic powers, from the majority; but if this is right, he probably cannot justify himself to those to whom he *needs* to justify himself without entering the community and thereby exploding anything that might count as a justification. He must make a move according to the prevailing norms of the community to which he wishes to justify himself, or he must act according to other norms.[72] If he opts for the former, he must end his strategy: his attempt to 'call' terrorism (by) anything but wrong or bad will go unheeded; if the latter, he should save his breath and stop trying to justify himself: either people will come to see the world his way, or they will not.[73] Further, even if he is successful in his rebellion, there is a good chance that our terrorist will not have (re)introduced exiled justice into the *polis*. He will simply have displaced one paradigm with another. He will not have stormed the palace so much as changed the guard.

But what about the possibility of introducing new elements into discourse – or using a new discourse altogether – with accordingly different apophantic powers borrowed from internal sentiment? If Homer can work within one discourse, and we within another, then there seems to be no barrier to there being any number of possible discourses. Yet to introduce a new element into an extant discourse, or, more radically, to try to institute an entirely new discourse, looks as though it comes close to the introduction of a private language: what looks like a possibility turns out not to be.

The more simple option is to attempt the introduction of a new element into an extant discourse which, if the graft is good, will unveil a hitherto unacknowledged moral value in a certain act or event. In this picture, let us say, this act can be

---

72 Wittgenstein, 1990, § 294.

73 Indeed – he might find himself in a position that cannot be justified. The radical implications of occupying such a position are considered by Lovibond: 'The anarchic spirit who undertakes too bold a programme of subversion endangers his own intellectual identity thereby, for he runs the risk of severing himself wholesale from all available models of sound judgement' (Lovibond, 1983, p. 121).

described as 'pitimmeral', a new term with a positive moral spin. For this new term to have any apophantic power, we must be able to say that it was understood by its hearer, since a term that is not understood has no apophantic power.[74] But the person introducing the new term must also understand it: that is, the new term would be meaningful nevertheless, if only to the speaker. If a person wanted to be able accurately to describe x (such as bombing) as pitimmeral, he would have to *understand* 'pitimmeral' – and if anyone did not share this understanding, that would be *their* problem. The question is whether there is anything that might meet this criterion – that the use of 'pitimmeral' would be meaningful, albeit perhaps for the moment idiosyncratically. I do not think that there is. In fact, not even the speaker would have much of an idea of what he meant by the moral terms he might introduce in this situation. Hence it would turn out to be difficult to sustain the thought that he could have introduced a new term without the moral connotations of extant discourse.

The reason for this is that, as Putnam points out, meanings are not in the head. *ergo* they must be outside of the head. Aside from the dubious possibility that there is some sort of sense to meaning by which a term gets its meaning thanks to its ability to signify a Form of some sort, the remaining possibility is that meanings are created in a public, 'inter-mental' context. Either way, there does not seem to be much in the Putnamian argument that would give succour to the terrorist: introducing new terms within a discourse, or introducing a whole new discourse that might, in the longer term, be able to prop up a new apophansis just is not in the gift of the individual. No one can simply decide that, henceforth, the meaning of a term is *PQR*. Meanings not being in the head, one does not *create* them – one *receives* them.[75] And since I am not willing to accept an oracular account of meanings, I am committed to the publicity account.[76] This implies a commitment to a certain genealogy, according to which the

---

74 At this point, one thinks of the discussion of the word *iki*, which describes a characteristic of Japanese art, in Heidegger's 'Dialogue on Language' (in Heidegger, 1982): 'How often did I hear the word on Kuki's lips, yet without experiencing what is said in it' (p. 13). Presumably, familiarity with the term would allow a person to talk about *iki* and the degree to which an artwork displays it – but *iki* would remain hidden from one who did not know the term.

75 Note the contrast in this picture with the traditional empiricist prioritisation of thought over language. In Lovibond's words, 'ordinary speech is conceived, not on a model suggested by natural science or technology, but on one suggested by art. The expression of thought in language is likened to its expression in any other linguistic medium: until it is embodied in the medium, it is without determinate content' (Lovibond, 1983, p. 28).

76 Some might argue that a sort of provisional private language could be constructed. On this picture, I could form my own meanings, and so effectively create my own discourse, as long as it was publicly accessible. Public accessibility would guarantee a criterion of correctness. However, I am reluctant to accept this. For one thing, it places too much emphasis on the contingent. What if no one cared about my new discourse, or everyone died except me? My discourse would still be publicly accessible in principle, but I would still only have my own memory to guarantee that I had remembered my own meanings aright – which is

moral constitution of the world is revealed by discourse, which itself depends on meaning. But the grand-daddy of them all is the public sphere. Apophansis depends on publicity; ultimately, morality is intersubjective. This is why, a few pages ago, I rejected the Humean idea that the 'new creations' of moral terminology could be derived from 'internal sentiment'.[77] Hume *is* subjective, and subjectivism is *wrong*.

(It is interesting to apply this analysis back to Aristotle in a manner that I indicated in the last chapter. For him, the difference between a political animal such as man and a gregarious animal such as a bee was man's ability to deliberate concerning good and evil. One is *politikon zōon* because one is *zōon logon ekhon*. Closer to the truth, though, is the suggestion *zōon logon ekhon* is an accurate description of a person because, at the very least, he is of *hoi polloi*. And this, even if not *political* as such, is at least *social* or '*poly*tical'. This also means that to do something deliberately, one must have a social context, since deliberate action presupposes at least the possibility of deliberation (*bouleusis*), which is impossible without comprehensible articulation (*logos*) – it is inconceivable that one could act deliberately without understanding *why* one acted thus, even if the explanation is trivial.)

Arguing that values and norms are available to us primarily (or only) because of the way that they are implicit in language obviously has serious implications. Not least of these is that the debate between independentists and dependentists seems to have been sidestepped. A quality such as 'good' can be a characteristic of a thing independently of us qua private individuals, but this does not commit us to the idea that an account has to be given of values in terms of the fabric of present-at-hand material *stuff* or immaterial Forms. As I said, a value is objective in the sense that it is not something that springs from our cerebellum but is something that is found in the world, and this world is constituted, discursively, 'for us'. But this does not mean that it is a part of enduring reality; without sentience of the right sort, there would be no value. A second implication is that, given that it is a part of the meaning of moral and evaluative terms that they have authority, and that this authority does not have to be traced any further than having understood a word, a curmudgeonly question such as 'Why be moral?' can be solved – or, better, avoided. Asking why one should be moral is tantamount to asking why one should understand. No answer can be given, but no answer is really necessary anyway.

On the other hand, a third implication is that there is no standard that could settle moral questions definitively. To an extent, certain moral debates may therefore be interminable, although no less meaningful for that: seeing matters aright would

---

no guarantee at all (cf. Wittgenstein, 2001, § 265). More directly, Putnam's point is not that meanings ain't just in the head: it is that they just ain't in the head – not the tiniest little bit.

77 Hume, 1994, app. 1, p. 135. I am ignoring the fact that Hume links these 'creations' to taste rather than reason because, as I argued in the last chapter, taste alone cannot give morality the authority that is expected. I should not necessarily be thought of as agreeing with Hampton that it is *reason* that gives authority, though. My argument here is the same as the one that I suggested in my discussion of Kant in Chapter 2: that it is *language* that does this, and that reason is based on language.

be a matter of sharing a point of view.[78] Given that morality depends on discourse rather than traditional 'facts', we have to accept that there is no pre-existent standard that might serve to limit what a nascent language might allow as 'moral'. In a pre-linguistic state of nature, for example, we would only need two people to create the public space necessary to come up with a rudimentary language. Presumably we would only *necessarily* need the same two people to thrash out a rudimentary moral code to describe the values and norms that their nascent discourse imparted to the world. In this world, *any* sort of scheme of moral concepts is possible as long as the two people have satisfied the necessary condition that they can articulate it by slotting it into a given language-game. Of course, in this state of nature, the two players are making up the rules of this language-game as they go along, so this will present no difficulty. The morally important point is that, once the publicity criterion has been satisfied, there is nothing to stop anything at all being permitted with all the moral backing in the world – literally.[79]

This sort of thought opens the way to the idea that there is an inbuilt authoritarianism to language that is contrary to individual autonomy, and thereby to individual moral agency, simply because external meanings dictate the parameters of meaningful thought. In using a discursive medium such as a language, one cannot help but subscribe to a preordained set of values, norms and so on. Language is necessary in framing comprehensible thought and cannot be privately concocted: hence it appears that it restricts intellectual and moral freedom, because external factors dictate *ab initio* what can and can not meaningfully be thought, and what the 'meaning' of those thoughts might be ('*This* is how we think. *This* is how we act. *This* is how we talk about it', in Wittgenstein's words[80] – and there is not much we can do about it). Augustine might display a preponderance of *will*-words to call things – but the will is not, when it comes to the crunch, *Augustine*'s.

To give a rough example: Aristotle uses the word 'slave' and this leads him to think 'tool' – an association that modern commonsense moral thought would hold to be morally tainted. However, Aristotle is not a bad man, nor is he making a moral mistake: it is just that 'slave' implies 'tool' in a morally unproblematic sense for him because this is how the language-game that he plays – let us call it 'Hellenic' – shapes his thought. The shift in thought between him and us is attributable to a shift in language: 'slave' does not *mean* the same any more: it does not have the same moral extension. But it is *language* that has shifted, beyond the control of any autonomous moral agent. Indeed, we can take this argument back so that we can bring it to bear on the consideration of reason as a moral tool (at least in the Kantian sense). Kant wanted the rational capacities that determine morality to be independent,

78 Cf, *Might there be External Reasons?* in McDowell, 1998, pp 100–101; see also *Are Moral Requirements Hypothetical Imperatives?* in ibid. p. 86.

79 This point bears with a point raised by Nietzsche: '*Multiplication table.*– One is always wrong, but with two, truth begins.– *One* cannot prove his case, but two are irrefutable' (Nietzsche, 1974, §260).

80 Wittgenstein, 1990, § 309.

so that at least in principle a rational animal brought up in isolation could still be doggedly good. But reason (*logos*) and deliberation imply language (again: *logos*). To be rational – to be able to deliberate and entertain articulate thoughts – one has to have been inculcated into a linguistic community – to play its language-game. The language-game we play will thereby determine where reason takes us.

It is also worth noting that the subordination of morality to language-game can account for moral inconsistency. For one thing, there is no obvious necessary reason to think that one should be engaged in just one game at a time; hence one might be unable to decide about something's moral value because there are two games to play. The possibility of playing two games – that is, participating in two discourses with two modes of apophansis – at once and exclusively of each other is not at all mysterious, and it should not impinge on the possibility that one may dart between them. Second, there is no reason to think that any *one* game might do the same thing at all times – think of Wittgenstein's example of the 'adding 2' game that suddenly becomes an 'adding 4' game. Nothing has gone wrong according to the rules of the game: there is no inconsistency. It is just that players of the game do something different according to circumstance. Analogously, in reply to Kant, it might be wrong to lie *now*, but not … (wait for it …) *now*; this would not require major explanation or suggest inconsistency. To make a judgement of inconsistency must come from outside of the rules of the game – one must be playing a game that prizes uniformity. What might found the 'must'? Only the norms of another game.

On this basis, the place of commonsense in moral thought becomes far more clear. Commonsense, on this picture, is simply a direct articulation of the norms inherent within a given discursive medium such as a language. Hence it was a matter of commonsense for Aristotle that slaves were tools and that Greeks should rule non-Greeks. It is equally a matter of commonsense today that terrorism is morally worse than democracy. *But no further metaethical explanation can be given*, because the discourse that moulds commonsense also moulds what a more rigorous metaethical system might tell us about morality – a value-judgement or norm is a precept of moral reason because it is built into the structure of how reasoning works – as well as bankrolling quasi-Humean apophansis. And there is also no need to worry too much about the suspicion that discriminating morally between *poleis* and terrorists might not be self-consistent: since morality trails discourse, and since there is no immediate reason to think that discourse should obey any rules comprehensible from outside of itself, it becomes much less of an admission of moral defeat to say that there *is no* single principle that can back the supposition.

Publicity, Commonsense and Critique

The importance of language and therefore of the public space in metaethics ties in with an important element of Heidegger's thought. '[L]anguage,' he writes, 'comes under the dictatorship of the public realm, which decides in advance what is intelligible and what must be rejected as unintelligible.'[81] Note how snugly this fits in with the demand that I articulated a while ago for publicity in meaning. Especially when we consider that moral deliberation surely must be articulate, and that the medium of articulation is intelligible language, the important role of the public in the formation of discourse and so of moral thought is clear. While we have to resort to the extra-cranial for meaning, Heidegger takes matters one easy step further: all our language, and so all our thought, is effectively imposed by the public.

Consistently throughout his career, for Heidegger, the subsumption of thought to language to publicity means that it is susceptible to the input of '*das Man*', the impersonal 'they'. Using a language inevitably means, in the language of *Being and Time*, surrender or swamping of personal authenticity. Insofar as it is a tool for expressing thoughts,[82] language *could* be used authentically; the problem is, though, that language is more than this: it determines the form that those thoughts are going to take right from the start. 'We not only *speak* language,' says Heidegger, 'we speak *from out of* it ... [I]t is *language* that speaks.'[83] In effect, our thoughts come second-hand: '[t]he "they" prescribes one's state-of-mind, and determines what and how one "sees"'.[84]

Worries along these lines might be read into an exhortation in Heidegger's address to German students on 3 November 1933: 'Let not propositions and "ideas" be the rulers of your Being'.[85] Discourse all too easily descends into inauthenticity through unthinking use; the word 'ideas' in this quotation can be read as standing for the everyday and unreflective moral truisms built into language rather than any authentic engagement with the world. To allow off-the-shelf bourgeois propositions, ideas, ideologies and creeds to 'rule' our Being forecloses authenticity. On this interpretation, Heidegger's involvement with Nazism ('The Führer alone is the present and future German reality and its law', the exhortation continues) was ostensibly part of an attempt to bring a little authenticity into European life – to 'rescue' it from the creeping technological inauthenticity of the modern world – notwithstanding that the attempt was suffused by political naïveté[86] about the 'inner truth and greatness' of National Socialism[87] and his own ability 'to lead the Leader'.[88] If authenticity

---

81   *Letter on 'Humanism'* in Heidegger, 1999b, H 149; 1999c p. 221.

82   *The Way to Language* in Heidegger, 1999c, *passim*.

83   Ibid., p. 411.

84   Heidegger, 1999a, H 170.

85   Cited in Wolin, 1998, p. 47.

86   Heidegger called his involvement his great blunder (*eine große Dummheit*). It is ambiguous whether the blunder was getting involved in the first place, or simply thinking that he might have been *able* 'to lead the Leader'.

87   Heidegger, 2000, H 152.

88   Cf. Heidegger's letter to the Rector of Freiburg University, in which he claims that he had detected the possibility that 'an autonomous alliance of intellectuals could deepen and transform a number of essential elements of the "National Socialist Movement" and thereby contribute in its own way to overcoming Europe's disarray and crisis of the Western Spirit'. In his 1966 *Spiegel* interview, Heidegger suggests that he had believed National Socialism

means rejecting the easy moral categories and 'idle talk' of *das Man*, it is easy to see the rationale behind an exhortation to abandon 'ideas'.

And this thought has implications for moral philosophy understood in a more conventional sense. It would appear that morality is not what we thought it was; commonsense morality is not morality with a commonsense twist, but – more or less – commonsense with a moral twist. Commonsense itself, and the metaethical thought that might grow from it, is more or less determined by others, though – it must be understood as *sensus communis*. Insofar as discourse is permeated by *das Man* to the extent that it is *das Man* that in the end determines what the moral ready-to-hand qualities of an act or event might be, the prospect of being able independently to reach a moral conclusion looks to be threatened. If being *zōon logon ekhon* depends on being some sort of *zōon protopolitikon*, there will always be a determinate role for others in decisions that are generally taken to be one's 'own'.

The problem that grows from this is that avoiding what Heidegger sees as the inauthenticity that comes from public language would appear to commit the agent to irrationalism and meaninglessness. This obliterates the possibility of a coherent morality as it is usually understood: either we speak from the point of view of *das Man*, or we do not speak at all and, by default, cannot have a *moral* defence against *anything*, including Nazism. This is a particular worry, given Heidegger's biography. On the one hand, we could frame comprehensible moral and normative thoughts – but this would mean that they were not *our* thoughts so much as (inauthentic) vocalisations of the norms built into language. On the other hand, an attempt to try to frame our thoughts in an authentic manner, rejecting readymade linguistic convention, is doomed to failure because such a programme would be forced into silence. Moreover, *trying* to be authentic must, surely, involve an idea of what authenticity and inauthenticity are which is not reliably authentic in the first place, since this idea would rely on 'propositions and "ideas"', and 'choosing' one over the other seems itself to rely on inauthenticity for the conceptual validity of what is chosen. At the very best, even if we entertain the possibility that an authentic moral standpoint is possible, it is not clear how we would be able to tell authenticity from inauthenticity.

Moral autonomy seems to be under threat: if we want a coherent morality, this has to be coupled with the recognition of the elimination of anything like an *auto* from *nomoi*. The big question, then, is whether and how it is that any kind of critique is possible. We need not share Heidegger's apparent worries about inauthenticity being a problem to suppose that the question is bogus. Reasonably frequently, there do seem to be people who are not overwhelmed by *das Man*. Presumably, Germans who became Nazis were participants in the same broad discourse or discourses as those who did not – the Nazi Heidegger taught consummate anti-Nazis such as

---

represented a stage in the evolution of the relationship between man and technology, although he claims in the same interview that his view of technology changed subsequently. Such an alteration, presumably, would have implied a re-evaluation of National Socialism (at least if we can treat Heidegger as having acted in good faith at least once during his career).

Arendt, Marcuse and Gadamer – so the question concerns how this might be. More disruptively, there do seem to be radical challenges to the *status quo ante* that come from within from time to time. Feeding into the next chapter, how a rebel, critic or terrorist might have escaped from *das Man* in the light of my argument to this point is a question to which I turn now.

Is there any basis for the still powerful intuition that a normative standard is attainable that might apply in all circumstances? From the argument so far, it looks as though we ought to shrug and chalk up something like Nazism or terrorism to simply being a product of a different moral game.[89] Allowing that the formation of norms depends on discursive context seems to be as much as to concede that no authoritative normative or evaluative stance is reliably available against the Nazi or the terrorist: we either play his game or we do not. We might try to persuade the players in the moral game to switch codes – but we ought not to think that there is any particular *moral* reason for this any more than we would think that there is an authoritative reason that might convince a rugby-player to switch from League to Union rules. (As Nietzsche points out, '*[e]very* morality is … a piece of tyranny against "nature", likewise against "reason": *but that can be no objection to it unless one is in possession of some other morality which decrees that any kind of tyranny and unreason is impermissible*'[90] – and *this* morality, by extension, will be vulnerable to the same critique.) A terrorist *could* be operating within a different paradigm, so could lay claim to just as much moral backing as we could lay against him. The only difference would be one of comprehension – whose moral language-game we understand – rather than of a matter of moral *right* and *wrong*. Equally, a preference for democracy over political violence would be a matter of language rather than objective morality. Is there any sense in which we can get out of this relativism?

Yet more seriously, it looks at the moment as though the position is that *any* attempt to provide a moral critique of anything must be inauthentic, just because to be moral it must use already-existing language. And yet there is a powerful intuition that something is wrong here. Heidegger's suggestion that 'ideas' be abandoned to the Führer itself looks desperately inauthentic by Heidegger's own standards.[91] Even if there is *something* to rejecting (bourgeois) 'ideas', it does not follow that the Führer should replace them. Not only is it the case that subscription to any mass movement such as the NSDAP and the unthinking, unspeaking obedience which that entails looks to be either inauthentic or downright neurotic; it is also the case that authenticity and at least *some* ideas look like the best defences against waking up one morning to find yourself a Stormtrooper. As long as not wanting to be a Stormtrooper can have an ethical dimension – as surely it can – it seems to be obvious that one can take an authentic ethical standpoint. So – surely – ethics and authenticity cannot be *always* incompatible.

---

89 Cf. Wittgenstein, 2001, § 241; Lovibond, 1983, ch. 14.

90 Nietzsche, 1990, § 188; emphasis mine.

91 Cf. Heidegger, 1999a, H 268 ff.

These problems can be solved, and the essence of the solution is the same for both. In the next chapter, again drawing on Heidegger, I will suggest how ethical critique can be grounded.

Chapter 5

Oughtobiography: Heidegger and Ethical Thought

I have difficulty in understanding how a young man can come to a decision to ride to the next village without being afraid that – leaving possible misfortunes quite out of account – even the span of a normal, fortune-favoured existence will be wholly inadequate for the trip.

Kafka, *The Next Village*

If I was present at the murder of others without risking my life to prevent it, I feel guilty in a way not adequately conceivable either legally, politically or morally … If human beings were able to free themselves from metaphysical guilt, they would be angels, and all the other three concepts of guilt would become immaterial.

Jaspers, *The Question of German Guilt*

In Chapter 4, I tried to show what morality is (and *is not*). I claimed that it is a creation of humans but of no individual human, and that the discursive ingredients of commonsense morality are, in essence, the basis of more traditional metaethics. The problem that this gave me was one of how to account for moral dissent and the possibility of critique of any notional moral system. Allowing that the terrorist or Nazi might somehow have come up with a moral discourse that was at least coherent, what – if anything – might we say in response?

In an attempt to come to terms with this twin problem, I want to make further use of Heidegger's thought; and as a spin-off of my argument, I will offer a demonstration that, courtesy of his approach to ontology and the analysis of Dasein, Heidegger is himself a profoundly ethical thinker, despite the fact that he does not concern himself with 'ethical problems' as the phrase is usually understood. What I am going to attempt in the next few sections is to show how Heidegger's ontological thought can sustain an ethical reading. What I think I will be able to demonstrate is that there is in Heidegger an ethic of modesty, even though, from time to time, removal of the patina from the argument will only be possible thanks to the addition of themes from other thinkers. One difficulty that I will face – a major part of the patina – is the famous opacity of Heidegger's thought; Alan Megill's characterisation of him as 'an imaginary novelist, clumsy in his use of language and prolific in his output'[1] is not without justice. Indeed, by the 1950s, Heidegger could be said to have been moving away not only from the easily *comprehensible*, but also from language per se: in the

---

1 Megill, 1987, p. 105.

essay *The Question of Being*, for example, he writes the word 'Being' as '~~Being~~'[2] almost as if he wants to leave only the shadow of the word. However, the key to a Heideggerian ethic is what necessitates this opacity. The difficulty in reading him is related to exactly what it is that I suspect makes his thought ethical in the first place.

There is good reason for his crossings-out. I will develop the theme more later, but it is worth noting as a preliminary that, if Heidegger is right about the apophantic role of discourse, an implication of this is that a word within discourse calls something out of Being-as-a-whole and makes it stand alone. For this reason, words can deal with the being of being*s*, but they are not nearly so good at dealing directly with Being *simpliciter*. In his attempt to think about Being, implicitly a part of his programme from the first words of *Being and Time*, Heidegger is in the position of trying to write *about* that which cannot be verbalised – to get behind language; and to this end he crosses out what he writes. Megill draws an illuminating comparison with Wittgenstein:[3] the famous last sentence of the *Tractatus Logico-Philosophicus* suggests that '[w]hat we cannot speak about we must pass over in silence'.[4] Heidegger, it would appear, attempts to write this silence in his dealings with what cannot be said. (This is obviously a flat refusal of Plato's position concerning writing and the priority of the (Formal) present-at-hand – that speech is a direct link to truth, and that writing is a mere receipt.[5]) The 'unverbalisable' will inform a good deal of what I have to say here about ethics.

The first thing I shall do in this chapter will be to address the matter of moral agency. How do creatures who like to think of themselves as moral agents stand ontologically in relation to the rest of the world? This is a question that I will answer in terms of Dasein. Next, I will raise the question of what is meant by the term 'ethics'. For reasons that I will mention at the time, I am not willing to admit that 'ethics' and 'morality' are terminologically interchangeable. Once I have done this, I need to provide a link between the ontological status of the agent and what I understand by 'ethics': this is something that I think I can do pretty painlessly. This link, I think, will open the way to the possibility of a critique of (internally coherent) moral systems. The form of this critique is something that I will also examine.

Agency and Dasein: the Break from Descartes

Since Heideggerian ontological thought will play an important part in this chapter, it is worth tracing now what this thought is and how it feeds into a radical difference from traditional ethical thought. By and large, the traditions of moral thinking that I have considered allow us to think of the moral agent as separate from the context of the world in which he operates. Although it is chronologically inaccurate, this is

---

2   In Heidegger, 1999b.
3   Megill, 1987, p. 170.
4   Wittgenstein, 1997, § 7.
5   Cf. *Phaedo*, in Plato, 1981, 275a.

a kind of Cartesianism. In Descartes's view, wherever and whenever I think, this can only be because I am. Whatever else might be false, one cannot doubt the 'I'. Roughly speaking, Descartes thinks that he can eliminate the universe and leave his thinking self untouched. Even if the *cogito* is in the world, this is a largely contingent matter: it can be 'taken out' of the everyday world rather as the conjuror's rabbit can be taken from the hat.

Not so, says Heidegger, whose response to the Cartesian approach changes throughout his career, but is never anything other than a rejection. Heidegger replaces the *cogito* with Dasein – literally, 'being there' – which is described as 'an entity which in each case I myself am'.[6] Dasein is not an entirely Heideggerian invention – Macquarrie and Robinson point out in an editorial footnote to *Being and Time* that the word had a place in traditional German philosophy as standing for 'almost any kind of being'[7] – but what is done with the idea *is* new. Heidegger takes the word at face value; as far as he is concerned, Dasein is not a being in its own right, separate from the world around it. Rather, 'there-ness' – the '*da*' of Da-sein – is of vital importance. Dasein is in-the-world fundamentally: it is ingrained in it. The hyphenation is all: the rabbit cannot be taken from the hat.

The difference is drawn explicitly around halfway through *Being and Time*:

> If the '*cogito sum*' is to serve as the point of departure for the existential analytic of Dasein, then it needs to be turned around, and furthermore its analytic content needs new ontologico-phenomenal confirmation. The '*sum*' is then asserted first, and indeed in the sense that "I am in a world" ... Descartes, on the contrary, says that *cogitationes* are present-at-hand, and that in these an *ego* is present-at-hand too as a worldless *res cogitans*.[8]

For Heidegger, the world is a presupposition of there being something like a *cogito*. In the quotation above, the phrase 'I am in a world' is of vital importance: the very possibility of my being depends on the world, in contrast to the 'worldless *res cogitans*' that I would be in the Cartesian picture.

By the time of his dismissal of Sartre in the *Letter on 'Humanism'*, Heidegger's position is (on the face of it) even further from the Cartesian tradition (and also significantly different from his own position in *Being and Time*):

> Sartre expresses the basic tenet of existentialism in this way: Existence precedes essence. In this statement he is taking *existentia* and *essentia* according to their metaphysical meaning, which from Plato's time on has said that *essentia* precedes *existentia*. Sartre reverses this statement. But the reversal of a metaphysical statement remains a metaphysical statement.[9]

---

6 Heidegger, 1999a, H 53.
7 Ibid., H 7, n. 1.
8 Ibid., H 211.
9 *Letter on 'Humanism'* in Heidegger, 1999b, H 159; 1999c p. 232.

Whatever their differences, though, what links these quotations is the idea that *essentia* cannot be thought independently of *existentia* (or vice versa). Trying to decide whether *existentia* or *essentia* has priority is still trying to make a decision within a context defined by Plato and refined by Descartes from which Sartre has not escaped. Cutting through all of this, Heidegger simply insists that the '-sein' of Dasein is always 'da' – *there*, out in-the-world and mediated by the world. It is for this reason that Heidegger renders the word 'existence' as 'ek-sistence'.[10] 'Existence' implies that Dasein could step outside of the world. By contrast, 'ek-sistence' rams home the point that Dasein's being is mediated by the world around it.

Like it or not, Dasein i s in-the-world, and *essentially* so; it is always *'there'*. This gives to Dasein its inescapable condition of 'thrownness': it is, as Heidegger spews, 'ahead-of-itself-in-already-being-in-a-world'.[11] Dasein i s only insofar as it has discovered itself as being in-the-world. Dasein's 'thrownness' into the world means that for Dasein to have 'discovered' itself fully, it must have done so within the context of the world.[12] Without this discovery, there is no Dasein: Dasein is a product of attention that is not yet its own (since the 'I' is nothing more than a characteristic of Dasein[13] – we are forbidden from claiming, with Descartes, that the existence of the 'I' underpins everything else that we might say) and its having come into its own awareness as a being-in-the-world. Certainly, Dasein recognises itself as *itself* rather than as something else, but this does not diminish the manner in which Dasein is not and cannot be immediately present to itself. Rather, its own b e i n g comes to light only through constant analysis of the world in which it i s. To talk about Dasein is to talk 'in terms of a *functional process* that constantly and cumulatively re-capitulates itself'.[14] Further, Dasein's reflective knowledge of itself is no different fundamentally from its knowledge of anything else: '[w]henever Dasein i s, it is as a Fact; and the factuality of such a Fact is what we shall call Dasein's *"facticity"*'.[15]

That there is no 'unthrown' or worldless *res cogitans* in Heideggerian ontology means that the world has ontological priority over Dasein – this is a point that will turn out to be important later – and that anyone who wants an authentic existential understanding of Dasein must turn his attention to the world into which Dasein is thrown, and also to the fact of its thrownness: the fact that it is nothing but a kind of 'having-been-thrown' ek-sistent entity.

Already, this line of thought suggests moral implications. Traditional moral thinking has tended to assume that its protagonists have a primary input into actions. At an extreme, this might be thought in terms of a Platonic or Kantian supersensible 'free will', but it need not be: there is a range of less metaphysically demanding

---

10 *On the Essence of Ground* in Heidegger, 1999b, H 37.

11 Heidegger, 1999a, H 192. I think that there is more than a parallel here with Husserl; Dasein, I think, could be said to be an 'unbracketed' product of ἐποχή. Unfortunately, though, I do not know nearly enough about Husserl for this to merit anything more than a footnote.

12 Ibid., H 135.

13 Ibid., H 117.

14 Olafson, 1995, p. 153; emphasis mine.

15 Heidegger, 1999a, H 56.

forms that this thought might take, such as the Aristotelian notion, already discussed, that *logos* can be an effective cause of action separately from *phusis*. Either way, mind matters and matter does not; it is this sentiment that bases my characterisation of traditional moral thought as Cartesian. This thought comes alongside a second: that moral questions are only really fit to be asked when things could be otherwise. A hurricane might be bad, but it is not *evil* because there is nothing deliberate (that is, Aristotle would say, nothing derived from the *logos*) about the devastation it causes. This implies some degree of independence of the moral agent from the world around him: even though the Aristotelian might admit that to act from deliberation is still to act from a cause, this does not detract from the idea that deliberative reason might still be a specific and *special* kind of cause that 'belongs' to the 'unencumbered' moral agent. But the idea that Dasein ek-sists – that it is in-the-world – pans out as meaning that as Dasein we have to abandon our ideas of the ontological priority of the 'I' and of unencumberedness. Or, put another way: 'an entity "within-the-world" has Being-in-the-world in such a way that it can understand itself as bound up in its "destiny" with the Being of those entities which it encounters in its own world'.[16]

Talk of destiny seems to do nothing except radicalise the argument that I presented in Chapter 4 concerning the serious antagonism between Heidegger and conventional 'moral' thought, which was taken to be more in thrall to commonplace language than to any traditional idea of an analytically released present-at-hand 'good' or 'evil'. Destiny seems somewhat bound to swipe all moral sense, and any *possibility* of moral sense, from Dasein. Heidegger's move means that there is no possibility of ac*tion* that is free from the influence of the world, because there is no independent ac*tor*. A Dasein that is dependent on the world is not just something that comes into being courtesy of that world but which can then go off to do its own thing; it remains tied to the world. And because of how tightly it is tied, it is difficult to swallow the idea of self-determination.

Humans are tied, on Heidegger's picture, to all kinds of worldly influences. (Of course, this point is entirely compatible with the argument of Chapter 4 if we bear in mind that discursively-established norms can also be a part of the world that shapes Dasein – this is another point that will get further attention later.) Now, Heidegger does not seem to be talking about destiny in the sense of cosmic predestination – the word appears in scare-quotes and so, perhaps, is used 'in its deconstructed sense to designate something other which resembles it'.[17] But its future is certainly not its own. And that, really, is quite enough to cause serious problems to anyone who wants to look at human affairs from a moral point of view.

So much, then, for Heidegger as a moral thinker. Not only does he provide grounds to think that reason might be the product rather than the raw material of a thought which turns out to depend on the 'they' of language, and so disrupt the idea

---

16 Ibid.

17 Derrida, 1989, p. 24. The quotation here is taken slightly out of context: originally it refers to Heidegger's use of the word '*Geist*' in *Being and Time* in relation to the problem of Heideggerian Nazism; however, I think that the point translates well enough.

of a morality that is as reliable as it is rational, but he seems also to have abolished the idea of the moral agent anyway: so even if there *was* some sort of 'morality' both comprehensible and authentic, we would be no better off; the 'unencumbered' moral agent – someone whose whole *being*, and not just his rational capacities, is independent of facticities such as the world or language – is nothing more than the shadow cast by an illusion. But still, Heidegger is an ethical thinker. More: despite the apparent moral impotence of Dasein, he is a *powerful* ethical thinker. How?

Writing about Ethics

The first thing to point out as I deal with this question is that I am not going to be using the word 'ethics' interchangeably with 'morality'. If I was, I would have to admit that Heidegger was no ethical thinker: indeed, the introductory chapter to *Being and Time* appears to invite the reader to dismiss ethics for not having interpreted Dasein with sufficient 'primordial existentiality'.[18] This appearance is deceptive, though: the problem is not with ethics qua moral philosophy – it is that ethics has hitherto lacked 'existential justification'; in this, he intimates, it is like just about every other field of study.[19] *Being and Time* can be seen as an attempt to provide an existential justification for other discourses.

How might we examine ethics *with* sufficient 'primordial existentiality'? The first thing to do is to re-evaluate what ethics *is*. The word is (fairly obviously) related to the Greek '*ēthos*', which gets transposed into the Latin '*mores*' – both have a meaning relating to character – which, in turn, gives us 'morality'. Morality is concerned with character; to be morally good is to be of good character. In this case, despite my desire to separate the two, there *is* indisputably an overlap between 'ethics' and 'morality'. On the face of it, the Heideggerian criticism of the notion of the 'unencumbered self' looks to have all but abolished the possibility that anything important might be contained in this concept. If there is no independent 'self', then the question of character seems to evaporate as being anything other than derivatively worth asking.

However, simply to stop at this point is a mistake. One thing to be considered is the advantage of *writing*, rather than *speaking*, about ethics and morality; it is important that account is taken of the difference between the written and spoken form of the word '*ēthos*'. In the Greek, the word is spelt with an *e psilon*: it appears, in written form, as ἔθος. However, the word *ēthos* is related to another word, spelt with an *eta* – ἦθος – which I will transliterate as ' *'ethos*'. The difference would be pronounced barely, if at all: and therefore it would be equally valid to appropriate either in such a way as to give us a word like 'ethics'. But *'ethos* can bear a meaning along the lines of 'custom' or 'accustomed place' as well as 'character'.[20] Hence

---

18 Heidegger, 1999a, H 16.

19 Ibid.

20 Liddell and Scott give 'custom, usage, manner, habit' for ἔθος and either 'an accustomed place' or 'custom, usage, habit' for ἦθος. Ἦθος seems to straddle position and *dis*position.

'ethics', if it has any meaning, can refer to an accustomed place just as much as it can refer to character or behaviour. Aristotle makes this point himself when he highlights the close link between moral goodness and habit.[21]

When, in the *Letter on 'Humanism'*, Heidegger suggests that 'ethics ponders the abode of human being',[22] he has in mind the word ἦθος: it is this spelling that he uses in the essay. Heidegger's statement has more than a hint of analytic truth to it, since *'ethos*, in a manner of speaking, *is* the 'abode of human being'. But what does this mean? A short answer is that human being's abode is that wherein it ek-sists. More needs to be said, though.

Although Dasein ek-sists in-*the*-world, it does not follow that Dasein discovers itself among or dwells within Being-as-a-whole. For Heidegger, the world in which Dasein ek-sists is, as I noted in the Chapter 4, mediated through discourse: it is *this* world into which Dasein finds itself as 'thrown' and which provides the context for Dasein's self-discovery. We do not live among Being, but among beings; '*Being*' – that is, Being-as-a-whole – '*is the transcendens pure and simple*'.[23] Because we live among beings rather than Being, Being withdraws from us: it is *not 'ethos*. This informs the crossed-out word, '~~Being~~', in the essay *On the Question of Being*:

> The crossing out of this word initially has only a preventive role, namely, that of preventing the almost ineradicable habit of presenting 'being' as something standing somewhere on its own that then on occasion first comes face-to-face with human beings.[24]

Because Being has withdrawn 'before' Dasein finds itself, any attempt to encompass it in words or concepts is to reduce it to *a* being, which it is not.

From the 'point of view' of Dasein, we are 'thrown' into a world that already contains (and, qua world, is manifested in) things like hammers and values. Because Dasein is being-in-the-world, it cannot separate itself from the values and (moral) institutions that are already there, 'awaiting' it. (This is related to Dasein's facticity and, arguably, lends a moral aspect to Dasein's ek-sistence – but it is not what traditional moral thought has in mind.) A quotation from MacIntyre sums up the situation: 'a man who tried to withdraw himself from his given position in heroic society would be engaged in the enterprise of trying to make himself disappear'.[25] We can strip away the bits about heroic society: the salient point is that someone who tries to live apart from the institutions around him would not only be drawn to intellectual incoherence as I argued in the last chapter. He would also be drawn to existential dissolution. (Bradley may be taken as making a similar point when he writes about 'my station and its duties'.[26]) Dasein finds and apprehends itself

---

21 Aristotle, 1976, II, i.
22 *Letter on 'Humanism'* in Heidegger, 1999b, H 187; 1999c, p. 258.
23 Heidegger, 1999a, H 38; emphasis and spacing in original.
24 *On the Question of Being* in Heidegger, 1999b, H 239.
25 MacIntyre, 2000, p. 126.
26 Bradley, 1962, *passim.*

'among', and draws itself *from*, a world – a *moral* world – that is already formed; it is *this*, not neutral nature or 'pure' being-as-a-whole, that Heidegger invites ethics to ponder.

This point constitutes a significant part of my contention that Heidegger is an ethical thinker. To think ethically is to be concerned with the 'abode' – the context – in which that thought takes place more than it is to be concerned with the character of the thinker. And this 'abode' includes the moral imperatives built into the world. Implicitly, *morality is among the things that ethics considers*: Dasein 'apprehends' morality as a piece of facticity. This is an important consideration in the separation of ethics from morality that I am proposing. (Of course, if we think of character as having at least something to do with human being – as surely we must – and if we combine this with the thought that human being's 'abode' is ek-static, we can draw a link between *ēthos* (wont) and *'ethos* (custom). Ethics as the study of character must, at some point, merit consideration of the point that the human being *with* that character ek-sists, and so it is linked with ethics qua accustomed place or abode. *'Ethos* still has priority over *ēthos*, though.)

There are other times when Heidegger's thought, though even more oblique than the above, suggests a close relationship between Dasein's being-in-the-world and ethical pondering. For example, the essay *Building, Dwelling, Thinking* calls dwelling the '*basic character* of Being'.[27] This means that for Dasein to grasp the meaning of Being – and the meaning of Being is, after all, the *leitmotiv* of *Being and Time* and, one way or another, of Heidegger's whole career – it must understand itself as something that *dwells*. Dwelling is more than a residence in passing, though. The Platonic soul or Cartesian *cogito* might live in the world, but neither *dwells* there; dwelling implies a deeply ingrained relationship that is much more than residency and tends towards Dasein's ek-stasis: '[m]an's relation to locales, and through locales to spaces, inheres in his dwelling'.[28] To think about the relationship of human being (not simply *a* human being or even human being*s*) to the world in which it i s, and in which it dwells, is, on this reading, an ethical matter.

It is this point that forms the foundation of the promised bridge between the analysis of Dasein and ethics. It is simply that Dasein could not b e without *'ethos*. At present, one could be forgiven for taking this as having either no moral message at all, or else a highly conservative one. Either way, there is little or no room in the picture for much in the way of ethical critique: even if one decides to embark on a programme of ethical research, it would appear that there is a Heideggerian insistence that this go no further than a kind of moral-existential psychoanalysis – an examination of the influences operating and forming the world in which one i s. However, I think that to draw this conclusion would be to have stopped short of a full realisation of the implications of Heidegger's characterisation of ethics and how it relates to Dasein. Pondering the abode of human being should not be seen, necessarily, as an intellectual stance that is limited to the norms built into the world

---

27 Heidegger, 1999c, p. 362.
28 Ibid., p. 359.

in which one i s. Indeed, I think that pondering the abode of human being is the key to the possibility of ethical critique that is possessed of the primordial existentiality that Heidegger implicitly demands at the beginning of *Being and Time*. The implications of this thought will occupy the remainder of the study.

Pondering the Abode: Authenticity and Finitude

Crucial here is the idea of authenticity; although it might appear that there is a caesura in my argument, it's one that I shall have to repair retrospectively as the argument progresses.

Heidegger's break from Cartesianism is such as to mean that 'Dasein' does not stand for an entity with determinate existence. This indeterminacy means that human Dasein has possibilities for being, and is free in relation to its future possibilities. Authentic Dasein is Dasein that has embraced its freedom.[29] By contrast, inauthentic Dasein is happy to go along with the everydayness of *das Man*. The 'advantage' of inauthenticity is that it is a good deal less arduous. It allows 'readymade' discourse to be determinate. This is not a characteristic of authentic Dasein. However, the fact that Dasein is inseparable from the world raises a problem in this sense. Being-in-the-world means being among the factical constituents of that world; and because Dasein is inseparable therefrom, the suspicion must be that there is something fishy about the freedom in authenticity. At the level of Dasein's freedom to 'choose itself' in relation to its future, it seems to be voluntaristic; but this voluntarism implies a separation from the world – it is certainly fairly queasily related to the notion that Dasein is 'bound up in its "destiny" with the Being of those entities which it encounters in its own world'.[30]

So what is the sense of the freedom to choose that is attributed to authentic Dasein? The answer is actually reasonably straightforward – at least in the qualified sense of the word that applies to Heidegger – but at this stage at least, it will appear to be yet another hurdle to the idea that Heidegger can serve as any kind of recognisably ethical thinker. Freedom, as far as Heidegger is concerned, is a matter of 'letting beings be'.[31] By 'letting be' he does not mean a kind of benign neglect – he means allowing things to be revealed as things. This reflects his use of the verb 'to be' as active-intransitive. In this sense, freedom is not caprice:[32] it can stem only from a recognition of the being of beings. Man is not free in the sense of having freedom at his disposal; his freedom lies in 'engagement with the disclosure of beings as such':[33] this means engagement with beings' potentialities. Of the beings which free Dasein lets-be, we should not forget human being itself. If freedom lies in letting beings be, it must also lie in letting human being reveal itself as what it is. In other

29 Heidegger, 1999a, H 193; also, see West, 1996, pp. 102–3.
30 Heidegger, 1999a, H 56.
31 *On the Essence of Truth* in Heidegger, 1999b, H83; 1999c, p. 125.
32 Ibid., Heidegger, 1999b, H 84; 1999c, p. 126.
33 Ibid., Heidegger, 1999b, H 84; 1999c, p. 126.

words, human freedom lies in reconciliation with human beings' potentialities for being – including its own. Freedom, then, is a matter of Dasein's possibilities-for-being – it is not a matter of choosing actively any one of those possibilities. Dasein's freedom is nothing more than that it is indeterminate. Man is free, that is, not when he does not face obstacles to his doing what he will; he is free just insofar as he could turn out to be (pretty much) anything.[34] Authenticity, as the characteristic of the free Dasein, is simply an embracing of the existential indeterminacy of Dasein in the face of its possibilities.

One of the possibilities for being of human Dasein is, paradoxically enough, its own non-being. Letting its being be, authentic Dasein will be in a situation in which it embraces its own finitude, and one sense of the finitude of human Dasein is simply that humans are mortal. So one of the ways in which authenticity manifests itself is in Dasein's having embraced its being-towards-death: its having recognised its own death as an 'uttermost possibility'.[35] Authentic human Dasein is Dasein that recognises that an aspect of its freedom is that it may die; hence it lets itself be what it is: mortal. But mortality is not the only sense in which Dasein is finite. The wider point is that, insofar as authentic Dasein embraces its own possibilities, this must provoke an embrace of all possible situations in which Dasein is not. In contemplating my own death (qua 'uttermost possibility') as a potentiality for my being, there is an implicit recognition of the world beyond that in which I am and, importantly, beyond what I know or can know. This is important. My own finitude means that there is an 'outer limit' to my being; but, idealism not being an option given Dasein's inseparability from the world around it, this limit also implies that there is something 'on the other side' of Dasein's non-being. Dasein bears the 'trace' (in the Derridean sense[36]) of the world I do not know.

What does this mean for ethics? Simply that in 'pondering my abode', I must take into account the limits of myself and my abode. Authentic understanding of (my own) Dasein demands the recognition of the possibility of Being-without-me and, by implication, the possibility of other worlds that I do not and cannot know. So although it is impossible for Dasein coherently to think of itself without a '*da*' in which it is, and this means that it is not possible for Dasein to separate itself from the world in which it is – a world that includes all manner of institutions including moral values – the authentic ethical pondering of this cannot be inured completely against the possibility of an 'otherwise'. Because, in Heidegger's words, 'Being is the transcendens pure and simple',[37] ethical pondering of the Dasein's abode and of its relationship with Being provides a counterpoint to all Dasein's possible worlds. (The claim that 'Dasein's understanding of Being pertains with equal primordiality both to an understanding of something like a "world", and to the understanding

---

34 Viz. Heidegger, 1999a, H 193.

35 Ibid., H 262–3 and *passim*.

36 Cf. *Différance* in Derrida, 1982; also McQuillan, *Five Strategies for Deconstruction* in McQuillan, 2000, pp. 18ff.

37 Heidegger, 1999a, H 38.

of the Being of those entities which become accessible within a world'[38] serves as neat support for this idea.) And because it provides an irreducibly transcendent counterpoint, it is possible for ethics, as it ponders its abode, to offer a critique of its own.

Pondering the Abode: Ethics and Infinity

I have already introduced Descartes as a contrast to the Heideggerian analysis of Dasein, and implied that traditional moral thinking has shown complicity in what is arguably a Cartesian alienation of the moral agent from the world around him and a moral prioritisation of the agent over the world. I want to push this idea a little further now by suggesting a direct difference between a 'Heideggerian ethic' and a more traditional ethic. This will turn out to have an implication for one of the perennial questions of moral philosophy: what does it mean to be good?

The first thing that I want to point out stems from the ties between Dasein and the world in which it is. Dasein is in the world by virtue of Care.[39] Heidegger notes that the 'existential meaning' of Dasein is 'Care'.[40] More: this Care is the essence of Being-in-the-world.[41] Somewhat irritatingly, Heidegger is reluctant to give a more substantial or less gnomic positive account of what he means by the word than this. What he offers is a negative account: Care does not have anything to do with worry (*Besorgnis*) or carefreeness (*Sorgslosigkeit*).[42] Care is not a matter of sympathy for a particular thing; the best sense to make of it is to allow that it informs the mode of a relationship with the world already there that makes sympathy possible. Dasein is *based in* Care:

> Care, as a primordial structural totality, lies 'before' every factical 'attitude' and 'situation' of Dasein, and it does so existentially *a priori*; this means that *it always lies in them*. So this phenomenon by no means expresses the priority of the 'practical' attitude over the theoretical. When we ascertain something present-at-hand by merely beholding it, this activity has the character of Care just as much as does a 'political action' or taking a rest and enjoying oneself. *'Theory' and 'practice' are possibilities of Being for an entity whose Being must be defined as "Care"* …
>
> Care is *ontologically 'earlier'* than the phenomena we have just mentioned …[43]

---

38 Heidegger, 1999a, H 13.

39 I have taken the liberty of capitalising the word to distinguish it from 'care' in the everyday sense. In their translation of *Being and Time*, on which I am relying, Macquarrie and Robinson do no such thing. But since I think that this leaves open the way to a confusion between the concept of *Sorge* and 'care' in the sense that it is more usually understood that Heidegger seems to have been at pains to avoid, I stand by my decision.

40 Heidegger, 1999a, H 41.

41 Ibid., H 193.

42 Ibid., H 192.

43 Ibid., H 193–4; emphasis mine.

Care is that mode through which Dasein finds itself and the foundation from which Dasein builds itself. In this sense, it is important to note that Care has ontological priority over Dasein and *precedes* the (hitherto unformed) self's constitution as being-in-the-world. Authentic Dasein does not say 'I care': '*Care does not need to be founded in a Self*'.[44] However, it does say something along the lines that 'The self that "I" am i s Care': '[w]hen fully conceived, the Care-structure includes the phenomenon of Selfhood'.[45]

Since it is due to Care that Dasein i s, Care is crucial for authentic Dasein. Because Dasein is, in Olafson's phrase, a matter of constant and cumulative recapitulation,[46] it has its basis in *constant* Care of its being-in-the-world.[47] Dasein that has allowed itself to 'forget' its grounding in Care does not stop being Dasein, of course – but for the sake of *authentic* Dasein, the Care-structure that founds Dasein must be constantly carried over into Dasein's apprehension of itself. Authentic Dasein being conceived as having embraced what it i s existentially, it follows that this involves the recognition that (a) it is ek-sistent, and (b) it i s through Care. In allowing itself to be cut off from its existential basis, Dasein is inauthentic. (In Sartrean terminology, it is living in a kind of bad faith.)

The ethical implications of this are notable. The prioritisation of Care over Dasein ensures that Dasein cannot authentically insulate itself from the *'ethos* in which it i s. Dasein, in order to be able to regard itself as authentic, must b e Care-ful of the world around it and 'embrace' this Care in its day-to-day being. In other words, authentic Dasein is constantly solicitous of its *'ethos*: the world in which it ek-sists. To carry Care over into authentic Dasein as heedfulness or solicitousness is an ethical demand. And because authenticity is not something that one can earn and then take for granted, it is an *ongoing* ethical demand: the demands of Care are not demands that can be satisfied. Dasein always i s in-the-world and must therefore always be Care-ful of its being-in-the-world. It must always be heedful of its *'ethos*. It is for this reason that, at least for authentic Dasein, there is an existential demand for ethics – abode-pondering – that is inexorable: notwithstanding how solicitous one is or has been in the past, one can never 'afford' to stop being heedful of *'ethos*.

What are the implications of this sort of argument? As I argued in Chapter 4, it is entirely possible for there effectively to be values and imperatives built into the world in which Dasein i s regardless of whether or not there is anything scientifically acceptable about such a claim. Now, insofar as traditional moral thinking has a tendency to conceive of the moral agent separately from the world, it can allow this agent to ignore the world around him if he chooses. There might be *moral* reason not to, but, existentially at least, there are no serious consequences to such a stance.

---

44 Ibid., H 323; emphasis in original.
45 Ibid.
46 Olafson, 1995, p. 153.
47 It would appear that the demand for Care qua solicitousness of the world could be read as informing the elision of epistemology and ontology in Heidegger to which I referred in Chapter 4.

This point stands *even if* values and imperatives are built into the phenomenological structure of the world.

By contrast, the Heideggerian denial of a free-floating moral agent who can separate himself existentially from this event means that an imperative built into the world in this way *cannot* be ignored. It is existentially impossible to cut oneself off from the world around one. Accordingly, as long as the world in which one is reveals itself through Care as having certain imperatives built into it, then one cannot claim that they are 'nothing to do with me'. Care reveals imperatives as parts of the world in which Dasein ek-sists. Simply because I know of something, it is a part of my *'ethos*: the place wherein I dwell.

Owing to the manner in which 'my' Dasein – the Dasein-that-is-me – is thrown into and drawn from the world around it, to ignore something, or to convince myself that I need pay no special heed to something because it is not to do with *me*, it must have already come into my purview. It is already a ground for Dasein. Whereas in the traditional moral picture I can say that something has nothing to do with me and be right if it cannot be causally traced to me, a Heideggerian approach forces the concession that by the time that I am aware of this something, it is part of the world – the world in which I 'already' am. *'Ethos* is, after all, fundamental to Dasein, and this is part of the fundament. And in this sense, it has a lot to do with me. Wilful ignorance is inauthentic: it ignores *'ethos* and is therefore unethical.

(Interestingly, it would be wrong-headed to think that the location of an event modifies this claim. Echoing a point made by Heidegger,[48] Hannah Arendt has pointed out that, at least phenomenologically, geography has been all but abolished:

> [E]ven the notion of distance ... has yielded before the onslaught of speed. Speed has conquered space; and ... it has made distance meaningless, for no significant part of a human life – years, months, or even weeks – is any longer necessary to reach any point on Earth.[49]

Telecommunications mean that something on the other side of the globe might be just as much a part of the world in which I am as something on the other side of the street. In effect, this means that, let something take place on the other side of the Earth, it can still be something which has something to do with me[50] – something of which, for the sake of authenticity, I ought (hypothetically 'ought', that is) to take account. The point stands iteration: simply knowing about something is enough to demolish the idea that it has nothing to do with me. (I do not have the space or expertise to work out the thought, which seems to be a good deal more complex, but I suspect that something similar must be said for events removed in time, too.))

Moral values can be built into the world from which, qua Dasein, I cannot separate myself. So can imperatives. As long as authentic Dasein must be heedful of its 'abode', though, it must also be heedful of these demands which are 'ahead' of it

---

48 *The Thing* in Heidegger, 1975, p. 165.
49 Arendt, 1998, p. 250.
50 See Brassington, 2002, for a discussion of what this implies politically.

in its *'ethos*. Moreover, it would be incoherent for Dasein to filter these imperatives: they are a part of the world in which ek-sistent Dasein finds itself. So it is impossible for Dasein to ignore the imperatives built into the world insofar as they constitute a part of Dasein's ek-stasis. On this basis, I think that it might be fair to impute some ethical sense to Henry's claim that 'There are no innocents', notwithstanding that it would be a sense radically different from what I believe Henry might have imagined.

For as long as the world in which Dasein ek-sists is at least partly constituted by imperatives of whatever sort, the ethical demands on Dasein are unsatisfied. Now, of course, it may be impossible practically to respond to any one of the imperatives confronting Dasein; and it is likely to be impossible to respond to every such imperative. Nevertheless, because, qua factical aspect of the world in which Dasein is, the imperative has priority over Dasein, this impossibility does not make it go away. It just lingers as an imperative that remains unfulfilled. But not to meet an imperative is negligence.

This practical negligence – the negligence of certain factical imperatives that arises as a result of limiting oneself to the possible – means that, ethically, there are no innocents. Note that this is an indication of the difference between ethics and morality, at least as it stands traditionally, which sanctions the 'filtering' of these imperatives. *Ought* implies *can*, and if an imperative cannot be met, its imperative power is diminished. But ethics cannot allow such filtering because the *oughts* that confront ek-sistent Dasein as it 'ponders its abode' are there irrespective of any *can*. Having said this, authenticity and ethical abode-pondering will not tell us *what* is to be done: it makes no directive claims at all. It simply demands that something's having come into our ethical purview is sufficient to establish that there is at least some sort of demand on us. Ethics is (at least as I use the word) simply a demand for solicitousness of the world, which may have woven into it any range of morally value-bearing features and moral imperatives. It might well be inauthentic to accept the morality built into the world 'sight-unseen' – pondering the abode implies pondering the limits to the abode, too, as I have already argued – but this does not sanction pretending that the demands 'already' constituting Dasein's world are not there.

Heidegger devotes a portion of *Being and Time* to what he calls *Schuldsein* – 'Being-guilty' – which adds another layer to what I am getting at here. By this, he does not mean guilt in a moral sense, in terms of good and evil (in the sense that one might be guilty of having broken a window), but in terms of a more pervasive ground upon which such terms can be founded:

> This essential Being-guilty is ... the existential condition for the possibility of the 'morally' good and for that of the 'morally' evil – that is, for morality in general and for the possible form that this may take factically. *The primordial 'Being-guilty' cannot be defined by morality, since morality already presupposes it for itself.*[51]

---

51 Heidegger, 1999a, H 286; emphasis mine.

As it happens, 'guilt' is not a particularly happy rendition of what Heidegger has in mind: he seems uncomfortable with the word '*Schuld*'. His insistence that 'Dasein does not load a "guilt"' – note the scare-quotes – 'upon itself through its failures or omissions'[52] testifies to this. All the same, the notion is, I suspect, germane to my intentions: Being-guilty is a condition of authentic Dasein.

The thought of Schuldsein involves something like the idea that one owes one's very Being to *'ethos*, filtered through Dasein. To owe is to be in debt (*Schuld*) – but this is not the sort of debt that can be made good. Nevertheless, authenticity means having to take account of this 'existential credit' and the fact that it is unshakeably burdensome. The suggestion that morality presupposes 'Being-guilty' should be taken, I think, as a hint that morality is concerned with how best (within the realms of the possible) to respond to the inexorable calls of *'ethos*. *Schuldsein* implies that although something may not be my *fault*, it is still a feature of the world in which I am. I might not be responsible *for* it, but, qua Care-ful Dasein, I am responsible *to* it. Ethically, in relation to the imperatives built into the world, authentic Dasein's position is like that of the Red Queen, for whom 'it takes all the running you can do to keep in the same place'.[53]

Authenticity means that the onus is on me, qua authentic Dasein-which-is-me, at least to be heedful of everything in the world; 'world' here is meant as that space within which I dwell.[54] If I want to be authentic, then I must get to grips with this world. This, in a nutshell, is why I think that Heidegger is an ethical thinker: he forces us to come to terms with *'ethos*, and will not let us escape from it. It is this kind of analysis that could stand a chance of giving to ethics the 'primordial existentiality' that *Being and Time* diagnoses as missing from it.

Morality and Authenticity: The Problem of Nazi Virtues

So: there are imperatives built into the world. These are not imperatives that are dictated by morality in the traditional sense: they are imperatives that traditional morality tries to accommodate. In becoming aware of a given act or event as a factical phenomenon, with an inbuilt and equally factical value, one has 'already' admitted it as a part of one's *'ethos*. One ek-sists within imperatives.

Of course, not all of these imperatives have an equal pull. At the same time that discourse allows things to be unveiled as things with a given imperative pull, morality, as a part of that discourse, arranges that pull. So, to give a rough-and-ready example, in the context of a discourse that holds that *ought* implies *can*, if something is impossible, it is stripped of its imperative pull, and if something that *appears* to be a duty turns out to be impossible, it is said quite properly not to have been a duty after all. The *ought/can* rule should not be taken as unquestionable, though: not all discourses necessarily make the same distinction, and not all need recognise the

---

52 Ibid., H 287.
53 Carroll, 1998, p. 145.
54 See Heidegger, 1999a, H 64 ff. for discussion.

propriety of denying that there might be an impossible duty. Antigone and Orestes both face impossible choices which they still must make – and herein lies their tragedy. For them, *ought* does not imply *can*, since they ought to obey two conflicting laws but cannot. Or think of the way that Oedipus ought not to marry his mother, but cannot but do so. 'Was I the sinner?' he asks; 'I have endured wrong undeserved; God knows nothing was of my choosing.'[55] There is a similarly tragic element to the story of Isaac and Abraham, for all that Kierkegaard insists otherwise.[56]

However they pan out, moral strictures and structures are part of Dasein's environment; authentic Dasein recognises its integration into its environment and so, *ex hypothesi*, with those moral dicta. This gives a strong reason to think that a criterion of authentic Dasein might be to have embraced whatever the moral rules might be as determined by the socio-historically contingent discursive climate within which we ek-sist – it is this that makes imperatives imperative, and grants them whatever pull they have. On top of this comes the argument of the last chapter, that goodness is a matter of whatever is defined as goodness by everyone and no one in particular. This means that 'good' can change according to the discursive framework in which Dasein ek-sists. It is possible from here to move towards an answer to one of the perennial questions of moral philosophy: *How should I be good?* However, The answer towards which I am moving is problematic – certainly if I want to remain true to my idea about leaving commonsense morality pretty much as I find it – and I will offer an example of what the problem is before I work it through.

Preparatory to looking at that problem in its full form, I want to look at a simpler situation. The situation I have in mind is something like the Eichmann case. We can accept that characteristics such as diligence and punctiliousness are praiseworthy, and that characteristics such as obedience and loyalty are virtuous characteristics in a civil servant. And yet in the Eichmann case, it is exactly these virtues that are problematic. I will assume, partly for the sake of charity, but partly also because I cannot imagine how things might be otherwise, that Eichmann did not set out to do something *evil*: rather, that he chose to obey certain fairly innocuous and occasionally praiseworthy imperatives such as 'follow orders', 'be efficient', and so on. In his own defence, Eichmann submitted that '[h]is guilt came from his obedience, and obedience is praised as a virtue … "I am not the monster I am made out to be," Eichmann said. "I am the victim of a fallacy."'[57] One is reluctant to say that Eichmann's problem was that he was just *too* good, though. So there has to be some way to account for this.

It is not difficult at all to nail what this is. We can accept that a characteristic might be a virtue, but that responding to an imperative such as 'be efficient' does not exhaust the moral situation. Allowing that the discursive climate in the Third Reich was not *radically* different from that to which we are more used – to a large

---

55 *Oedipus at Colonus*, in Sophocles, 1974, ll. 271, 513–15.

56 Kierkegaard, 1985, *passim*.

57 Arendt, 1994, pp. 247–8.

extent, the Nazi evil was banal[58] – it is plain that there would have been any number of imperatives factically woven into the world that Eichmann ignored. These were just as much built into his abode (*'ethos*) as the efficiency imperative. Indeed, he must have been aware of what was afoot – he had been at Wannsee, for example. His failure lay in thinking that his moral responsibility stopped, *à la* Hegel, with what was directly under his control. This allowed him to be a good civil servant in a narrowly defined sense while ignoring other aspects of the world as having nothing directly to do with him.[59] This was inauthentic: it is not possible authentically to close one's mind to the suffering of millions and the massive imperative that this must carry in any recognisable moral system.

Something very similar can be said about events such as the Milgram experiments.[60] It is obvious that there were factical characteristics of badness in the tasks expected of the naïve participants. More than this: the experiment was designed around the presentation of the world in such a way as to *convey* this badness to entirely normal people. Nevertheless, Milgram himself notes that the participants, directed apparently to administer painful electric shocks to unseen others, 'protested even while they obeyed'.[61] This means that they must have been aware that there was something worthy of protest in what they were doing. But it was also a part of the world that they chose to negate by concentrating on the task in hand: one of the other things that Milgram records is that the participants went to extraordinary lengths to perform the required task well at the expense of taking into account the wider context in which it was performed. This, I would charge, is unethical, in the sense that it was an attempt to deny an aspect of Dasein's being-in-the-world apropos of a plain imperative to disobey.

The Milgram participants and Eichmann alike fell victim to a *mens rea* fallacy: thinking that it was the narrowly defined intention that was important, separately from its circumstance. I argued in Chapter 2 how this was, at least, possible, inasmuch as it amounts to willing one thing without willing another, even though the first entails the second. But when Dasein is in-the-world and that world contains things like the Final Solution or the infliction of shocks on 'innocents', such a narrowing of moral horizons is not authentically sustainable. What I defended above was the *psychological* possibility of a purification of intent (the phrase is Rachels'[62]): at that point in the argument I could not mount the *ethical* critique of the strategy that I am suggesting now. This ethical critique is that, because we ek-sist in a world (and a world, moreover, that is phenomenologically rich and messy, not stripped-down

---

58 Arendt, 1994.

59 In *Modernity and the Holocaust*, Zygmunt Bauman makes the point that '[t]here seems to be less hope than before that the civilised guarantees against inhumanity can be relied upon to control the application of human instrumental-rational potential once the calculation of efficiency has been awarded supreme authority in deciding political purposes' (Bauman, 2000, p. 116).

60 Viz. Milgram, 1974, *passim*.

61 Ibid., p. 10 .

62 Rachels, 1986, p. 92.

and purified of unclear programmes and imperatives), we cannot just stand aside from the *'ethos* that we inhabit when it displays characteristics which we might find distasteful. This point harks towards Jaspers' conception of metaphysical guilt: in simply knowing about something bad, we have a metaphysical responsibility to it that is not annulled or exhausted by any more systematic and rigorous moral programme that we may adopt.[63] As with Heidegger's *Schuldsein*, 'metaphysical guilt' does not seem like exactly the right term – but this is a rather pettifogging point.[64]

The demands of *'ethos* cannot necessarily be disciplined into a moral system and they 'pre-date' any programme of action, because they 'pre-date' the moral agent existentially. The ethical failure of someone like Eichmann means that whatever success he might have had concerning one imperative is negated by the failure to act in response to a moral obligation built into the world to which he was responsible despite not having a formative role therein.[65] Obedience and efficiency may be virtues, but it cannot have been possible for a duty not to kill or a duty to save not to have outweighed such a virtue without any difficulty at all, or need for consideration of the relative merits of obedience over (this) disobedience. Knowledge of the extermination programme presents a massive imperative in its own right.

Interestingly, this response to the Eichmann and Milgram examples represents a rehabilitated form of Aristotelianism. For Aristotle, 'goodness' was subordinate to questions of what is right for a particular person by nature. The Heideggerian argument I have been pushing in this chapter is that one's 'nature' is ek-sistent and inseparable from the world around it. Being a *morally* good person might involve adherence to the prescriptions of a particular moral code. But in the Aristotelian sense, human nature now being defined in terms of its ek-sistence and relation to *'ethos*, to be a good human involves recognition that one is by nature in the midst of various imperatives. And because *'ethos* has priority over the moral, in the sense that any given metaethical theory chases and gives account for imperatives *ex post facto*, it is inauthentically doctrinaire to sacrifice its imperatives at the moral altar. In this sense, it is possible to accuse Eichmann of having been a bad person on the basis that he cut himself off from his ek-sistent nature.

---

63 Jaspers, 2000, esp. p. 26.

64 Jaspers seems to have Heidegger in mind in this passage about the wilful ignorance and horizon-closing of certain Nazi fellow-travellers, which I think is relevant – the interruptions in square brackets are mine: 'A professor speaks: "We are the Fronde within the Party. We dare frank discussion [Heidegger declared that his *Nietzsche* lectures showed his opposition to National Socialism]. We achieve spiritual realisations. We shall slowly turn all of it back into the old German spirituality." [Think of the *Introduction to Metaphysics* and Derrida's meditation on '*Geist*' (Derrida, 1989), or Heidegger's claim that '[o]nly our German language has a deep and creative philosophical character to compare with the Greek' (Heidegger, 2002a, p. 36)] ... Many intellectuals went along in 1933, sought leading positions and publicly upheld the ideology of the new power [the Rectoral address springs to mind], only to become resentful later when they personally were shunted aside' (Jaspers, 2000, p. 62).

65 My contention that imperatives pre-date Dasein is something that I have tried to reflect in the construction 'responsibility *to*'.

Admittedly, this may not look like much – but when ethics is defined in terms of a sensitivity to and heedfulness of *'ethos*, it does not need to provide any imperatives of its own in a conventional moral sense. Instead, the ethical sensitivity of authentic Dasein will be receptive to the powerful (if sometimes confusing) imperatives built into the world in which it i s. These imperatives arise without prejudice from any particular traditional metaethical theory – say, one that weighs heavily in favour of a reasonably precise bureaucratic duty rather than a more inchoate responsibility to the wider world – and its tendency to mould imperatives to its own measure. As I have just said, the ethical failure of an Eichmann lies in his bringing a moral prejudice to pre-articulate *'ethos*.

So much for this simple preparation. I want now to look at a scenario that is, I think, a good deal more disturbing. It is a scenario in a possible world that presents itself with imperatives built in that are genuinely different from those to which we are accustomed. An extreme version of this might be seen in Will Self's novel *Great Apes*, in which it is considered a form of abuse for a daughter *not* to have been the object of her father's sexual attention[66] – but we do not have to be so hallucinatory. For my scenario, I propose a visit to Twin Earth, a virtual facsimile of Earth. (From this point on, the words that refer to things on Twin Earth will have the prefix 'tw-': hence Twin Earth becomes 'Twearth', and so on.) The difference between Earth and Twearth is that history turned out differently, and the Nazis won the war. The discourse that guarantees moral apophansis having been 'Nazified', and other discourses having been successfully expunged, agents on Twearth would ek-sist within a different system of morality. And so words like 'Jew' would have a 'moral meaning' comparable to that of 'Nazi' on Earth.

On Twearth is a person called Twiain: my genetic and neurological double. The factical constitution of the world being different under the Nazi discourse prevalent on Twearth, Twiain would not ek-sist within the same *'ethos* as me. Learning about the Final Solution, Twiain might admit that it was unpleasant work, but that it was necessary and good. Twiain's grandfather, an SS guard in the 1950s, had found his work distressing and problematic, but this was because he remembered the days before the Nazi revolution, and it is difficult entirely to forget the moral framework within which one has grown up. Discourse, and thereby, the world, having been Nazified since then, Twiain might understand this, but still be revolted by the thought of sympathy to Jews. What are we to make of this person?

The responses that I am forced to give if I want to be consistent with my argument in the last chapter and a half are counterintuitive and disturbing. For one thing, I think that Twiain would assent to a phrase such as 'Nazism is good', and that, since there is nothing to a moral statement except discursively upheld apophansis, it would be t r u e, in the sense that the moral epithet reflected discursively bankrolled features of the world and had been correctly applied thereto. And growing out of this point is a second: if Twiain did all the things that Nazis are supposed to do, there would not be much of a moral argument that we (on Earth) could present against him

---

66 Self, 1998.

– and, correspondingly, Tweichmann could send people to Auschwitz with a clear conscience: he might even sneer at Eichmann for having missed the bigger picture. In a moral argument, it would be pointless to argue that 'good' *really* means what we are used to and not what Twearthians are used to, because such a claim would be false. 'Good' would be apposite to some things on Earth, and some other things on Twearth. Is this all that there is? Fortunately for anyone who wants to avoid moral quietism or nihilism, I do not think so: I shall now suggest why.

Ethics and Krisis

As the situation stands, it is not obvious that I can say more than that, in the world in which *I* am, there is something morally repugnant about Nazi morality; but I have to admit that my Nazi *doppelgänger* could say, and very probably *would* say, the same thing about my anti-Nazi sympathies. I cannot escape the feeling that this person could genuinely hold a set of moral beliefs with which I disagree fundamentally and yet be no worse a person for it morally: echoing Dancy, the point is that my disagreement with Twiain is one concerning *what* he believes, not *that* he believes.[67] Indeed, I suspect that I should admit that if this is worrying, it is so only on the basis of the adoption of exactly the 'God's eye' view of morality from which I have distanced myself.[68] Nevertheless, I suspect that *ethically* there might be something to be said that can allow something more than a quietistic response to Nazi morality. Although I suspect that the sketch of the next few paragraphs might appear to be woefully inadequate, it does, I think, at least mark out the direction that a critique of any moral system (and all moral systems) can take.

The problem that I face is one that arises through adherence to an argument inspired by Heidegger. If there is a solution, consistency suggests that I ought to look first to Heidegger. And it does turn out to be through him that I can suggest a solution; I think that I have already touched on what it might be when I made earlier points about authentic Dasein having accounted for its own death and the possibility of worlds that it can never know. Supposing that Nazism was successful, on the

---

67 I restrict this, for the sake of simplicity, to moral beliefs. I am aware that Nazi beliefs involved the idea that there was a Judaeo-Bolshevik plot, that there was a serious physiological difference between races that could be scientifically demonstrated, and so on. These beliefs are demonstrably false: there is something present-at-hand on which to disagree, even if, as with hammers in the last chapter, the present-at-hand cedes priority to the other aspects of the world as phenomenologically understood. The question of divergent moral beliefs is more interesting just because, *ex hypothesi*, there is nothing on which to disagree. Hence I can say that I disagree and that I think the beliefs are false – but this is not something that I can ever demonstrate satisfactorily.

68 In Chapter 4 I made reference to McDowell's use of Cavell in *Virtue and Reason* and *Non-Cognitivism and Rule-Following* (both in McDowell, 1998, pp. 60–61, 206–11) as being able to cast light on what is going on in moral debate: it is worth repeating this reference here.

argument I have presented so far, it would have inculcated a certain set of values and norms into the discursively supported world. There would be no moral fact of the matter beyond this: there *is* nothing present-at-hand to settle moral disputes in the way that there is a fact of the matter that can settle whether the metal in the crown is gold. Nevertheless, as I have already argued, Twiain's belief would be supported by nothing more than discourse; and reflection on this should be enough to destabilise his certainty. Of course, exactly the same applies to us and to our moral standards: they, too, cannot call on anything more than discourse as a guarantor. This should be taken as a warning against *any* moral dogmatism, regardless of whether or not we agree with it. I will return to this point.

Twiain, our putative 'good Nazi', would assent to a statement to the effect that Nazi moral beliefs were true. But Heidegger argues that '[t]ruth is un-truth'.[69] As discourse brings something to light from obscurity it makes it true: strictly speaking, as I noted in Chapter 4, *aletheia* – truth – means 'wresting from oblivion' or 'bringing to light'. However, in wresting beings from obscurity, two things happen. First, Being slips into oblivion; therefore any statement covers at least as much as it uncovers – even when it is true. Second, because that which is uncovered is as inseparable from the 'knower' as the 'knower' is from the world, it is always subjective and partial; Dasein cannot get a God's-eye view of the world in which it i s. Consideration of Dasein's existential situation leads to the conclusion, then, that knowledge of beings is always fragmentary[70]. Both these strands force an admission that the familiar world is not all that might be. Although it is not existentially possible for Dasein to separate itself from the world in which it i s, consideration of its being-in-the-world denies that there is any ground for complacency. This consideration is ethical 'pondering of the abode of human being'. Everything worldly is open for criticism; authenticity and authentic pondering of finitude are inseparable from *krisis*.[71]

Thus when Richard Wolin claims that Heidegger's equation of truth and un-truth leads him to 'extreme judgmental incapacities',[72] he is right in a sense, but arguably he misses the consequence of the claim. Certainly, if by 'judgement' he means the ability to say definitively and correctly that *this* is right and *this* is wrong, he is right. But his point lacks pertinence. The main reason for this is that correctness does not exhaust Heidegger's understanding of truth: for him, a close association of truth with correctness is concomitant with a particular moment in the history of metaphysics, according to which truth is separate from appearance. But if we understand '*aletheia*', thence 'truth', as *uncovering*, there is – admittedly – no reason to deny the *association* of truth and correctness, but also no reason to suppose that

---

69 *The Origin of the Work of Art* in Heidegger, 2002b, p. 36; 1999c, p. 185.

70 *On the Essence of Truth* in Heidegger, 1999b, H 89; 1999c, p. 130.

71 I have chosen this, rather than a more conventional, spelling because I do not want to be thought of as being Jeremiad or nihilistic. All that I am advocating is the idea that moral opinions should always be thought of as being on trial – this is one of the senses of the word 'κρίσις'. I believe that I am doing nothing more than echoing the ring of the hammer in the subtitle to Nietzsche's *Twilight of the Idols*.

72 Wolin, 1990, p. 122.

'truth' *just means* 'correctness'.[73] Two rival judgements can claim truth with equal legitimacy; but truth, correspondingly, cannot be taken as definitive and exhaustive.[74] It follows from this, though, that a thoughtful person will have to admit a limit to his own judgements: whatever truth he might assign them is not the whole story. Correspondingly, if 'judgement' is taken to mean '*final* judgement', Wolin is again right. But no judgement can be final. This does not count against the ethical demand for *krisis* – judgement – at all times, though: in fact, for the authentic Dasein, the ethical space for *krisis* will never be filled.

For this reason, I would suggest that, although Heidegger might be read as offering succour to just about any *moral* discourse by eliminating any extra-discursive standard of truth – all instances of uncovering must, on Heidegger's account, be counted as true: an account that removes any criteria for judgement[75] – he offers none at all *ethically* – that is, in terms of pondering Dasein's abode and its limits. He does not claim that all that is untrue is true (a claim that would inflate the idea of judgement to the point of bursting), nor that all truth is false (a claim that would deflate judgements), but that all truth is *un*-truth. This is a claim that calls for modesty in making judgements: any statements we might make or beliefs that we might have, though formative of Dasein, are 'incomplete'. Inevitably, truth (in the sense of something definitive and total) is something 'deferred' – something unattainable to Dasein.

The good Nazi might be 'secure' in his beliefs; but this should not be taken as meaning that he can afford not to entertain alternative possibilities for Being: that he should be happy with this security. The same, of course, goes for the liberal. However, a recognition of the provisional nature of judgements and beliefs and a corresponding refusal to make absolute claims to truth begets a kind of de facto liberalism – indeed, a liberalism that is stronger than its traditional likeness, since it does not draw from any moral dogma. Heideggerianism forces us to judge, but then to judge the judgement. Though Gadamer is a critic of Heidegger, he articulates a position that can come to his defence: such a *krisis* 'has logically the structure of a question. The essence of the question is the opening up, and keeping open, of possibilities.'[76]

For this reason, the assertion that truth is un-truth should alert us to a means of defence against any kind of totalitarianism. It does not allow one a free hand to cook up whatever 'truths' one might wish (notwithstanding the last chapter's arguments about the difficulties in this anyway). Even though any programme of truth is destined to be 'incomplete', there is a difference between making an untrue statement and *lying*. A statement that aims at truth cannot contain all that there is to say, regardless of whether or not it is mistaken. A lie, on the other hand, has pretensions to build

---

73 Cf. *On the Essence of Truth* in Heidegger, 1999b.

74 Cf. *The Question Concerning Technology* in Heidegger, 1999c, esp. p. 332, for elaboration of this theme.

75 See Tugendhat, *Heidegger's Idea of Truth* in Wolin, 1998.

76 Gadamer, 2004, p. 298.

empires – in the end, this is what lies are for – and so has to maintain the charade that its claims are beyond question. And the stronger the dogmatic certainty of a statement – certainly a moral statement – and the less ground it concedes to the possibility of its antithesis, the more one should suspect its pretensions. When a statement goes so far as to suggest that there is an imperative to act in a given way that is not wholly dependent on the contingencies of a given discourse, and which is therefore not to be criticised – this sort of statement is of the kind that would wither under the light and heat of a distant candle.

Although authentic Dasein might make t r u e claims in relation to the discursively constituted world in which it ek-sists, these claims must be made tentatively, in the awareness that any instance of uncovering simultaneously covers alternative points of view and Being-as-a-whole. Authentic Dasein never quite allows itself to believe what is unveiled as telling the whole story. So if Twiain is committed to the totalitarianism in which he finds himself, this is an ethical failure: because ethical pondering bears the trace of the 'otherwise', ethics will not tolerate totalitarianism.

(In this, we may compare Nietzsche's diagnosis of '[a] very popular error: having the courage of one's convictions; rather it is a matter of having the courage for an *attack* on one's convictions!!!'.[77] Other aspects of Nietzschean thought are similarly worth noting here as appreciably similar to the Heideggerian line I am taking. As West points out, the analysis of Dasein implies that 'the world' is as inseparable from the idea of consciousness as Dasein is inseparable from the world; 'Heidegger's radical challenge to the objectivism of western metaphysics could not be more apparent':[78] Nietzsche's attack on Platonism chimes into this. One of the upshots of the attack is that the objectivity of judgements is threatened:

> From now on, my dear philosophers, let us beware of the dangerous old conceptual fable which posited a 'pure, will-less, painless, timeless knowing subject', let us beware of the tentacles of such contradictory concepts as 'pure reason', 'absolute spirituality', 'knowledge in itself' … Perspectival seeing is the *only* kind of seeing there is, perspectival 'knowing' the *only* kind of 'knowing'.[79]

The rejection of any 'knowing' that is not 'perspectival' will not allow hubris: it forces the knower to admit that his 'knowledge' is conditional on other possible perspectives being abandoned. It forces the realisation of the possibility of other, differently constituted, worlds. One's moral 'knowledge', whether that be individually or culturally ordained, is *only* a perspective. Granted, one might know the discursively upheld *Sittlichkeit* of the world in which one ek-sists; but ethical pondering means also that one realises that it is '*only*' discursively upheld. Dasein does not learn any 'objective' moral truths from the ethical contemplation of its 'abode'.)

---

77 Cited in Nietzsche, 1974, § 296*n*; also in Kaufmann, 1974, p. 423.
78 West, 1996, p. 102.
79 Nietzsche, 1996, III, § 12.

Naturally, a sustained critique of Dasein and its *'ethos* is probably not something that can be sustained in day-to-day existence. Nevertheless, it would be well to remember that there *are* other possibilities for Being than those that a r e presently. And there *are* precedents for thinking that it might be possible to get behind the constraints of everyday discourse, and so to be jolted into a consideration of the norms carried within language. Deleuze and Guattari argued, for example, that because of his apparent prioritisation of form over content within language, the schizophrenic was 'free';[80] Foucault would seem to have been in agreement with the idea when, in his introduction to their *Anti-Oedipus*, he renamed it *An Introduction to the Non-Fascist Life*.[81] In Foucault's own work he nods approvingly towards de Sade, Nietzsche and Artaud for disrupting the parameters of commonplace thought.[82]

In a less extreme sense, it would appear that something comparable could be said of other media: particularly, the same could be said of various forms of art. 'Being' was written as 'B̶e̶i̶n̶g̶' at least partly because the attempt to put it into a word strips that word of exactly that which it is supposed to be conveying. It is non-articulable: no word can get behind the wordy-worldly as Heidegger wants to do. However, art can convey an impetus to thinking that is not necessarily articulate – this point is something like the one recently made by Bryan Magee.[83] For example, Artaud writes that his Theatre of Cruelty:

> was created to restore an impassioned compulsive concept of life to theatre, and we ought to accept the cruelty on which this is based in the sense of drastic strictness, the extreme concentration of stage elements.
>   This cruelty will be bloody if need be, but not systematically so, and will therefore merge with the idea of a kind of severe mental purity, not afraid to pay the price one must pay in life.[84]

His intention, it would appear, was to make his audience sit up – to disrupt that which might otherwise pass without thought. For this reason, though it cannot present norms, art can, even if momentarily, cure us of the tendency to mistake the world in which we a r e for something that exhausts all that might b e. It need not be literal, and so it can convey an inarticulate feeling.

This ability is exemplified in haiku. This one is chosen pretty randomly from Basho:

Darkening waves –
Cry of wild ducks
Faintly white[85]

---

80 Cited by Itkonen, 1988, p. 317.
81 In Deleuze and Guattari, 1996, p. xiii; also Foucault, 2002, p. 108.
82 Foucault, 1997a, pp. 279–89.
83 Magee, 2005, *passim.*
84 *The Theatre of Cruelty: Second Manifesto* in Artaud, 1999, p. 81.
85 Basho, 1985, § 60.

The poem is not really about anything; closer to the truth, though, would be a claim that it is not about *any thing*, which is not the same. In its Zen simplicity, it encourages a sensitivity to that which cannot be put into words: it is exactly this sort of un-wordy contemplation that ethics, qua contemplation of 'abode', demands, because of the proximity of this 'abode' to discourse.[86] This done, it invites authentic Dasein to contemplate the limits of its *'ethos*.

Being pulled up short by a text, a painting, a drama, or whatever, reminds us that there are alternatives from our customary worldviews.[87] This accords with Artaud's view, and it also helps explain Heidegger's contention that '[t]he tragedies of Sophocles ... preserve the *'ethos* in their sayings more primordially than Aristotle's lectures on "ethics"'.[88] Art promotes contemplation of the abode of Dasein; since this is what ethics is, it follows that art can promote ethics. An authentic awareness of *'ethos* and the realisation that it hangs on nothing more than discourse brings modesty: it does not offer its own morality or falsify existing morality, but it does remind Dasein of its limits. In this, it affords authentic Dasein the tools of critique, since authentic Dasein will bring to its self-apprehension a state of *krisis*. If poetry, or art more generally, has the ability to provoke an inarticulate ethical thinking, the position is something rather close to Shelley's claim that the poet is the unacknowledged legislator of mankind;[89] his thought, which is rather like the argument I am pushing here, is that poetry 'awakens and enlarges the mind itself by rendering it the receptacle of a thousand unapprehended combinations of thought'.[90]

More radically, the thought ties in with Marcuse's critique of 'one-dimensional' society. This is a society marked by 'one-dimensional' thinking: a thought process which is relentlessly positive, insofar as it is hypnotised by the established and the given, rather than thought which criticises the basis of that establishment and that givenness.[91] In Marcuse's critique, the concentration on, say, the science of the present-at-hand as opposed to speculative metaphysics results in a 'purged language, purged not only of its "unorthodox" vocabulary, *but also of the means for expressing other contents than those furnished to the individuals by society*'.[92] On the other hand, he thinks, slang can achieve the same as art, insofar as it opens the possibility of critique because it is the creation and creative use of language, unimpeded by the prevailing consensus. I suspect that Marcuse may be unique in having based a scathing social critique at least partially on the word 'boob-tube'.[93]

---

86 Cf. *'... Poetically Man Dwells ...'* in Heidegger, 1975, esp. pp. 227 ff.

87 Cf. Gadamer, 2004, pp. 270 ff.

88 *Letter of 'Humanism'* in Heidegger, 1999b, H 184; 1999c p. 256.

89 *A Defence of Poetry* in Shelley, 1991, l. 1114.

90 Ibid., ll. 304–5.

91 Marcuse, 1994, *passim.*

92 Ibid., p. 174; emphasis mine. This clearly echoes Heidegger's critique of modern technology: 'Science always encounters only what its kind of representation has admitted beforehand as an object possible for science,' he suggests in *The Thing* (Heidegger, 2001, p. 168). There is a similar strain in *The Question Concerning Technology.*

93 Ibid., p. 86.

Self, World and Other

The appropriation of Heidegger by ethical thought, then, demands an openness to possibility: although Heidegger *could* be used by the Nazis or any other such movement – his insistence that Dasein cannot be separated from its milieu opens the way for cultural chauvinism – he can also offer tools to critics. (Richard Rorty suggests a possible alternative biography of a 'Heidegger' not particularly different from the Heidegger I am considering here, in which his skills are put to anti-Nazi use.[94]) What is uncomfortable about a Heideggerian approach is that it does seem to allow that one might be obligated to whatever milieu it is in which one finds oneself even while its critic. It would appear that, for the sake of authenticity, one must obey even while one protests (and in this, compare Kant, whose enlightened despot 'would dare to say: *Argue as much as you like and about whatever you like, but obey*'[95]). The only consideration that tempers this unhappy conclusion is that one is rarely, if ever, a participant in just one discourse. The world is too incoherent a place, the discourses through which one might ek-sist too polysemic, for Dasein ever to be able rigidly to say that it i s *this* but not *that* or ek-sists within *this* but not *that* discourse: Dasein i s in-the-world; the world is propped up by discourse; and there are several discourses. And, for this reason, there is always likely to be leeway for Dasein to be authentic (and to b e authentically) in any number of differing, sometimes competing, ways.

But there is one more element that might be worth bringing to light in this context. Ethics, I have argued, does not impart any norms of its own: it just demands a sensitivity to and a confrontation with those that are built into our environment (*'ethos*). This is a claim that I want to modify a little now – at least tentatively.

The Heideggerian approach that I have suggested brings a need for a sense of modesty in one's assertions. However, it also brings with it a demand for modesty in respect of oneself. A part of Levinas's ethical opposition to Heidegger is that the concentration on Being implies that it 'subordinate[s] the relation with someone, who is an existent, (the ethical relation) to a relation with the *Being of the existent*'.[96] Levinas's worry is that Heidegger objectifies the Other, diminishing his radical and irreducible alterity and that this objectification is a greater threat to the ethical relation between subjects than even something like torture.[97] Once the Other has been reduced to the status of simply another thing that one may encounter in the world, and assuming that it is permissible to treat non-personal objects as means to an end, then there is no barrier to using persons as means. Taken in conjunction with Heidegger's own claim that the death camps were not essentially different from mechanised agriculture, this is a worrying point.

---

94 *On Heidegger's Nazism* in Rorty, 1999.

95 *An Answer to the Question: What is Enlightenment?* in Kant, 1995, p. 59.

96 Levinas, 1969, p. 45.

97 It is interesting to compare this to de Beauvoir's commentary on the Marquis de Sade (1972, p. 41): 'mais je pense que l'idée [du meurtre] lui répugne sincèrement …'. His victims must still be *subjects*.

However, it need not be – or, at least, not in the sense that Levinas would have it. For one thing, Levinas seems to be an uncritical prisoner of the prioritisation of persons over things. But this is to *assume* that a Dasein that authentically ponders its abode will take at face value the traditional prioritisation of *logos* over *phusis*. I can see no reason why it should. Certainly, there might be a cultural prejudice along these lines, but it is not compelling in a way that would make it immune to ethical criticism. It might be that, within my milieu, there is a prioritisation of *logos* over *phusis*. But, of course, things might be different: whatever the relation might be, authentic Dasein cannot afford to take this as read. Pondering the norms built into the world in which I ek-sist should demonstrate that there is nothing at all to back up the prioritisation. It would only be absolutely reliable as long as there was a Platonic or divine guarantor – and there is none. *Pace* Dostoyevsky, given that God is dead, *nothing* is permitted. This is the major difference between a Heideggerian-based ethic and traditional ethics: it does not presume that everything that is not forbidden is permitted, since there is no one to permit.

So even if Levinas is correct to think that analysis of the being of the existent reduces the Other, more still has to be said for the critique to be powerful. This is quite aside from the fact that Levinas is *wrong* to accuse Heidegger of a 'thingification' of the Other in the first place. Heidegger is clear that concentrating on the being of the existent does *not* reduce the Other to anything; 'he is *never* apprehended as a human-Thing present-at-hand … *The Other is encountered in his Dasein-with-the-world*',[98] says *Being and Time*. Note the verbs: one might *apprehend* a present-at-hand thing, but one *encounters* an Other. There is no reason to think that the encountered Other might *ever* be apprehended.

It is true that *Being and Time* does seem to hint that whatever is not present-at-hand is ready-to-hand; this hint is, I suspect, an important aspect of Levinas's worry that Heidegger 'thingifies' the Other and makes him ready-to-hand. But the idea that one *encounters* rather than *apprehends* the Other hints that the proper way to think of persons is precisely *not* to regard them as mere 'things' – to regard them as *neither* present-at-hand *nor* ready-to-hand. Moreover, I have already suggested that this easy division of the world into presence- and readiness-at-hand is not sufficient to account for the phenomenological richness of the world; so even if Heidegger *did* make such a division, I think that one can remain broadly true to Heideggerianism while still insisting on something more complex. That is, even if Heidegger does promote the idea that, if he is not present-at-hand, the Other must be ready-to-hand, I see no reason why we should accept it.

So we have a twofold modesty here. First, there is nothing to back up the commonsense thought that persons have moral priority over things. But this does not mean that persons are existentially *reduced* to things. The prioritisation could remain within *moral* discourse. But ethically? This difference vanishes once we begin to ponder our worldly abode: to take account of the fact that moral discourse could easily be otherwise – that it is not guaranteed by any absolute standards. So nothing

---

98 Heidegger, 1999a, H 120; emphasis mine.

is *reduced* to *anything*. Only tentatively can Dasein rely on a priority of *logos* over *phusis*. Since Dasein cannot separate itself from its world, this alters its capacity to make capital of the world around it; the world is not at Dasein's disposal. Second, both Others and others feature in the facticity of the world in which Dasein i s. There is no question of authentic Dasein being able to analyse Others out of existence, then, without having acted in bad faith to its own ek-sistence.

We can factor this response back to the comment about mechanised agriculture and the death camps. The horror of our response would seem to be preconditioned by the notion that industrial agriculture is generally permissible – albeit with reservations, this tends to get our assent – and that therefore Heidegger's statement *raises* the death camps to that level. We seem reluctant to reverse the claim, though. Why not say that the death camps were horrible, and that mechanised agriculture, in its commodification and 'enframing' of the world – the term is a motif in *The Question Concerning Technology*[99] – is playing the same game (albeit to a different degree)? In reducing the world to a 'standing-reserve', humanity forgets its close relationship *with* the world and so makes itself, qua humanity, vulnerable to its own enframing. So much could be said by elements of the Green movement today, which might find itself indebted to Heidegger. Heidegger may have been guilty of brutality in his choice of words, but the sentiment is surely defensible – somewhere else, though.

Democracy, Terrorism and Existence

In Chapter 4, I tried to show that the *moral* difference between terrorism and democracy was attributable to the parameters of discourse. Each notion has a chain of associations and imperatives linked with it. As I argued in Chapter 1, there may be significant moral overlaps between the terrorist and the civil-social politcian – but the way that discourse evolves brings with it a sort of moral apartheid, which need not be particularly coherent, but which keeps the two distinct. The problem faced in this chapter was that this looked to be at odds with the commonsense idea that there might be a moral fulcrum of some sort. If all morality is reduced to discourse, it becomes difficult to say what is morally wrong with something that is apparently coherent: if, somehow, someone *did* manage to produce his own moral discourse, anything might go. At the same time, there was a related problem concerning how we might be able to offer a critique without risking incoherence. On a simple presentation of the problem, to allow critique might allow too much; to labour the impossibility of escaping the contemporary discourse allows too little.

I have located the solution to this problem by offering an account of ethics that has been unravelled with the help of the analysis of Dasein's being-in-the-world that is aired (first and foremost) in *Being and Time*. The Delphic instruction *gnothi heauton* leads to the recognition that one i s in-the-world; self-understanding reveals

---

99   In Heidegger, 1999c.

an intimate ek-static relationship with the surrounding world. Important in this ek-stasis is the discourse that supports the world in which Dasein is. I have already noted the pertinent Wittgenstinian maxim that '[t]he limits of my language mean the limits of my world'.[100] This is the point that the Heideggerian analysis of Dasein could make. However, there is no reason to stop *thinking* here. Philosophy 'runs out' at the limits of language; but to recognise the ends of philosophy is implicitly to grasp the possibility of a 'beyond'. Being exhausts philosophy, not the other way around (which is perhaps why philosophy has neglected it). For Dasein to know itself fully and authentically means that it must remind itself of the possibility of its own absence. This knowledge could be moral-phenomenological as easily as it could be mortal: Dasein, to know itself, must recognise its integration with such givens as morality, but must also recognise that the world could be otherwise, signalling the absence of the Dasein which I am.

Contemplation of the moral 'elsewhere' means that, even though Dasein cannot wrench itself from the factical milieu of its ek-sistence, it can still provide itself with a counterpoint to the world in which it is. Such a counterpoint will not provide it with any norms – ek-sistence will not tell us that terrorism is something to eschew or that saving kittens is good – but it gives us pause in our moral certainties. It gently demands humility. The power of the ethical is precisely that it does *not* give a 'Thou shalt'. There is no empire of ethics – no *imperator*, no imperative – but that ethics instigates the subversion of every empire[101] because it recognises that the moral empire has boundaries, and that there might be something beyond them – even if this something is inconceivable.

Continual critique of this type is probably not something that could reasonably be expected in everyday life. But who says that ethics should be reasonable? An imperative such as 'Be reasonable!' is a part of the *'ethos* in which Dasein is. And as a *part* of the *'ethos*, it should not be taken as the existential be-all and end-all: 'good', authentic Dasein will criticise it, as it criticises all imperatives. (Bauman cites the Talmud: 'Is the law for saints?'[102] Whatever else the law might be, it is not 'total'.) Nevertheless, as I have argued, I think that art is one of the things that can provoke ethical reflection; it can instigate the little tremors that allow at least the possibility of the moral equivalent of the 'butterfly effect'.

Cataclysms have the same effect, of course: they can demonstrate the limits of the *status quo*. Might not the terrorist be a kind of artist, then? 'What do the victims matter if the gesture is beautiful?' Laurent Tailhade asked.[103] Could not the odd bomb be valuable if it succeeds in awakening contemplation of one's place in the world? This would not justify it, of course – the ethical 'precedes' justice – but it might mark the 'great noontide' of a paradigm. Terrorism disrupts our cosy morality in the same way that ethics can (and perhaps should).

---

100 Wittgenstein, 1997, 5.6.
101 Cf. *Différance* in Derrida, 1982, p. 22.
102 Cited in Bauman, 1993, p. 81.
103 Primoratz, 1990, p. 135.

The difference, though, is that the terrorist *is* trying to build an empire. His action might be productively disruptive, but this is not *why* he carried it out. To disrupt is one thing, but violence interposes the agent on the world around him; even the Situationist who wants to prompt cultural disorientation implicitly tries to impose the maxim 'be critical!'. Authentic Dasein, on the other hand, knows that to be so convinced of something that death might be invoked to enforce it seems to be massively self-important (and foolhardy); in the face of the Heideggerian argument concerning the partial nature of truth and the necessary tentativeness in making moral claims, such impositions are unsustainable.

Moreover, insofar as the terrorist *does* tend to reduce populations to masses, he does ignore the irreducible Other, treating him instead as either a part of a present-at-hand crowd, or else as a ready-to-hand other – a resource for his use and exploitation. Neither attitude is compatible with authenticity. Imagine that a bomb goes off in a crowded room. Maybe everyone in that room had committed a crime that deserved retribution: even in commonsense moral terms, there are no innocents here. Still, no one commits a crime en masse. To treat of a group en masse is to reduce each person therein to nothing more than their membership of a group: it is bureaucratic and efficient, but it surely does not deal with the *moral* evaluation of each member of the group. It tries to totalise the untotalisable Other. But, on the basis that the Other is a part of the world in which Dasein i s, such a move can only be seen as inauthentic.

This point does not rule out violence: the gleeful account of the grisly execution of Damiens the regicide given by Foucault at the start of *Discipline and Punish*[104] suggests as much. In this case, a simple execution would, ultimately, have done the trick. But Foucault's implicit suggestion is that Damiens's fate was tailored to fit *him*; as such, it pays a kind of dark respect to him as an individual, as an Other who remains Other. This respect came to an end with the efficiency of the guillotine; this quick, painless and efficient means of disposing of the criminal is no longer the execution of an enemy (*polemios*): it is the execution of a *task*. Levinas can be read in this light: he writes that '[t]o inflict suffering is not to reduce the Other to the rank of object, but on the contrary is to maintain him superbly in his subjectivity'.[105] The terrorist pays no such account of the Other; but since he lives in a world in which there a r e Others – that is, since the existence of Others is a fact of *'ethos* – mass terrorism is unethical.

What is Wrong with Terrorism(?)

And so I have come back to my starting point: the moral difference between civil society and terrorism. One uncomfortable conclusion is that *there is no cast-iron, copper-bottomed or gold-plated moral condemnation that could be applied to Henry or to any other criminal. Nor can we say that what he did was contemptible because of the contempt we feel.* Chapters 2 and 3 should have disposed of these comforting

104 Foucault, 1991, pp. 3–6.
105 Levinas, 1969, p. 239.

thoughts. What is at the basis of moral assertions and moral apophansis is the way that discourse works, and while these assertions and moral revelations are not under the control of any individual, they are also not something that one could 'discover' in the traditional metaethical sense. It is the discourse that contains morality that lays the conditions for Dasein's discovery of itself (among the worldly) in the first place. What is wrong with terrorism – and what is permissible about democracy – is (if I may be excused) noThing.

Still, the ethical point is this: even though the morality upon which Dasein is built is inescapable, there remains the contemplation of the abode of Dasein. This contemplation cannot help but to involve the 'otherwise-than'. Contemplating the abode of Dasein means contemplating the 'edge' of Dasein – which means admitting the possibility of an inaccessible 'outside edge'. It also means admitting that any moral dictum is only ever partial – and so should only be made tentatively. And so, even though Heidegger was unwilling to 'redonner un sens au mot "Humanisme"',[106] I think that this marks him out as being able to out-humanise the most entrenched humanism. He calls for modesty. Heidegger cannot provide a morality; but his ek-centricity, simultaneously subverting and founding all morali*ties*, opens the way for an ethical rigour that outpaces all morali*ty*.

---

106 *Letter on 'Humanism'* in Heidegger, 1999b H 147; 1999c, p. 219.

Bibliography

Included in the bibliography is a number of books and articles that, while not cited directly, have been important in the development of the arguments presented in this volume.

Allen, L. and Gorski, R. (1990) 'Sex Difference in the Bed Nucleus of the Stria Terminalis of the Human Brain', *Journal of Comparative Neurology*, **302** (4).
––––– (1991) 'Sexual Diamorphism of the Anterior Commisure and Massa Intermedia of the Human Brain', *Journal of Comparative Neurology*, **312** (1).
––––– (1992) 'Sexual Orientation and the Size of the Anterior Commisure in the Human Brain', *Proceedings of the National Academy of Sciences*, **89** (15).
Allen, L., Richey, M., Chai, Y. and Gorski, R. (1991) 'Sex Differences in the Corpus Callosum of the Living Human Being', *Journal of Neuroscience*, **11** (4).
Allison, H. (1995) *Kant's Theory of Freedom*, Cambridge: Cambridge University Press.
Anscombe, G. (1979) *Intention*, Oxford: Blackwell.
Arendt, H. (1994) *Eichmann in Jerusalem: A Report on the Banality of Evil*, New York: Penguin.
––––– (1998) *The Human Condition* (2nd edn), Chicago: University of Chicago Press.
Aristotle (1882) *Psychology*, trans. E. Wallace, Cambridge: Cambridge University Press.
––––– (1974) *Categories/ De Interpretatione*, trans. J. Ackrill, Oxford: Clarendon.
––––– (1976) *Ethics*, trans. J.A.K. Thomson, Harmondsworth: Penguin.
––––– (1992) *The Politics*, trans. T.A Sinclair and T.J. Saunders, Harmondsworth: Penguin.
Artaud, A. (1999) *The Theatre and its Double*, trans. V. Corti, London: Calder.
Augustine (1898) *Confessions*, London: Walter Scott.
––––– (1995) *Confessions*, ed. G. Clark, Cambridge: Cambridge University Press.
Barker, E. (ed.) (1960) *Social Contract*, London: Oxford University Press.
Basho. (1985) *On Love and Barley: Haiku*, trans. L. Stryk, Harmondsworth: Penguin.
Bauman, Z. (1993) *Postmodern Ethics*, Oxford: Blackwell.
––––– (2000) *Morality and the Holocaust*, Cambridge: Polity.
de Beauvoir, S. (1972) *Faut-Il Brûler Sade?*, Paris: Gallimard.
Benjamin, W. (2000) 'Critique of Violence', trans. E. Jephcott and K. Shorter, in McQuillan, M. (ed.), *Deconstruction: A Reader*, Edinburgh: Edinburgh University Press.
Blackburn, S. (1984) *Spreading the Word*, Oxford: Clarendon.

────── (1993) *Essays in Quasi-Realism*, New York: Oxford University Press.

Bradley, F. (1962) *Ethical Studies*, London: Oxford University Press.

Brassington, I. (2002) 'Global Village, Global Polis', in Moseley, A. and Norman, R. (eds), *Human Rights and Military Intervention*, Aldershot: Ashgate.

Carroll, L. (1995) *The Hunting of the Snark*, Harmondsworth: Penguin.

────── (1998) *Alice's Adventures in Wonderland / Through the Looking-Glass*, Oxford: Oxford University Press.

Collins, P. (2002) *Banvard's Folly*, London: Picador.

Cullity, G. and Gaut, B. (eds) (1998) *Ethics and Practical Reason*, Oxford: Clarendon.

Dancy, J. (1993) *Moral Reasons*, Oxford: Blackwell.

Davidson, D. (1963) 'Actions, Reasons and Causes', *Journal of Philosophy*, **60** (23).

────── (2001) *Inquiries into Truth and Interpretation*, Oxford: Clarendon.

Deleuze, G. and Guattari, F. (1996), *Anti-Oedipus: Capitalism and Schizophrenia*, trans. R. Hurley, M. Seem and H. Lane, London: Athlone.

Derrida, J. (1981) *Dissemination*, trans. B. Johnson, London: Athlone.

────── (1982) *Margins of Philosophy*, trans. A. Bass, Brighton: Harvester.

────── (1988) 'The Politics of Friendship', *Journal of Philosophy*, **85** (4).

────── (1989) *Of Spirit: Heidegger and the Question*, trans. G. Bennington and R. Bowlby, Chicago: University of Chicago Press.

────── (1994) *Specters of Marx*, trans. P. Kamuf, New York: Routledge.

────── (2000) *Politics of Friendship*, trans. G. Collins, London: Verso.

Dworkin, R. (1992) 'Liberal Community', in Avineri, S. and de-Shalit, A. (eds), *Communitarianism and Individualism*, Oxford: Oxford University Press.

Ettinger, E. (1995) *Hannah Arendt / Martin Heidegger*, New Haven: Yale University Press.

Ewin, R. (1972) 'What is Wrong with Killing People?', *The Philosophical Quarterly*, **22** (87).

Foucault, M. (1991) *Discipline and Punish*, trans. A. Sheridan, Harmondsworth: Penguin.

────── (1997a) *Madness and Civilisation*, trans. R. Howard, London: Routledge.

────── (1997b) *The Order of Things*, London: Routledge.

────── (2000) *Essential Works 1954–1984, vol. 1: Ethics*, ed. P. Rainbow, Harmondsworth: Penguin

────── (2002) *Essential Works 1954–1984, vol. 3: Power*, ed. J. Faubion, Harmondsworth: Penguin.

Gadamer, H.-G. (1986) *The Idea of the Good in Platonic-Aristotelian Philosophy*, trans. P. Smith, New Haven: Yale University Press.

────── (2004) *Truth and Method*, trans. J. Weinsheimer and D. Marshall, London: Continuum.

Gibbard, A. (1990) *Wise Choices, Apt Feelings*, Oxford: Clarendon.

Gorski, R. (2000) 'Sexual Differentiation of the Nervous System', in Kandel, E. et al. (eds), *Principles of Neural Science*, New York: McGraw-Hill.

Hampton, J. (1998) *The Authority of Reason*, Cambridge: Cambridge University Press.

Harman, G. (1984) 'Is there a Single True Morality?', in Copp, D. and Zimmerman, D. (eds), *Morality, Reason, Truth*, Totowa: Rowman & Littlefield.

Havelock, E. (1963) *Preface to Plato*, Oxford: Blackwell.

Hegel, G. (1991) *Elements of the Philosophy of Right*, trans. H. Nisbet, Cambridge: Cambridge University Press.

Heidegger, M. (1975) *Early Greek Thinking*, trans. D. Krell and F. Capuzzi, New York: Harper & Row.

———— (1982) *On the Way to Language*, trans. P. Hertz, San Francisco: Harper and Row.

———— (1991a) *Nietzsche, vol. 1: The Will to Power as Art*, trans. D. Krell, New York: HarperCollins.

———— (1991b) *Nietzsche, vol. 2: The Eternal Recurrence of the Same*, trans. D. Krell, New York: HarperCollins.

———— (1991c) *Nietzsche, vol. 3: The Will to Power as Knowledge and as Metaphysics*, trans. D. Krell, New York: HarperCollins.

———— (1991d) *Nietzsche, vol. 4: Nihilism*, trans. D. Krell, New York: HarperCollins.

———— (1999a) *Being and Time*, trans. J. Macquarrie and E. Robinson, Oxford: Blackwell.

———— (1999b) *Pathmarks*, trans. W. McNeill, Cambridge: Cambridge University Press.

———— (1999c) *Basic Writings*, ed. D. Krell, London: Routledge.

———— (2000) *Introduction to Metaphysics*, trans. G. Fried and R. Polt, New Haven and London: Yale Nota Bene.

———— (2001) *Poetry, Language, Thought*, trans. A. Hofstadter, New York: Perennial Classics.

———— (2002a) *The Essence of Human Freedom*, trans. T. Sadler, London: Continuum.

———— (2002b) *Off the Beaten Track*, trans. J. Young and K. Hayes, Cambridge: Cambridge University Press.

———— (2004) *The Essence of Truth*, trans. T. Sadler, London: Continuum.

Hobbes, T. (1994) *Human Nature and De Corpore Politico*, Oxford: Oxford University Press.

———— (1999) *Leviathan*, Cambridge: Cambridge University Press.

Hodge, J. (1995) *Heidegger and Ethics*, London: Routledge.

Homer (1991) *Odyssey*, Harmondsworth: Penguin.

Honderich, T. (1989) *Violence for Equality*, London: Routledge.

Hume, D. *Of the Original Contract*, in Barker, 1960.

———— (1965) *Of the Standard of Taste and other Essays*, Indianapolis: Bobbs-Merrill.

———— (1985) *A Treatise of Human Nature*, Harmondsworth: Penguin.

—— (1994) *An Enquiry Concerning the Principles of Morals*, La Salle: Open Court.

—— (1998) *Dialogues and Natural History of Religion*, Oxford: Oxford University Press.

Itkonen, E. (1988) 'A Critique of the "Post-Structuralist" Concept ion of Language', *Semiotica*, **71** (3/4).

Jaspers, K. (2000) *The Question of German Guilt*, New York: Fordham University Press.

Kain, P. (1988) *Marx and Ethics*, Oxford: Clarendon.

Kant, I. (1930) *Lectures on Ethics*, trans. L. Infield, London, Methuen.

—— (1993) *Grounding for the Metaphysics of Morals*, trans. J. Ellington, Indianapolis: Hackett.

—— (1995) *Political Writings*, ed. H. Reiss, Cambridge: Cambridge University Press.

—— (1998) *The Metaphysics of Morals*, trans. M. Gregor, Cambridge: Cambridge University Press.

—— (1999) *Prolegomena to any Future Metaphysics*, trans. G. Hatfield, Cambridge: Cambridge University Press.

—— (2003) *Critique of Pure Reason*, trans. N. Kemp Smith, Basingstoke: Palgrave Macmillan.

—— (2004a) *Critique of Practical Reason*, trans. M. Gregor, Cambridge: Cambridge University Press.

—— (2004b) *Religion within the Boundaries of Mere Reason*, trans. A. Wood and G. di Giovanni, Cambridge, Cambridge University Press.

Kaufmann, W. (1974) *Nietzsche: Philosopher, Psychologist, Antichrist*, Princeton: Princeton University Press.

Kenny, A. (1993) *Wittgenstein*, Harmondsworth: Penguin.

Kierkegaard, S. (1985) *Fear and Trembling*, trans. A. Hannay, Harmondsworth: Penguin.

—— (1989) *The Sickness Unto Death*, trans. A. Hannay, Harmondsworth: Penguin.

King, M. (2001) *A Guide to Heidegger's Being and Time*, Albany: State University of New York Press.

Korsgaard, C. (1986) 'The Right to Lie: Kant on Dealing with Evil', *Philosophy and Public Affairs*, **15** (4).

Lacoue-Labarthe, P. (1990) *Heidegger, Art and Politics*, trans. C. Turner, Oxford: Blackwell.

Laqueur, W. (1977a) *Guerrilla*, London: Wiedenfeld and Nicolson.

—— (1977b) *Terrorism*, London: Wiedenfeld and Nicolson.

Leiter, B. (2001) 'Moral Facts and Best Explanations', *Social Philosophy and Policy*, **18** (2).

Levinas, E. (1969) *Totality and Infinity*, trans. A. Lingis, Pittsburgh: Duquesne University Press.

―――― (1981) *Otherwise than Being or Beyond Essence*, trans. A. Lingis, Dordrecht: Kluwer Academic Publishers.

Little, M. (1994a) 'Moral Realism I: Naturalism', *Philosophical Books*, **35** (3).

―――― (1994b) 'Moral Realism II: Non-Naturalism', *Philosophical Books*, **35** (4).

Locke, J. (1967) *Two Treatises of Government*, Cambridge: Cambridge University Press.

Lovibond, S. (1983) *Realism and Imagination in Ethics*, Oxford: Blackwell.

Lyotard, J.-F. (1990) *Heidegger and 'the jews'*, trans. A. Michel and M. Roberts, Minneapolis: University of Minnesota Press.

Macfarlane, L. (1974) *Violence and the State*, London: Nelson.

Machiavelli, N. (1995) *The Prince*, trans. G. Bull, Harmondsworth: Penguin.

Mackie, J. (1977) *Ethics: Inventing Right and Wrong*, Harmondsworth: Penguin.

MacIntyre, A. (2000) *After Virtue* (2nd edn), London: Duckworth.

Magee, B. (2005) 'Philosophy's Neglect of the Arts', *Philosophy*, **80** (313).

Mandela, N. (1994) *Long Walk to Freedom*, London: Little, Brown.

Mapel, D. (2001) 'Revising the Doctrine of Double Effect', *Journal of Applied Philosophy*, **18** (3).

Marcuse, H. (1965) 'Repressive Tolerance' in Wolff, R. et al., *A Critique of Pure Tolerance*, Boston: Beacon Press.

―――― (1994) *One-Dimensional Man*, London: Routledge.

Marx, K. and Engels, F. (1975) *Collected Works: vol. 3*, trans. M. Milligan and D. Stuik, London: Lawrence and Wishart.

McDowell, J. (1998) *Mind, Value and Reality*, Cambridge, Mass.: Harvard University Press.

McNaughton, D. (1995) *Moral Vision*, Oxford: Blackwell.

McQuillan, M. (ed.) (2000) *Deconstruction: A Reader*, Edinburgh: Edinburgh University Press.

Megill, A. (1987) *Prophets of Extremity*, Berkeley: University of California Press.

Mehta, J. (1971) *The Philosophy of Martin Heidegger*, New York: Harper and Row.

Milgram, S. (1974) *Obedience to Authority*, London: Tavistock.

Mill, J. (1985) *On Liberty*, Harmondsworth: Penguin.

Miller, A. (2003) *An Introduction to Contemporary Metaethics*, Cambridge: Polity.

Miller, F. (1997) *Nature, Justice and Rights in Aristotle's* Politics, Oxford: Clarendon.

Milton, J. (2000) *Paradise Lost*, Harmondsworth: Penguin.

Moore, G. (1968) *Principia Ethica*, Cambridge: Cambridge University Press.

Moss, D. (1997) 'Politics, Violence, Writing: The Rituals of "Armed Struggle" in Italy', in Apter, D. (ed.), *Legitimization of Violence*, London: Macmillan.

Nietzsche, F. (1968) *The Will to Power*, trans. W. Kaufmann, New York: Vintage.

―――― (1969) *Thus Spoke Zarathustra*, trans. R. Hollingdale, Harmondsworth: Penguin.

―――― (1974) *The Gay Science*, trans. W. Kaufmann, New York: Vintage.

—— (1990a) *Beyond Good and Evil*, trans. R. Hollingdale, Harmondsworth: Penguin.

—— (1990b) *Twilight of the Idols / The Anti-Christ*, trans. R. Hollingdale, Harmondsworth: Penguin.

—— (1992) *Ecce Homo*, trans. R. Hollingdale, Harmondsworth: Penguin.

—— (1994) *Human, All Too Human*, trans. M. Faber with S. Lehmann, Harmondsworth: Penguin.

—— (1995) *The Birth of Tragedy*, trans. C. Fadiman, New York: Dover.

—— (1996) *On the Genealogy of Morals*, trans. D. Smith, Oxford: Oxford University Press.

—— (1997) *Untimely Meditations*, trans. R. Hollingdale, Cambridge: Cambridge University Press.

Nozick, R. (1974) *Anarchy, State and Utopia*, New York: Basic Books.

Nussbaum, M. (1986) *The Fragility of Goodness*, Cambridge: Cambridge University Press.

Olafson, F. (1995) *What is a Human Being?: A Heideggerian View*, Cambridge: Cambridge University Press.

Paine, T. (1985) *Rights of Man*, Harmondsworth: Penguin.

Plato (1921) *Sophist*, trans. H. Fowler, London: Heinemann.

—— (1973) *Phaedrus and Letters VII & VIII*, trans. W. Hamilton, Harmondsworth: Penguin.

—— (1981) *Five Dialogues: Euthyphro / Apology / Crito / Meno / Phaedo*, trans. G. Grube, Indianapolis: Hackett.

—— (1987) *The Republic*, trans. D. Lee, Harmondsworth: Penguin.

Platts, M. (1979) *Ways of Meaning*, London: Routledge.

Pöggeler, O, 'Heidegger's Political Self-Understanding', in Wolin, 1998.

Primoratz, I. (1990) 'What is Terrorism?', *Journal of Applied Philosophy*, **7** (2)

Prins, H. (1990 *Bizarre Behaviours: Boundaries of Psychiatric Disorder*, London: Tavistock.

Putnam, H. (1985) 'The Meaning of "Meaning"', in *Philosophical Papers vol. 2: Mind, Language and Reality*, London: Cambridge University Press.

—— (1998) *Reason, Truth and History*, Cambridge: Cambridge University Press.

'R.A.T.' (1971?) *The Bomb Throwers*, [York?]: Organisation of Revolutionary Anarchists.

Rachels, J. (1986) *The End of Life*, Oxford: Oxford University Press.

Redhead, M. (1997) 'Nietzsche and Liberal Democracy: A Relationship of Antagonistic Indebtedness?', *The Journal of Political Philosophy*, **5** (2).

Rorty, R. (1999) *Philosophy and Social Hope*, Harmondsworth: Penguin.

Rousseau, J.-J, *The Social Contract*, in Barker, 1960.

—— (1999) *Discourse on Inequality*, trans. F. Philip, Oxford: Oxford University Press.

de Sade, D.-A.-F. (1965) *Three Complete Novels: Justine / Philosophy in the Bedroom/ Eugénie de Franval and Other Writings*, trans. R. Seaver and A. Wainhouse, London: Arrow.

Sallis, J. (ed.) (1993) *Reading Heidegger: Commemorations*, Bloomington: Indiana University Press.

Sartre, J.-P. (1965) *Nausea*, trans. R. Baldick, Harmondsworth: Penguin.

—— (1995a) *Being and Nothingness*, trans. H. Barnes, London: Routledge.

—— (1995b) *Truth and Existence*, trans. A. van den Hoven, Chicago: University of Chicago Press.

—— (1996) *Sketch for a Theory of the Emotions*, trans. P. Mairet, London: Routledge.

—— (1997) *Existentialism and Humanism*, trans. P. Mairet, London: Methuen.

Sayre-McCord, G. (ed.) (1988) *Essays in Moral Realism*, Ithaca: Cornell.

Shaw, B. (1946) *Man and Superman*, Harmondsworth: Penguin.

Schopenhauer, A. (1969) *The World as Will and Idea, vol. 1*, trans. E. Payne, New York: Dover.

—— (1995) *On the Basis of Morality*, trans. E. Payne, Indianapolis: Hackett.

Sedgwick, P. (1981) 'Illness – Mental and Otherwise', in Caplan, A. et al. (eds), *Concepts of Health and Disease*, London: Addison-Wesley.

Self, W. (1998) *Great Apes*, Harmondsworth: Penguin.

Shelley, P. (1991) *Selected Poetry and Prose*, London: Routledge.

Sher, G. (1987) *Desert*, Princeton: Princeton University Press.

Singer, P. (1973) *Democracy and Disobedience*, Oxford: Clarendon.

—— (1983) *Hegel*, Oxford: Oxford University Press.

—— (1996) *Practical Ethics*, Cambridge: Cambridge University Press.

Smart, J. and Williams, B. (1993) *Utilitarianism: For and Against*, Cambridge, Cambridge University Press.

Sophocles (1974) *The Theban Plays*, trans. E. Watling, Harmondsworth: Penguin.

Steinberg, J. (1978) *Locke, Rousseau, and the Idea of Consent*, Westport: Greenwood Press.

Sturgeon, N. (1988) 'Moral Explanations' in Sayre-McCord, 1988.

Svavarsdóttir, S. (1999) 'Moral Cognitivism and Motivation', *The Philosophical Review*, **108** (2).

Tenenbaum, S. (2003) 'Quasi-Realism's Problem of Autonomous Effects', *The Philosophical Quarterly*, **53** (12).

Unger, P. (1996) *Living High and Letting Die: Our Illusion of Innocence*, New York: Oxford University Press.

Walker, R. (1989) *The Coherence Theory of Truth*, London: Routledge.

Ward, J. (1995) *Heidegger's Political Thinking*, Amherst: University of Massachusetts Press.

West, D. (1996) *An Introduction to Continental Philosophy*, Cambridge: Polity Press.

Wheen, F. (2000) *Karl Marx*, London: Fourth Estate.

Wiggins, D. (1987) *Needs, Values, Truth*, Oxford: Blackwell.

Wilkins, B. (1992) *Terrorism and Collective Responsibility*, London: Routledge.

Williams, B. (1993a) *Moral Luck*, Cambridge: Cambridge University Press, 1993.

—— (1993b) *Shame and Necessity*, Berkeley: University of California Press.

—— (1993c) *Ethics and the Limits of Philosophy*, London: Fontana.

Wittgenstein, L. (1980) *Culture and Value*, Oxford: Blackwell.

—— (1990) *Zettel*, Oxford: Blackwell.

—— (1997) *Tractatus Logico-Philosophicus*, London: Routledge.

—— (2000) *The Blue and Brown Books*, Oxford: Blackwell.

—— (2001) *Philosophical Investigations*, Oxford: Blackwell.

Wolff, R. (1970) *In Defence of Anarchism*, New York: Harper Torchbooks.

Wolin, R. (1990) *The Politics of Being: The Political Thought of Martin Heidegger*, New York: Columbia University Press.

—— (1998) *The Heidegger Controversy: A Critical Reader* (2nd edn), Cambridge, Mass.: MIT Press.

Wollstonecraft, M. (1992) *A Vindication of the Rights of Woman*, Harmondsworth: Penguin.

Wright, C. (1992) *Truth and Objectivity*, Cambridge, Mass.: Harvard University Press.

Young, J. (2002) *Heidegger's Later Philosophy*, Cambridge: Cambridge University Press.

Index

NOV 1 3 2007

0 1341 1027932 7

2007 10 18